Edited by
Rolando Bussi

Designer
Giorgio Linares

Italian texts translated by
William Terry Mc Clintock

Films
Zincografica Vaccari, Modena, Italy

Composition
Fotolinotipia Borghi s.n.c., Modena, Italy

Printed in Italy by
Edizioni Panini s.p.a.
41100 Modena - Italy
Viale Emilio Po, 380
Tel. 059/331133
Telex 510650 EDIPAN I

Manufactured in Italy by
ARBE Industrie Grafiche, Modena
October 1988

© Copyright Edizioni Panini s.p.a.

All rights reserved

Distributed in U.S.A. by
Princeton Architectural Press
New York

First Exhibition:
New York, Urban Center
November-December 1988

EVERYDAY MASTERPIECES
memory & modernity

a study of an international vernacular architecture between the two world wars

Joselita Raspi Serra
Françoise Astorg Bollack
Tom Killian

with Paolo Mascilli Migliorini and Nicoletta Zanni

Edited by Joselita Raspi Serra

EDIZIONI PANINI

HONORARY COMMITTEE

Dr. Sergio Romano
Ambassador of Italy to Moscow

Senator and Prof. Giulio Carlo Argan
University of Rome

Prof. Roberto Racinaro
Rector of the University of Salerno

Prof. Paolo Fusaroli
Rector of the University of Trieste

Dr. Sergio Balanzino
General Director for Cultural Relations,
Ministry of Foreign Affairs

Dr. Francesco Corrias
Consul General of Italy to New York

Hon. Dott. Amelia Ardias Cortese
Assessor of Education,
Region Campania

Dr. Elisabetta Kelescian
Ministry of Foreign Affairs

Prof. Gian Claudio Macchiarella
Director of Istituto Italiano di
Cultura, New York

Ms. Frances Halsband
President of the Architectural League of New York

Prof. James Beck
Chairman of the Department of Art History and Archaeology, Columbia University

Dr. Christopher Eggemberger
Pro-Helvetia Association, Zurich

Hon. Vincenzo Corghi
President of the Italia-URSS Association

Dr. Antonina Manina,
Ščusin Museum, Moscow

EXECUTIVE COMMITTEE

Françoise Astorg Bollack, New York
Fabio Ciofi, Rome
Ulrich Franzen, New York
Maristella de Panizza Lorch, New York
Frederiecke Taylor, New York
Rosalie Genevro, New York
Tom Killian, New York
Antonina Manina, Moscow
Joselita Raspi Serra, Rome
Nicoletta Zanni, Trieste
Paolo Mascilli Migliorini, Naples

Secretariat, care of the Dipartimento di Analisi delle Componenti Culturali del Territorio, University of Salerno
Dr. Margherita Platania
Mrs. Gigliola Genise
Mr. Luigi Pinto

ACKNOWLEDGEMENTS

Avellino, Carmine Colucci
Bari, Carmelo Calò Carducci private collection
Bologna, Anna Maria Matteucci
Florence, Biblioteca della Facoltà di Architettura, Ezio Godoli
Gorizia, Laura Brandi
Lausanne, Jacques Gubler
Milano, Carla Menozzi Andreani, Davide Campari S.p.A., Fulvio Irace, Piercarlo Lingeri, Ente Triennale di Milano
Naples, Marcello Avena, Biblioteca Nazionale, Giuseppe Caramanna, Bruno Cotronei, Giovanni de Franciscis, Leonardo Di Mauro, Gennaro Napoli, Maria Luisa Scalvini
Neuchâtel, Cecilia Oesch
New York, The late Arthur Drexler, Ulrich Franzen, Sarah Landau, Beth Sullebarger
Rome, Antonello Busiri Vici, Giorgio Cafiero, Giorgio Calza Bini, Leda Cattini Vaccaro, Enrico Crispolti, Gigliola Del Debbio, Ecole Française, Paola Libera, Cristina Loi, Giuseppe Massara, Studio Moretti, Anna D'Este Pascoletti, Vieri Quilici, Raffaella Raspi, Massimo Ridolfi, Simonetta Tozzi, Cesare Valle
Rovereto, Municipality, Mazzoni Depero Collections
Trieste, Flavia Benuzzi, Giuseppe Cotroneo, Decio Gioseffi, Maria Laura Jona, Luciano Maffeo, Marco Pozzetto
Venice, Roberto Masiero, Eugenio Vassallo
Zürich, Stanislaus von Moos, Otto Stern

AUTHOR'S ABBREVIATIONS

F.A.B.: Françoise Astorg Bollack
T.K.: Tom Killian
P.M.M.: Paolo Mascilli Migliorini
J.R.S.: Joselita Raspi Serra
N.Z.: Nicoletta Zanni

CONTENTS

Index of the photographic itinerary and of the thematic essays	pag. 8
Preface	pag. 9
Being in the Everyday (J. Raspi Serra)	pag. 11
A "Decent Table" (T. Killian)	pag. 13
The Temple and the Aeroplane: a formal study of three buildings (F. Astorg Bollack)	pag. 15
Photographic itinerary	pag. 21
Thematic essays (F. Astorg Bollack, T. Killian, P. Mascilli Migliorini, J. Raspi Serra, N. Zanni)	pag. 137
European Modern Architecture: A Chronology 1896-1933 (J. Raspi Serra, N. Zanni, P. Mascilli Migliorini)	pag. 171
American Modern Architecture: A Chronology 1918-1933 (F. Astorg Bollack, T. Killian)	pag. 187
INTERVIEWS: with Alberto Sartoris, conducted by J. Raspi Serra and N. Zanni (February, 1988) with a biographical sketch edited by M. Sommella;	pag. 195
with Denise Scott Brown, conducted by T. Killian and F. Astorg Bollack (May, 1988)	pag. 203
New York from Classic to Moderne local Architects remember	pag. 211
Folk Modern/Moderne Sauvage (T. Killian)	pag. 219
The Past Present (J. Raspi Serra)	pag. 221
Tradition and Innovation in the Modern Architecture (N. Zanni)	pag. 223
The Architecture of Machines (P. Mascilli Migliorini)	pag. 227
Bibliography	pag. 231
Photographic References	pag. 241

The object of this research is related to the studies on Paestum and the Doric revival (1986); it is also linked to the suggestion of the spreading of architectural taste and elements through the «underground paths» a new way to investigate about art's problems.

Joselita Raspi Serra

EVERYDAY MASTERPIECES
memory & modernity

The exhibition has been promoted and organized by the Dipartimento di Analisi delle Componenti Culturali del Territorio of the University of Salerno, in collaboration with the Ministry of Foreign Affairs, the Architectural League of New York, the Istituto Italiano per gli Studi Filosofici, the Center for International Scholarly Exchange of Barnard College, Columbia University, the Associazione Italia-U.R.S.S., and the University of Trieste.

The exhibition was conceived and organized by Joselita Raspi Serra, Françoise Astorg Bollack, Tom Killian, Nicoletta Zanni, and Paolo Mascilli Migliorini.

INDEX OF THE PHOTOGRAPHIC ITINERARY
AND OF THE THEMATIC ESSAYS

Classical and modern as pure contrast 1a; 1b
Classical and modern as complementary 1c

PERSISTENCE OF THE CLASSICAL IN MODERN ARCHITECTURE 2a; 2b
Variations on the theme of the colonnade 3a; 3b
a) the temple 4a; 4b
b) the portico 4c; 4d
c) the pier wall 5a; 5b
d) the freestanding colonnade 6a; 6b
e) the centered facade with portico: the pavilion 7a; 7b; 7c
the centered facade 8a; 8b
Variations on the issue of symmetry: the urban facade
a) the centered facade with wings 9a; 9b
the centered facade with portico 9c
the curved facade 10a; 10b; 10c; 10d; 11a; 11b; 12a; 12b
b) the multi-centered facade or building 13a
the bent temple 13b; 13c
c) the curved corner as a center 14a; 14b; 14c
the curved corner 15a; 15b
d) the centered facade with dematerialized corners 16a; 16b
the centered facade: vertical center/horizontal edges 17a; 17b; 18a; 18b
e) the urban facade: return to essentiality 19a; 19b
the urban facade: modern combinations 20a; 20b
the facade as a city wall with towers 21a; 21b; 21c

THE ELEMENTS
a) heraldic elements 22a; 22b; 23a; 23b; 24a; 24b; 24c; 25a; 25b; 26a; 26b
b) rustication 27a; 27b; 27c; 27d; 28a; 28b; 28c; 28d
lettering as rustication 29a; 29b
the strip window as rustication 30a; 30b; 30c; 31a; 31b
the tuscan/rustic order 32a; 32b
c) the giant order 33a; 33b; 34a; 34b; 35a; 35b; 36a; 36b
d) the half round bay 36c; 37a; 37b; 37c
e) the half round bay as heraldic element 38a; 38b

"ARCHITECTURE PARLANTE" 39a
modern dispersion: buildings as vehicles 39b; 39c
dinamic composition: building as ships 40a; 40b; 40c; 41a; 41b; 42a; 42b; 42c

THE PICTURESQUE COMPOSITION 43a; 43b; 44a; 44b; 45a; 45b; 46a; 46b; 47a; 47b

THE NEW "QUARTIER" 48a; 48b; 48c; 49a; 49b; 49c; 49d
horizontal banding: form and space 50a; 50b
the centered facade 51a; 51b; 51c
the multi-centered building: recessed center 52a; 52b; 52c
building as garden (balconies, trellises) 53a; 53b; 53c
return to essentiality 54a; 54b; 55a; 55b; 56a
the play of volumes 56b; 56c; 57a
caming back to the beginning 57b

PREFACE

The "Classical", transmitted by the Doric architecture of the 18th century and the beginning of the 19th, reappeared, integrated with modern forms, in buildings in Europe and North America. There is a continuous rhythm of remembered and transformed elements in the everyday lexicon making a new language denoting the character of the epoch and revealing the underground paths of modern architecture. This international exhibition will present, through a series of examples of European and North American architecture, often unknown and unpublished, an uncodified culture, indicating the itinerary of a spontaneous language which links Europe and North America with a true international presence.

The buildings, built mostly during the period 1920-1940, are modern in style while at the same time exhibiting elements which refer to classical architecture. With few exceptions these buildings are the work of unknown or little known architects (most of the exceptions are either from the USSR or Italy where the strictures of the Modern Movement against classical references were not dominant). The exhibition also includes a number of classical works from the period 1750-1850: images of the memory, often the beginning of a new formal character.

The exhibition has two principal intentions: one, to demonstrate the continuing presence of classical references in Modern Architecture; and two, to present the work of little known or very often forgotten architects which merits more attention, both for its intrinsic worth and because it tests the integration of the modern and traditional, stylistically and urbanistically. This work demonstrates the existence of a world wide vernacular modern architecture, a true International Style.

This new approach is necessarily and intentionally incomplete. It must be considered a probe. Once one looks beyond the "geniuses", the amount of material is overwhelming: the real aspect of our towns.

J.R.S., F.A.B., T.K.

BEING IN THE EVERYDAY

Territory is not only a geographical space, territory is a temporal area in which the reality of history is fulfilled, a whole gamut of small and great things, beautiful and ugly, famous and modest, each vibrating with the same accord, tied to the same woes, upset by the same questions.

Territory is a design in time made of tesserae impressed with the mould of the epoch, marked by the force of events.

It is the everyday of that moment.

The everyday is not a non-value, but one of the opportunities of time in which all thoughts, all language, all forms of art of the moment show themselves. The truth of existence is in the common participation in Heidegger's «not-hiding of the being», typifying the moment.

Conventional criticism is accustomed to an autonomous and selective interpretation, to the subtle exaltation of its own aesthetic ego, to the illusion of being able to discount reality and memory — the past is for many a license to indulge in flights of interpretation. Conventional criticism selects events and individuals: «This gives rise to a habit of not taking actual things too seriously anymore, this gives to the "weak personality" as a result of which the actual and enduring make only a minimal impression; in externals one finally becomes ever more casual and indolent and widens the critical gulf between content and form to the point of insensitivity to barbarism, if only the memory is stimulated ever anew, if only ever new things to be known keep streaming in to be neatly put on display in the cases of that memory.» [1].

Often historians do not give us history: there is an intellectual narcissism which assigns places, tasks, separates the high from the low, removes the tensions and the hopes from the moment under scrutiny.

The reality of the everyday is broken and only heroes emerge.

But the origin is one and the same, whether it is for the curve of steel or for the slow arch of masonry.

And always the tension of being justifies and validates both expressions, in a unity in which the idea acquires a value only if it is reflected in the vernacular. In the recomposition of this plot the vocabulary of the everyday enunciates poetic form, revealing its contents, proving its historical reality.

In the ancient and modern panorama the life of the architectural elements gives a clue for the reconstruction of the fabric, for the preservation of the footprints of history and for a new reading of the original character of an epoch.

Episodes and tendencies re-emerge in everyday architecture as on a written page. It is almost a game to reconstruct the origins of transformed elements which, just as the simple and yet essential words which so often occur in a medieval codex, speak to us of the intellectual tensions felt and suffered.

At the edges of piazzas, along the streets of the periphery, the ordinary buildings, like papers in an archive, transmit in forms, colors and materials the modernity felt from the beginning of the century in buildings and architectural discourse.

Ordinary buildings codify facts and choices, without tension, revealing tendencies and interests in their counterparts.

The classical and the traditional, the antiquarian and the mass production, the style and the non-style, the individual and the standard, the use of color and the absolute white, horizontality and regional character, monumentality and machine symbolism... all are elements which are to alive in the debate; thoughts leaving their marks in the great myth stilled personalities, showing the contradictions of an oversimplified historical construction, clarifying participations and abstentions. *Sotto voce* these elements show themselves in countless ordinary aspects of the city, eternal living memory of history.

And the epoch tells as always its tale to posterity, thanks to the anonymous voices, so often uncultured, of the witnesses. [2]

J.R.S.

---

1 F. Nietzsche, *On the Advantage and Disadvantage of History for Life*, p. 25.
2 For the importance of vernacular architecture see Scully, 1986, pp. 17, 23, and *Perspective in Vernacular Architecture*, II, ed. by C. Wells, 1986, *passim*.

A "DECENT TABLE"

Walter Benjamin has quoted Georg Lukács to the effect «that in order to make a decent table nowadays a man must have the architectural genius of a Michelangelo»[1] (WALTER BENJAMIN, *Illumination,* 1973, Schocken, New York, p. 113). This, of course, is not a plea for «artistic furniture», that is for great artists — today's Richard Meiers, *et. al.* — creating the settings we see in *House and Garden* and *Casabella,* but rather a lament for the sorry state of the world today.

The so called primitive societies have done without artists. The Navajo blankets in our great museums and private collections were made by everyone (all of the women in the tribe), just as everyone in the primitive society made his own house. «When one is faced with a society which is still alive and faithful to its traditions, the impact is so powerful that one is quite taken aback: ... the houses were majestic in size in spite of their fragility, and were the result of the utilization of materials and techniques which we in the West are acquainted with in small-scale forms: they were not so much built as knotted together, plaited, woven, embroidered and mellowed by use... the village rose round its occupants like a light flexible suit of armour, closer to Western women's hats than to Western towns...
The circular arrangement of the huts around the men's house is so important a factor in their social and religious life that the Salesian missionaries in the Rio das Garcas region were quick to realize that the surest way to convert the Bororo was to make them abandon their village in favour of one with the houses set out in parallel rows. Once they had been deprived of their bearings and were without the plan which acted as confirmation of their native lore, the Indians soon lost any feeling for tradition...» (CLAUDE LEVI-STRAUSS, *Tristes Tropiques* (1955), 1981, Atheneum, New York, p. 215 and pp. 220-21).

Humans vaunt their intellect when in fact that intellect developed because of the humans' weakness in the face of competition for survival. We have progressed, as we never cease to congratulate ourselves; we have progressed to achieve a world, a society, which everyone who cherishes the label intellectual regards as a mess.
But just as technologists always propose more technology to correct the imbalances wrought by technology, intellectuals propose further intellectualization, that is further separation of the hand and brain. The artist, the architect, of course, is the brain part. Others do the work, often badly as this separation increases. As Lukács' remark makes clear, the intellectually less developed are no longer capable of making a decent table, and too many tables are needed for the intellectuals to supply them. Those who acquire a Meier table do so because it is rare (i.e., costly). It sets them apart. As long as originality is regarded as the issue, as long as the expression of an artist's creative genius is the focus of attention, society's needs will not be addressed.
«L'homme c'est rien; l'oeuvre c'est tout» (FLAUBERT).

Attention must be shifted away from the artists (who are only needed because the mass of people are adrift) to the making of a viable world, i.e. one which functions beautifully as everyone who vacations on a Greek island, or some other «primitive» counterpart, dreams of.

«... we have spent much energy and furty in recent centuries in destroying oral culture by print technology so that the uniformly processed individuals of commercial society can return to oral marginal spots as tourists and consumers, whether geographical or artistic. The eighteenth century began to spend its time at the Metropolitan Opera as it were. Having refined and homogenized and visualised itself to the point of self-alienation, it hied off to the Hebrides, the Indies, the Americas, the transcendental imagination, and especially to childhood, in search of natural man...» (MARSHALL MCLUHAN, *The Gutenberg Galaxy*, (1962) 1965, University of Toronto Press, p. 212).

Miami Beach, The Grand Concourse in the Bronx, the colonial *quartiers* of Rabat or Cairo may not be up to the Greek island (but are we so sure they aren't architecturally?) but they are worlds made by ordinary men with ordinary talents — certainly not Michelangelos — and if what we want is a better world, they merit our attention! Of course, for those who love these buildings, they are sufficient, like any true art work, but in order to see them one must jettison the art history progression dominant in criticism today.

«Thus, when Lotte Brand Philip undertook to reorient the analytical task with regard to the Ghent Altarpiece, the resistance was intense. Her argument was that Hubert van Eyck was the author of the alterpiece, only not of its painted surface, but rather of its frame.
The idea that authorship might displace itself outward to the frame does terrible things to the system of positivist relationships out of which the art historian works. Because authorship would then be made to flow from the bounded pictorial image into that great sea of anonymous artisanal practice that formed the shop systems of the arts. Authorship, with all its decorum and priorities, would collapse under this weight...

The notion of the painting as a function of the frame (and not the reverse) tends to shift the focus from being exclusively, singularly, riveted on the interior field. Our focus must begin to dilate, to spread...» (ROSALIND KRAUSS, «Sincerely Yours», 1982. *The Originality of the Avant-Garde and Other Modernist Myths*, 1985, The M.I.T. Press, Cambridge, Mass. & London, pp. 190-91).

T.K.

THE TEMPLE AND THE AEROPLANE: A FORMAL STUDY OF THREE BUILDINGS

Jacques Henri Lartigue, Glider constructed by Maurice Lartigue, Chateau de Rouzat (1909). New York, The Museum of Modern Art.

Temple of Poseidon
Paestum, Italy
c.460 - 450 B.C.

«Nothing old is ever reborn. But it never completely disappears either. And anything that has ever been always reemerges in a new form». (ALVAR AALTO, *Painters and Masons*, 1921; quoted in *Sources of Modern Architecture, Studies on Alvar Aalto*, by DEMETRI PORPHYRIOS, Academy Editions, 1982).

In its long tradition, classical architecture perfected a compositional discipline as well as a rich idiom of tectonic elements — rustications, fluting, mouldings, etc.
In the late 19th century, the Great Tradition, as it was filtered through Beaux Arts classicism, grew increasingly perfunctory, and the demands of modern architecture were a welcome, necessary breath of fresh air. Architecture was cleansing itself, reaching back to a source, completing a journey started in the 18th century, at Paestum.
At the beginning of the 20th century, the architects engaged in the polemics of modernism were evolving a style based on new materials and construction methods. Many others, however, were unwilling to abandon the classical tradition and to embrace the ascetic principles of modern architecture; caught between the Temple and the Aeroplane, they looked for solutions that reconciled those two seemingly intractable opposites.

First, let us define the two parts of the equation — Classical and Modern.
In *The classical language of architecture* Sir John Summerson offers this definition:
«A classical building is one whose decorative elements derive directly or indirectly from the architectural vocabulary of the ancient world — the 'classical' world as it is often called: these elements are easily recognizable, as for example columns of five standard varieties, applied in standard ways; standard ways of treating door and window openings and gable ends and standard runs of mouldings applied to all those things».
And further: «... we must also accept the fact that classical architecture is only recognizable as such when it contains some allusion however slight, however vestigial, to the antique 'orders'. Such an allusion may be no more than some groove or some projection which suggests the idea of cornice or even the disposition of windows which suggest the ratio of pedestal to column, column to entablature.»
Classical architecture, the temple, is rooted, self contained, symmetrical, finite, vertical. A classical building STANDS: by means of columns and articulated walls, arches and vaults, blocks of masonry carry loads from the roof to the ground. A classical building is self contained, symmetrical, finite, vertical. It is humanistic. It speaks about HERE.
A modern building, on the other hand, as it was defined in the '20's and '30's, explodes to embrace the infinite; it is asymmetrical, dispersing, horizontal; it is not humanistic, but looks to the machine and the products of industry for its legitimacy; it speaks about MOVEMENT. To quote from Henry-Russell Hitchcock and Philip Johnson in *The international style*: «There is, first, a new conception of architecture as volume rather than as mass. Secondly, regularity rather than axial symmetry

serves as the chief means of ordering design. These two principles, with a third proscribing arbitrary applied decoration, mark the productions of the international style.»

Beyond the discipline of «regularity» as prescribed by Hitchcock and Johnson, modern architectural composition owes much to the aesthetics of the De Stijl movement and its images of picturesque compositions of planes balanced in space.

The three buildings analyzed here, built between 1928 and 1938 may, at will, be seen as essentially classical or essentially modern, just as the drawing of a vase may reveal two human profiles facing each other. Similarly our three buildings allow different readings which reveal contradictory symbols, integrated, synthesized and kept in

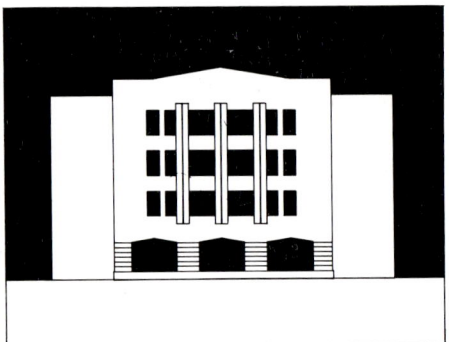
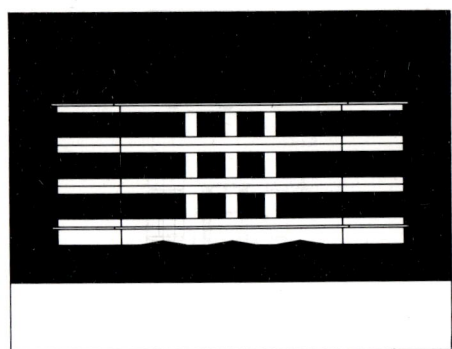

La Vigneronne Touraine
(F. BOLLACK)

tension in a whole.
What is modern about these buildings, and what is classical?
How are the elements of each language fused into a whole?
And why, in the first place, is this architecture worth taking seriously?
Let us look at our three buildings.

La Vigneronne Touraine **(16 b)**, a wine co-op in the south of France, was built in 1933[1] by George Salomon (1899-1976), a graduate of the Ecole Speciale d'Architecture in Paris[2].

It is a complex building which combines a classical composition with the signs of modernity. The symmetrical organization of a main *corps de logis* protruding over recessed wings, a simple tertiary composition, reveals itself to be a subtle counterpoint of tertiary and binary rhythms. At the center three triangular piers frame full width windows meant to be perceived as holes: we can thus read a loggia. However, the center is unexpectedly occupied by a solid — one of the three triangular piers — and the void slides beyond the boundaries of the portico itself, for the first windows outside the loggia are not separated from the piers by any masonry jamb. Then as one progresses toward the edges of the main block, the masonry jamb between the next two vertical windows — not a pier any more but not quite a wall yet either — provides a subtle transition between the hollow center and the solid walls which frame it. In these walls, forming the corners of the *corps de logis*, the windows are treated as punched openings, not as voids in a post and lintel system: the wall reasserts itself. This is not the condition at the corner of the wings where the edges are dematerialized — by rounding the corners in the area of the strip window on the left, and allowing the window to wrap around the corner on the right.

A flat cornice wall inflected into a pediment crowns the composition and wraps around the whole building.

The vertical emphasis of the three triangular piers flanked by two pairs of vertical windows is interwoven with two strong horizontal elements: the windows which are meant to read as a connected strip by the application of color banding (a part of the original design since it shows in an early photograph), and the line of the balconies which weave in and out of the piers — the impression of weaving is further reinforced by the triangular shape of the balconies at the center.

The emblematic elements of the classical tradition are there: a plain unadorned podium on which rests a three story classical temple with pediment, colonnade and rustications. However the archetype is subtly perverted with visual signs which are the hallmark of a modern building: the strip window, dematerialized corners, and a definite horizontal emphasis.

Henry Hohauser's[3] 1211 Pennsylvania Avenue in Miami Beach, **(1c)**, built in 1939[4], a fertile year for late Art Deco work, uses the compositional principles and

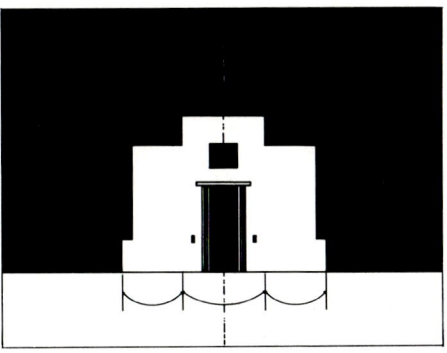
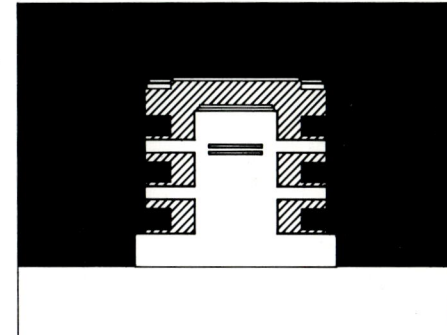

1211 Pennsylvania
Avenue - Miami Beach
(F. BOLLACK)

images of earlier European work[5]. It is decidedly a modern building although not devoid of classical references as around the entrance. The organization of the main elevation around a strong vertical *corps de logis* is beautifully accomplished.

The core of the building is a simple three story cube and, as in much similar work of the '30s, the architect has paid special attention to the issue of frontality and to the treatment of the corners. The corners are dematerialized by the use of corner windows which seem to be folded about the vertical edge that provides their axis of symmetry, the square corner post being set back not to be confused with the wall. The corners are further dematerialized by the treatment at the cornice where they have been cut back, revealing an «inner» cube with rounded edges. Thus the inner cube seems to be the core which holds the tightly applied planes of the outer cube. The center block which forms the entrance motif is a carefully balanced play of horizontals and verticals — the balconies vs. the center volume itself, the horizontal fins and lintel vs. the two story center panel and its pilasters. This massive expressionist volume with its miniature giant order framing the entrance presents an image quite different from the streamlined international style of the main body of the building: it is as though one style had been collaged onto another. Could it be that the architect felt the need to dignify a modern building with a neoclassical and expressionist entrance? Whatever the answer, the more traditional front seems to protect the modern cube.

A comparison with *La Vigneronne Touraine* might be instructive: whereas at *La Vigneronne Touraine* the architect organizes the building elements according to a Classical system of composition with parts related to each other in a hierarchical order, here the classical elements exist only as a vestige (the applied giant order at the entrance for example). Hohauser has played with signs and images exclusively: the image of the International Style; the image of the pediment; the image of speed (implied in the use of horizontal fins); the image of weightlessness (the cantilevered balconies).

Alberto Sartoris «Building for an Artisans' Community» **(7a)** at the 1928 Turin

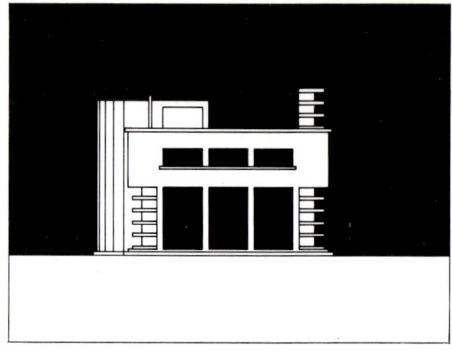

Comunità Autonome
Artigiane - Turin
(F. Bollack)

exhibition brings together the two poles of his education: his study at the Ecole des Beaux Arts in Geneva in 1919[6], and his involvement in the avant garde of modern achitecture.

The front façade is a perfect example of dual reading. If we choose to see a classical building, it is a two story pavilion, where the first floor portico is raised above the ground by a very attenuated stylobate. The second story, crowned by the most vestigial cornice, consists of three attic windows, not strip windows since the three ground floor pillars reassert themselves as part of the wall between each window, and since the group of three is limited to the extent of the portico below.

The fact that this open center, consisting of the portico and attic windows, is framed on the secod floor by masonry gives one possible clue for the interpretation of the horizontal blocks at the corner of the building at the ground floor. As they are located under the part of the second floor which is solid wall, they may be interpreted as rustications, reversed rustications however, where the usual (negative) joints between the stones are turned into the (positive) slabs. Their placement further reinforces their interpretation as rustications since, traditionally, the base of a building was where the architect sought to make the mass of the stone explicit by emphasizing its joints.

If we choose to see a modern building, the many visual *double entendres*, the ambiguities, reveal another mode. The four piers are more pilotis than columns, the rustications become speed fins, and a continuous masonry sill connects the three attic windows, emphasizing their horizontality. The «rustication fins» are interestingly recessed in both directions — they do not line up with the corner of the second story above, and they are recessed from the face of the adjacent pier — which reinforces the impression that the «garden goes under the house»: we are looking at a «house on pilotis»[7].

The volumetric composition, which is almost pure De Stijl is another modern element: its three discrete solids — the main building block, the half round bay, and the mast with horizontal fins — all address different views: in their spatial balance, they remind us of a drawing by Theo Van Doesburg[8].

In this building the integration of the modern and the classical is achieved not by weaving or layering as it is in *La Vigneronne Touraine* or at 1211 Pennsylvania Avenue, but by the use of «dual reading elements» which in turn affect the interpretation of the overall composition.

What we see at work in the three buildings we have examined is an inclusive process of accumulation, addition, integration: modern elements are woven in, added to, layered on the classical framework.

This integration is achieved by the use of «dual reading elements» (speed fins which may be read as rustication or pilotis which may be read as piers for example), by the use of a weaving process whereby modern symbols (the strip window for example, or horizontality) are threaded onto a classical framework (as at *La Vigneronne Touraine*), or by successive layering as at 1211 Pennsylvania Avenue where each thin layer admits of a different interpretation.

In general the center, or forward part, of a building will fulfill its representational function by being the most grounded and classical whereas the edges, or layers further from the viewer will demonstrate the highest degree of modernity (horizontality, dematerialized corners).

The consistent characteristic of these buildings is that in the battle of the future versus the past, the architect's position is inclusive: he gives us the best of both worlds.

We have analyzed three buildings located in Italy, the United States and in France: this book shows many more in other countries: why is it that this architecture is so international, when there is no evidence to show that it was a conscious movement? First of all, the many Exhibitions[9] of the beginning of the century proposed alternatives to avant garde modernism: these exhibitions were well publicized by architectural journals. Then, there are the combined factors of architectural education and of the irresistible promise of liberation that modernity offered.

An architect who graduated in the '20s and the '30s received an education structured on the Beaux Arts model: architects in Europe would have gone either to the Ecole itself or to a school, such as the Ecole Speciale d'Architecture de Paris (from which Robert Mallet Stevens and George Salomon graduated) whose curriculum was modelled on the Ecole's. Architects in the United States were equally under the Ecole's influence: Raymond Hood, who was a key figure, studied at the Ecole, whereas others such as Marvin Fine studied under a Beaux Arts architect (in his case Paul Cret).

Countries such as Morocco, or Egypt, were still under direct European influence (Morocco for example was then a French Protectorate where new buildings were often designed by architects from «La Metropole» — the main land — some of them Premiers Grands Prix de Rome).

The other factor — the irresistible promise of liberation that modernity offered — was also present internationally. There we must remember that the industrial revolution, the first world war, had brought changes of unbelievable magnitude: society had changed, the aeroplane more than any object symbolized the new age (it appears in Le Corbusier's early books with the regularity of an obsession). The old world was simply no longer adequate.

In this — international — climate, whereas the avant garde architect by stating the problem in terms of the new (new materials, new production methods, new means of locomotion) rendered inevitable a «revolutionary» architecture, the architects of our buildings assimilated the new and revolutionary with the memory of the antique, ensuring a vital cultural continuity.

F.A.B.

[1] This information was kindly provided to us by Mr. A. Brun, Director of La Vigneronne Touraine, in a letter dated October 13, 1980. «The Cave Vigneronne Touraine was built in 1933 by the Architect Salomon, D.E.S.A., Marseille with the contractor G. Laville from Avignon.
Starting capacity: 50,000 Hl.
No renovations except for the tanks. In 1940 a part was added under the Architect's supervision: a storage tank allowing a total capacity of 80,000 Hl.» (our translation)
Mr Brun indicates that some additional work was done under the supervision of Mr. Enjouvin, D.E.S.A., Marseille with the contractor Imberti from Pertuis in 1966, and later in 1979.
We are grateful to Mr Brun and to La Vigneronne Touraine for this information.
[2] Georges Salomon was born in 1899 and died in 1976.
He obtained his architectural degree form the Ecole Speciale d'Architecture (D.E.S.A.).
His works include: La Vigneronne Touraine, in La Tour d'Aigues, Vaucluse, France — 1933 — *Silo à Grain (Grain Silo), in Saint Vallier, Drome, France — 1933-34 — *Silo à Grain (Grain Silo), in Valencienne, Drome?, France — 1933-34 — *Silo à Grain (Grain Silo), in Chabeuil, Drome, France — 1933-34 —.
*We are indebted for this informations to the book *Rhône-Alpes* published by the Editions de l'Equerre in 1982 (in french).
This book was brought to our attention by Anne Astorg.
[3] Henry Hohauser was born May 27, 1895 in New York City, and died March 31, 1963 in Lawrence, Long Island, New York.
It is possible that he graduated from Pratt Institute in Brooklyn, N.Y.

For these facts we are indebted to the book: *Modern/Moderne/Modernistic Miami Beach Hotel Architecture/Circa 1940* by Jewel Stern/Project Skyline, published by the Museum of Modern Art, Oxford, 1982, and first published by the Akron Art Institute.
Refer to this book for additional information about buildings in Miami Beach and their architects.
[4.] *Portfolio, Miami Beach,* Art Deco Historic District; Editor: Barbara Baer Capitman; Publisher: Bucolo Preservation Press, 1979.
[5.] See *Dessins sur le thème 'Une Cité Moderne'*, circa 1924, by the architect Robert Mallet-Stevens, especially «L'Hotel».
These were published anew in: *Robert Mallet Stevens, Architecte* by Editions Archive d'Architecture Moderne, in 1980.
[6.] For additional biographical information as well as for other works of Alberto Sartoris, refer to: - Pamphlet Architecture #10, *Alberto Sartoris, Metafisica delle Architetture*; published by Pamphlet Architecture Ltd., a nonprofit Corporation — New York 1984 — English translation by Ty Geltmaker and Diane Ghirardo; *Progetti e Assonometrie di Alberto Sartoris* published by Officina Edizioni, Rome, in 1982 (in italian).
[7.] See *Le Corbusier et Pierre Jeanneret, oeuvre complète de 1910-1929,* published by W. Boesiger and O. Stonorov, 1956 edition by Les Editions Girsberger — Zurich, p. 128:
«Les cinq points d'une architecture nouvelle» (the five points of a new architecture).
1. Les pilotis
… La maison sur pilotis! La maison s'enfonçait dans le sol: locaux obscures et souvent humides. Le ciment armé nous donne des pilotis! La maison est en l'air, loin du sol; le jardin passe sous la maison, le jardin est aussi sur la maison, sur le toit.»
The pilotis.
… The house on pilotis! The house was sinking into the ground: dark quarters, and often humid. Reinforced concrete gives us the pilotis! The house is in the air, far from the ground; the garden passes under the house, the garden is also on the house, on the roof, (our translation).
[8.] In a biographical note written on the occasion of a show of Alberto Sartoris' drawings at Pratt Insitute (curator: Livio Dimitriu), Dennis Doordan indicates that in 1921 Alberto Sartoris «began to correspond regulary with Theo Van Doesburg».
[9.] Most notably:
1925: Exposition des Arts decoratifs et Industriels Modernes, Paris.
1930: Stockholm Exhibition (whose theme was «Housing, Transportation, Furnishings»). See for a very insightful comment on this exhibition *The Architecture of Erik Gunnar Asplund* by Stuart Wrede, published by the MIT Press, Cambridge Massachusetts and London, England, 1980, pp. 127-138.
Regarding the Stockholm exhibition, it is interesting to note that Francis Keally, the architect of the Brooklyn Public Library **(9c),** wrote a review of it in the December issue of The American Architect in December 1930 (entitled «My Impression of the Stockholm Exhibition»).
1927: Weissenhof Siedlung in Stuttgart.
1924: For Siedlungen built in Germany between 1924 and 1927, see *Wohnbauten und Siedlungen aus Deutscher Gegenwart* by Walter Müller-Wulckow, published by Karl Robert Langewiesche in the collection «Die Blauen Bücher» (in german).
1937: Exposition Internationale des Arts et des Techniques de la Vie Moderne, Paris.
For the impact of exhibitions on american architects, see «EXHIBITIONS» in the chapter «The City as Theater», in the book *New York 1930, Architecture and Urbanism between the two world wars* by Robert A.M. Stern, Gregory Gilmartin, and Thomas Mellins, published by Rizzoli International Publications, Inc., 1987.
See the book *Exposition Internationale des Arts et des Techniques de la vie moderne, Paris 1937, Cinquantenaire* published by the Institut Français d'Architecture/Paris-Musées, 1987 (in french).

EVERYDAY MASTERPIECES
Photographic itinerary

CLASSICAL AND MODERN AS PURE CONTRAST
GRAVITY VS. ANTI-GRAVITY

1a
Counter-constructive analysis of ta Maison particulière
1923
Theo van Doesburg (1883-1931)
van Doesburg Collection, Rijksdienst Beeldende Kunst (AB 5122), The Hague, Holland

1b
Temple of Poseidon
Paestum, Italy
c. 460-450 B.C.

CLASSICAL AND MODERN AS COMPLEMENTARY
GRAVITY AND ANTI-GRAVITY

1c
Apartment building
1211 Pennsylvania Avenue, Miami Beach, Fla.,
U.S.A.
1939 (MDPL)
Henry Hohauser (1895 or 1896-1963)

PERSISTENCE OF THE CLASSICAL IN MODERN ARCHITECTURE
OVERT

2a
Bronx County Building
Grand Concourse, Bronx, New York, U.S.A.
design 1931 or 1932, built 1933 (cornerstone) -
1934 (Stern)
Freedlander (1870-1943) & Hausle

VS. TRANSFORMED

2b
Villa
31 rue de la Haye, Casablanca, Morocco
c. 1930-1940

VARIATIONS ON THE THEME OF THE COLONNADE

3a
Project (facade) for the competition for the pavilion of the U.S.S.R. at the Exposition des Arts décoratifs et industriels modernes, Paris, 1925
1924
Ivan Aleksandrovič Fomin (1872-1936)
Gnima, Moscow, U.S.S.R.

3b
School for Rhythmic Gymnastics (Dalcroze Institut)
Hellerau, Dresden, D.D.R.
1910-1911
Heinrich Tessenow (1876-1950)

28

THE TEMPLE

OVERT VS. TRANSFORMED

4a
Maritime Terminal
Trieste, Italy
1926-1928
Umberto Nordio (1891-1971)

4b
Bus Kiosk
Porte de la Villette, Paris, France

THE PORTICO

OVERT VS. TRANSFORMED

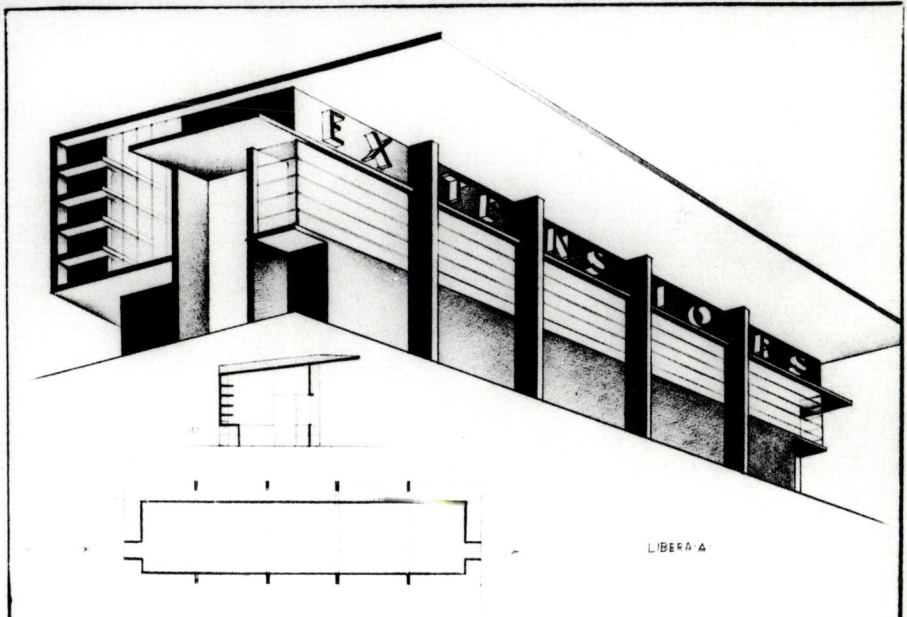

4c
Unexecuted project for the New Theater of Udine
Udine, Italy
1934
Cesare Pascoletti (1898-1986)

4d
Project for a pavilion for the exhibition «Extensiors»
Iª Esposizione Italiana di Architettura Razionale
Rome, Italy
1928
Adalberto Libera (1903-1963)

THE PIER WALL

OVERT VS. TRANSFORMED

5a
Post Office Madison Square Branch
East 23rd St., New York, U.S.A.
1935 (cornerstone) - 1937 (Stern)
Lorimer Rich

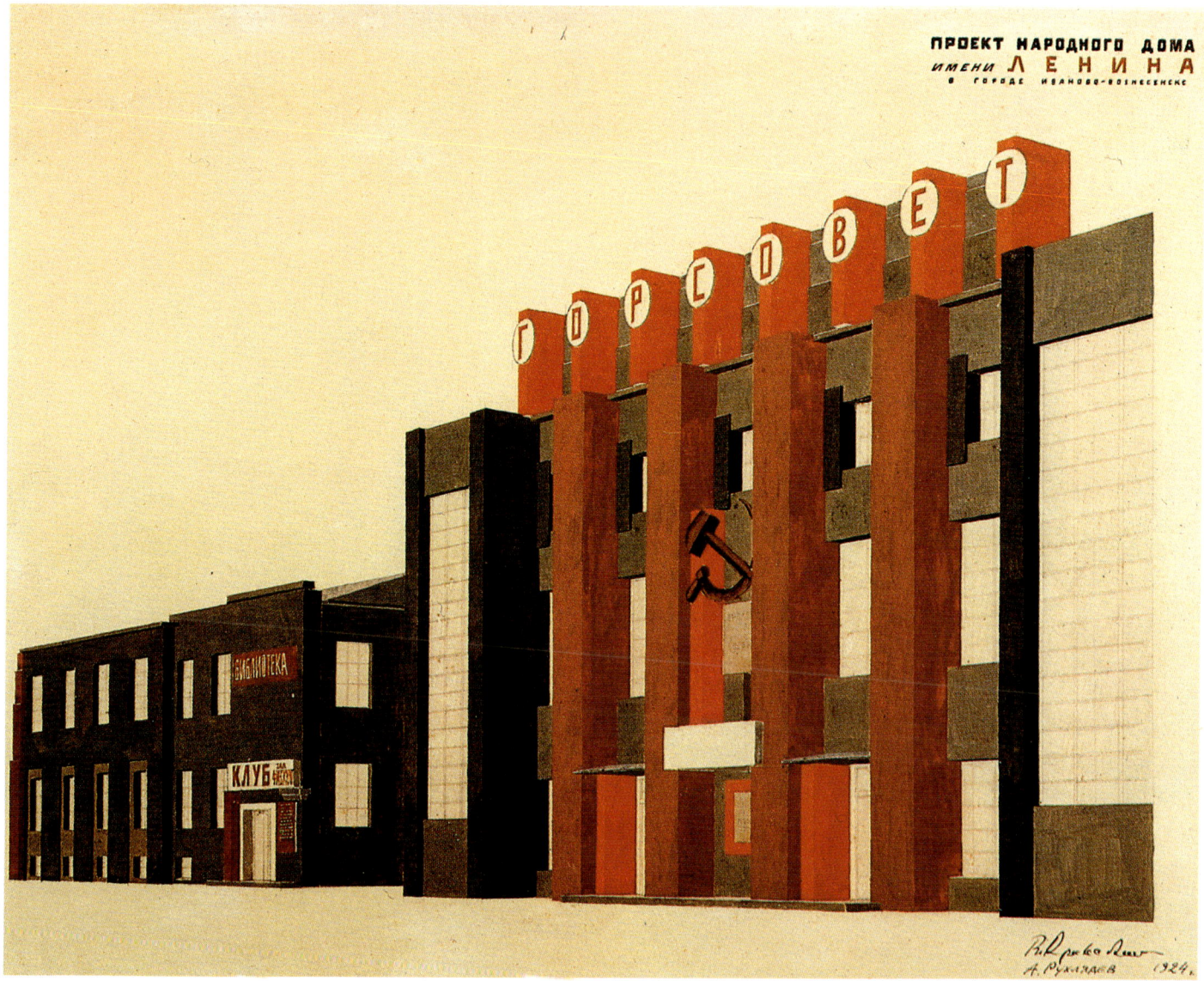

5b
Project for the V.I. Lenin Working People's
House competition
Ivanovo - Voznesensk
1924
Vladimir Fedorovič Krinskij (1890-1971)
Gnima, Moscow, U.S.S.R.

6a
Town Hall
Villeurbanne (Lyon), France
competition 1930, built 1931-1934
Robert Giroud (1890-?)

THE FREESTANDING
COLONNADE

6b
Padiglione della Stampa
V Triennale di Milano, Milan, Italy
1933
Luciano Baldessari (1896-1982)

7a
Building for the Comunità Autonome Artigiane
Esposizione del Valentino, Turin, Italy
1928
Alberto Sartoris (1901)

THE CENTERED FACADE
WITH PORTICO:
THE PAVILION

7b
Design for a gateway to a city
c. 1800
Staatliche Schlösser, Sans-Souci (Inv. no. 899)
Potsdam, D.D.R.
Friedrich Gilly (1772-1800)

7c
Villa Lazienkowskiego
Warsaw, Poland
1784

THE CENTERED FACADE

8a
Union Railroad Terminal
Cincinnati, Ohio, U.S.A.
1929-1933 (Wilson)
Fellheimer & Wagner

8b
The Cisternone
Livorno, Italy
1829-1842
Pasquale Poccianti (1774-1858)

VARIATIONS ON THE ISSUE OF SYMMETRY: THE URBAN FACADE

THE CENTERED FACADE WITH WINGS

9a
UOP Fragrances Factory (formerly Knickerbocker Laundry)
Dreyer Ave., Long Island city, Queens, New York, U.S.A.
1931 (BDR) - 1932 (Stern)
Irving M. Fenichel

9b
Dulwich Art Gallery, second project, western perspective
London, England
1811 (July 12th)
John Soane (1753-1837)
Sir John Soane's Museum, London, England

THE CENTERED FACADE
WITH PORTICO

9c
Public Library
Grand Army Plaza, Brooklyn, New York, U.S.A.
1937-1941 (Stern)
Alfred Githens, Francis Keally

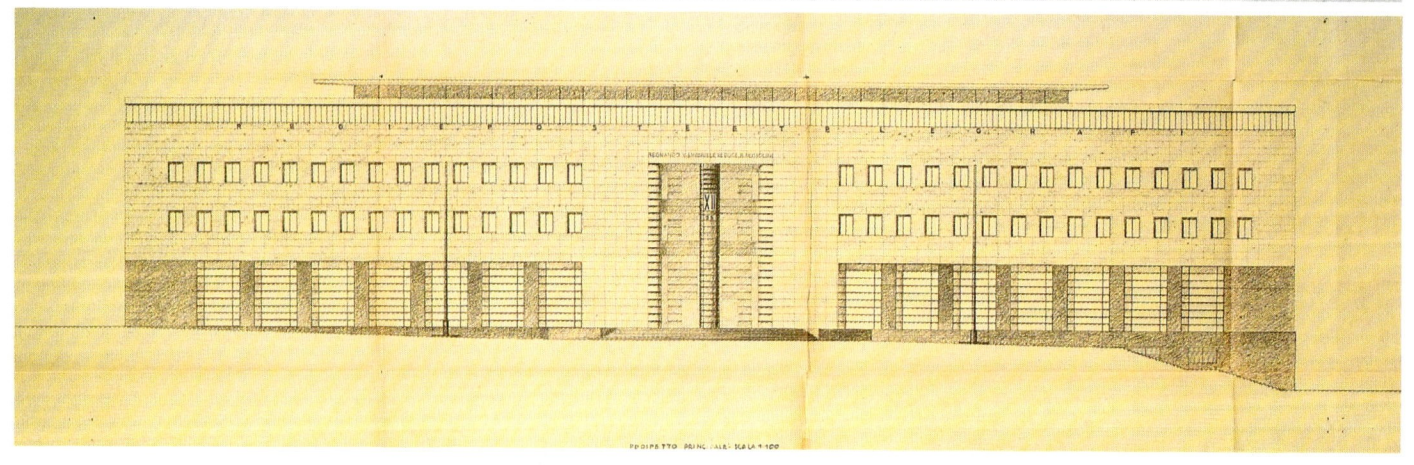

THE CURVED FACADE

10a-10b
Central Post Office
Naples, Italy
1929-1935
Giuseppe Vaccaro (1896-1971), Gino Franzi (1898-1973)

10c
«Les Tilleuls» (La Rotonde)
11-19 rue Charles Giron, Geneva, Switzerland
1928-1929
Maurice Braillard (1879-1965)

10d
Project for a Circus, plan of the second solution
Etienne-Louis Boullée (1728-1799)
Bibliothèque Nationale, Cabinet des Estampes,
Ha 55, n. 22, Paris, France

THE CURVED FACADE

11a
Casa della Giovane Italiana
Gorizia, Italy
1934
Gino Miozzo (1898-1969), Francesco Mansutti (1899-1969)

11b
Palazzo delle Corporazioni
Cosenza, Italy
1936
Mario De Renzi (1897-1967), Giorgio Calza Bini (1909)

THE CURVED FACADE

12a
Post Office in the Milvio Quarter
Viale Mazzini, Rome, Italy
1932
Armando Titta

12b
Villa Jeanne Michele
Marrakesh, Morocco
c. 1930-1940

46

THE MULTI-CENTERED
FACADE OR BUILDING

13a
Apartment building
Lungotevere Flaminio 78-80, Rome, Italy
c. 1936
Gra

THE BENT TEMPLE

13b-13c
Tunnel Garage
Broome St., New York, U.S.A.
1922 (facade)
Hector Hamilton (BDR)

THE CURVED CORNER
AS A CENTER

14a
Hecht Warehouse
Washington D.C., U.S.A.
1937 (Greif)
Abbot, Merkt & Co.

14b
Bank of England, Lothbury front
London, England
1795
John Soane (1753-1837)
Sir John Soane's Museum (DR, xii,1.1.),
London, England

14c
Covered Market
Via Carducci, Trieste, Italy
1935
Camillo Iona (1886-1974)

THE CURVED CORNER

15a
Apartment building
1150 Grand Concourse, Bronx, New York,
U.S.A.
1937 (Sullivan)
Hyman I. Feldman (1899-?)

15b
House of the Mchat
Brjusovskij Alley, Moscow, U.S.S.R.
1928
Aleksej Viktorovič Ščusev (1873-1949)
Gnima, Moscow, U.S.S.R

THE CENTERED FACADE
WITH DEMATERIALIZED
CORNERS

16a
Apartment building
Via Morghen 37, Naples, Italy
1937

16b
La Vigneronne Touraine (wine cooperative)
La tour d'Aigues, Vaucluse, France
1933 (owner)
Georges Salomon (1899-1976) D.E.S.A.

THE CENTERED FACADE:
VERTICAL CENTER/
HORIZONTAL EDGES

17a
Apartment building
Viale Michelangelo 50, Naples, Italy
1939
Ferdinando Chiaromonte (1902-1985)

17b
Apartment building
Via Tasso 203, Naples, Italy
c. 1938
Tommaso Cotronei (1902-1984)

THE CENTERED FACADE:
VERTICAL CENTER/
HORIZONTAL EDGES

18a
Apartment building
1500 Grand Concourse, Bronx, New York,
U.S.A.
1935 (Sullivan)
Jacob M. Felson (1866-1962)

18b
Botanical Institute
Città Universitaria, Rome, Italy
1932-1935
Giuseppe Capponi (1893-1936)

THE URBAN FACADE: RETURN TO ESSENTIALITY

19a
Warehouse (destroyed)
Gerard Avenue, Bronx, New York, U.S.A.
after 1931
Irving M. Fenichel (attributed)

19b
Entrance Gateway
Tyringham Hall, Buckinghamshire, England
1793-1801
John Soane (1753-1837)

THE URBAN FACADE: MODERN COMBINATIONS

20a
Women's Prison
Würzburg, Germany
1809
Peter Speeth (1777-1831)

20b
Tiffany & Co. Store
57th St. & Fifth Avenue, New York, U.S.A.
1939-1940 (Stern)
Cross & Cross

THE FACADE AS A CITY
WALL WITH TOWERS

21a
Project for «Intérieur de ville de guerre»
Etienne-Louis Boullée (1728-1799)
Bibliothèque Nationale, Cabinet des Estampes
(Ha 55, pl. 31), Paris, France

21b
Karl Marx-Hof
Vienna, Austria
1927
Karl Ehn

21c
Building of the Gioventù Italiana del Littorio
(G.I.L.)
Foro Italico, Rome, Italy
c. 1937
C. Costantini (?- 1986)

64

THE ELEMENTS
HERALDIC ELEMENTS

22a
Garage Citroën
Latina, Italy
Oriolo Frezzotti (1888-?)

22b
The Oath of the Horatii
1782
Jacques-Louis David (1748-1825)
Musée des Beaux-Arts, Lille, France

HERALDIC ELEMENTS

23a
Greystone Hotel
Collins Avenue, Miami Beach, Fla., U.S.A.
1939 (MDPL)
Henry Hohauser (1895 or 1896-1963)

23b
«Vue d'un Rocher élevé dans le centre du Camp
de Fédération...Lyon le 30 Mai 1790...»
1790
Claude Cochet le Jeune (1715-1790)
Musée Carnavalet, Pc. Hist. 11 B, Paris, France

HERALDIC ELEMENTS

24a
Essex House Hotel
Collins Avenue, Miami Beach, Fla., U.S.A.
1938 (MDPL)
Henry Hohauser (1895 or 1896-1963)

24b
Kirchgemeindehaus Wipkingen mit Post und
Wohnungen
Rosengartenstrasse 1, Zürich, Switzerland
1930-1932
Vogelsanger, Maurer

24c
Nelson's Pillar
1818
Francis Johnston (1761-1829)
Murray Collection, National Library of Ireland
(A.D. 2088), Dublin, Ireland

HERALDIC ELEMENTS

25a
Pan Pacific Auditorium
7600 Beverly Boulevard, Los Angeles, Calif., U.S.A.
1935-1938 (Gebhard)
Wurdeman & Becket

25b
Villa
Avenue Mohammed V, Safi, Morocco
c. 1930-1940

HERALDIC ELEMENTS

26a
Project for a pavilion of building materials
I Esposizione Italiana di Architettura Razionale
Rome, Italy
1928
Guido Frette (1901-1986)

26b
Ferdinand Buisson High School
Boulogne, Seine, France
1932 (cornerstone)
Cauvet & Ogé (cornerstone)

74

RUSTICATION

27a
Rose Court Apartments
Bennet Avenue, New York, U.S.A.
1936 (BDR)
Horace Ginsbern (1900-1969) (BDR) with
Marvin Fine (1904-1981)

27b
Apartment building
1791 Grand Concourse, Bronx, New York, U.S.A.
1936 (Sullivan)
Edward Franklin

27c
Barrière des Ministres
1785-1789
Claude-Nicolas Ledoux (1736-1806)

27d
Entrance to an Arsenal (model)
1785
Carl August Ehrensvärd (1745-1800)
Marin Museum, Karlskrona, Sweden

RUSTICATION

28a
Montezemolo Barracks
Via A. Baiamonti, Rome, Italy
c. 1938
Vittorio Cafiero (1901-1981)

28b
Newgate Gaol (demolished in 1902)
London, England
1769
George Dance the Younger (1741-1825)

28c
Hôtel des Monnaies (lateral facade)
Rue Guénégaud, Paris, France
1768-1775
Jacques-Denis Antoine (1773-1801)

28d
Butler Brothers Warehouse
Jersey City, N.J., U.S.A.
c. 1905
Jarvis Hunt (C. Wyatt)

LETTERING AS RUSTICATION

29a
Project for a building in Piazza San Babila
Milan, Italy
1934
Aldo Andreani (1887-1971)

29b
Design for the Campari Pavilion
1931
Fortunato Depero (1892-1960)

THE STRIP WINDOW
AS RUSTICATION

30a
Starrett-Lehigh Building, Warehouse
W. 26th to W. 27th St.,
Eleventh to Twelvth Aves.
New York, U.S.A.
c. 1930-1931 (Stern)
R.G. & William Cory with Y. Matsui

30b-30c
Apartment building
127-129, Avenue Moulay Hassan I, Casablanca,
Morocco
1934 (cornerstone)
J. Balois & P. Perrotte (cornerstone)

THE STRIP WINDOW
AS RUSTICATION

31a
Fiat Garage
Ave. Lalla Yaquote & Mutapha El Maani
Casablanca, Morocco

31b
Ibex House
42 Minories, EC3
London, England
1937
Fuller, Hall and Foulsham (Jones & Woodward)

THE TUSCAN/RUSTIC ORDER

32a
Spear & Company Store
22 West 34th St., New York, U.S.A.
1933-1934 (Stern)
De Young & Moscowitz

32b
House of the Director, detail of the portico
Salt Works
Chaux, Arcs et Senans, France
1775-1790
Claude-Nicolas Ledoux (1736-1806)

THE GIANT ORDER

33a
Apartment building
Via Barnaba Oriani 91, Rome, Italy
1936
Bianchini

33b
Villa
Via Aniello Falcone, Naples, Italy
1938
Tommaso Cotronei (1902-1984)

THE GIANT ORDER

34a
Daché Building (destroyed)
East 56th St., New York, U.S.A.
1936 (BDR) — 1937 (Stern)
Shreve, Lamb & Harmon (BDR)

34b
J. Kurtz & Sons Department Store
162 Jamaica Avenue, Queens, New York,
U.S.A.
Built 1931
Allmendinger & Schlendorf (LPC)

THE GIANT ORDER

35a
Cinema
Amiens, France

35b
Colonia Marittima «Villa Rosa Maltoni
Mussolini»
Calambrone, Tirrenia, Italy
1925-1933
Angiolo Mazzoni (1894-1979)

36a
Apartment building
Cairo, Egypt
c. 1930-1940
R. Antonius, architect/engineer (cornerstone)

36b
Apartment building
Heliopolis, Egypt

THE GIANT ORDER

THE HALF ROUND BAY

36c
Villa
Rabat, Morocco
c. 1930-1940

THE HALF ROUND BAY

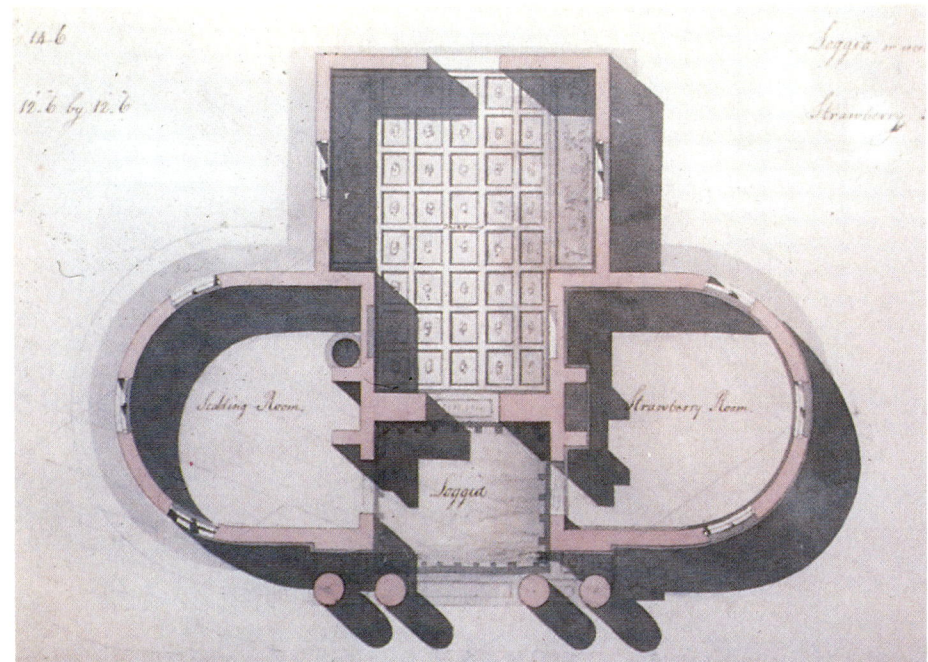

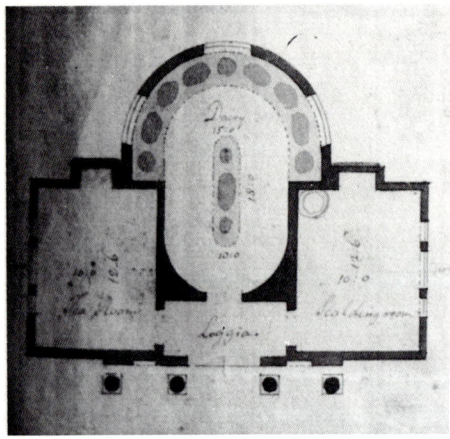
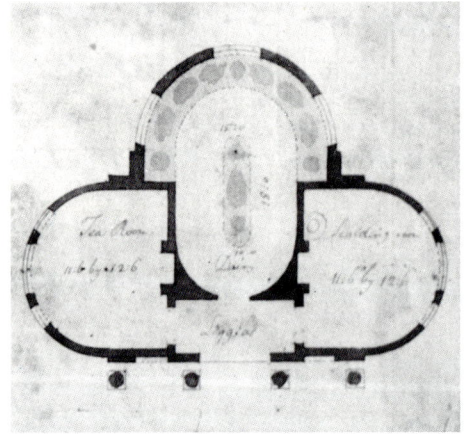

37a-37b
Hammels Park dairy, Hertfordshire, plan
1783
John Soane (1753-1837)
Sir John Soane's Museum (Al Designs for various Buildings by John Soane Architect, 1789-1794, Item 6 and 7), London, England

Rustic dairy, two alternatives
1781
John Soane (1753-1837)
Victoria and Albert Museum (3306,161) London, England

37c
Perrigny-Poste 1, Railroad Switching Station
Dijon, France

THE HALF ROUND BAY
AS HERALDIC ELEMENT

38a
Traffic Tower project
Berlin, Germany
1924 (Schulze)
Ludwig Mies van der Rohe

38b
Ristorante Cora
Fiera Campionaria di Bari
Bari, Italy
Nicolaj Diulgheroff (1901-1982)

"ARCHITECTURE PARLANTE"

39a
Motorboating Association
A.M.I.LA Club
Tremezzo, Italy
1926-1927
Pietro Lingeri (1894-1968)

MODERN DISPERSION: BUILDINGS AS VEHICLES

39b
Maison destinée aux Surveillants de la Source de la Loue, vue perspective
in Claude-Nicolas Ledoux, *L'architecture...*,
1804, pl. 6
Claude-Nicolas Ledoux (1736-1806)

39c
Heliotherapeutic Colony
Cattolica, Italy
1933
Clemente Busiri-Vici (1877-1965)

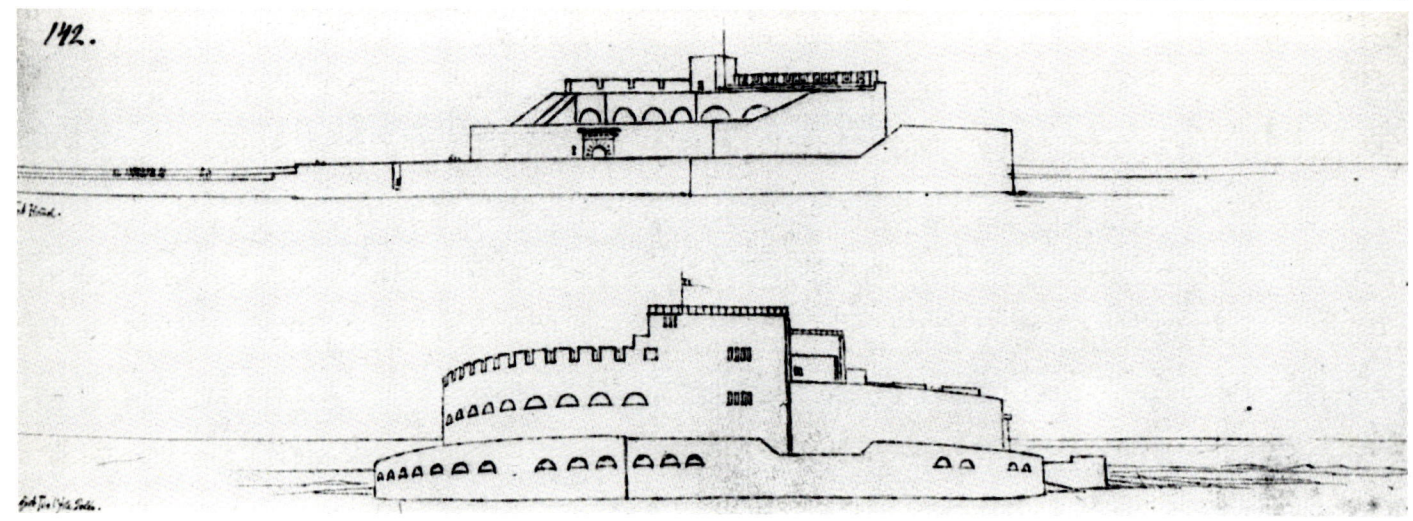

DYNAMIC COMPOSITION:
BUILDING AS SHIPS

40a
Fort Hommel und Fort sur l'Isle Pelee
1797
Friedrich Gilly (1772-1800)
Destroyed, formerly in the Technische
Hochschule, Charlottenburg, Berlin, B.D.R.

40b
«G. Nicelli» Airport
Venice, Lido, Italy
1932

40c
Castello d'acqua decorated by a public fountain
1780
August Cheval de St. Hubert (1755-1798)
Accademia di Belle Arti, Parma, Italy

DYNAMIC COMPOSITION:
BUILDING AS SHIPS

41a
Apartment building
1360 Montgomery St., San Francisco, Calif.,
U.S.A.
1937 (Gebhard)
J.S. Malloch developer/contractor

41b
Maritime Museum
San Francisco, Calif., U.S.A.
1936?-1939 (Gebhard)
William Mooser & son

DYNAMIC COMPOSITION:
BUILDING AS SHIPS

42a
Italian Pavilion at the Chicago World's Fair
1933
Adalberto Libera (1903-1963), Mario De Renzi (1897-1967)

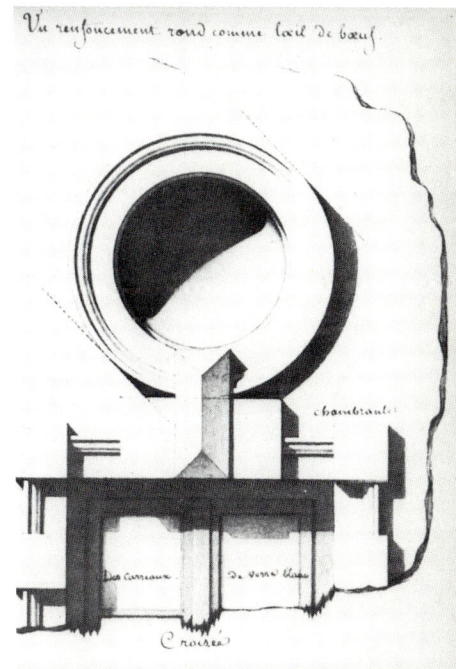

42b
Coca Cola Bottling Co.,
Los Angeles, Calif., U.S.A.
1936-1937 (Gebhard)
Robert V. Derrah

42c
«Un renfoncement rond comme l'oeil de boeuf»,
in JEAN-JACQUES LEQUEU, *Architecture civile*, pl.
21,59
Jean-Jacques Lequeu (1756-1825)
Bibliothèque Nationale, Cabinet des Estampes
(Ha 80, pl. 21, 59), Paris, France

THE PICTURESQUE COMPOSITION

43a
Pavilion of Bellevue
«Le Rendez-vous de Bellevue est à la pointe du Rocher»
Jean-Jacques Lequeu (1756-1825)
Bibliothèque Nationale, Cabinet des Estampes, Fonds Lequeu (Ha 80 fol., pl. 55), Paris, France

43b
Project for the competition for the Central Telegraph and Broadcast Station
Tverskaja Street (now Gor'kij Street)
1925
Aleksej Viktorovič Ščusev (1873-1949)
Gnima, Moscow, U.S.S.R.

44a
Casa del Combattente
Piazza Oberdan, Trieste, Italy
1929-1934
Umberto Nordio (1891-1971)

44b
Harmonious scale of buildings, unified with reflected structures: union of dynamic and static forms
1927-1928
Jakov Georgievič Černichov (1899-1951)
Černichov Family, Moscow, U.S.S.R.

45a
Union of single elements of a structure in a harmonious building. Visual characteristic of simplified structures with soft tonalities
1932
Jakov Georgievič Černichov (1899-1951)
Černichov Family, Moscow, U.S.S.R.

45b
Miroiterie (mirror shop)
Rabat, Morocco
c. 1930-1940

46a
Building of the Opera Nazionale Balilla (O.N.B.)
Gorizia, Italy
1928
Umberto Cuzzi (1891-1973)

46b
Project for the competition of the Lenin Working People's House
Ivanovo-Voznesensk
1924
Il'ja Aleksandrovič Golosov (1883-1945)
Gnima, Moscow, U.S.S.R.

47a
Warsaw Ballroom (formerly Hoffman's Cafeteria)
Collins Avenue, Miami Beach, Fla., U.S.A.
1940 (MDPL)
Henry Hohauser (1895 or 1896-1963)

47b
Casa della Gioventù in Trastevere
Rome, Italy
1933-1937
Luigi Moretti (1907-1973)

48a
Le Village de Maupertuis, vue perspective
c. 1800
Claude-Nicolas Ledoux (1736-1806)
Archives de Seine-et-Marne, Paris, France

THE NEW "QUARTIER"

48b
Bernstein Apartments
530-550 15th St., Miami Beach, Fla., U.S.A.
1938 (MDPL)
Henry Hohauser (1895 or 1896-1963)

48c
Townhouse Development
Elmhurst, Queens, New York, U.S.A.
1931-1940 (BDR)
George X. Mathews, developer/contractor

49a
Dade Boulevard Fire Station
Miami Beach, Fla., U.S.A.
c. 1939
R.L. Weed & E.T. Reeder

49b
Propylées de Paris, «vue perspective»
in Claude-Nicolas Ledoux, *L'architecture...*,
1847, pl. 157
Claude-Nicolas Ledoux (1736-1806)

49c
Don-Bar Apartments
1571-1573 Pennsylvania Avenue, Miami Beach, Fla., U.S.A.
1937 (MDPL)
Albert Anis (1889-1964)

49d
Maison de campagne, «vue perspective»
in Claude-Nicolas Ledoux, *L'architecture…*,
1804, pl. 29
Claude-Nicolas Ledoux (1736-1806)

HORIZONTAL BANDING:
FORM AND SPACE

50a
Townhouse
East 74th St., New York, U.S.A.

50b
Kesandra & South Shore Apartments
1525-1531 & 1535-1539 Pennsylvania Avenue,
Miami Beach, Fla., U.S.A.
1935 (MDPL)
Roy France (1888-1972)

51a
Apartment building
1425 Meridian (left) & 735 14th Place (right),
Miami Beach, Fla., U.S.A.
1425 Meridian 1936 (?) (MDPL)
Henry Hohauser (1895 or 1896-1963)

THE CENTERED FACADE

51b
Apartment building
7159 and 7163 Eastlawn St., Cincinnati, Ohio, U.S.A.
c. 1945-1950

51c
«Maison Bélanger», Paris
in J.Ch. Krafft, N. Ransonnette, *Plans...*, n.d., pl. 4
1787
François-Joseph Bélanger (1744-1818)

52a
Claire Apartments
1350-1354 Euclid Avenue, Miami Beach, Fla.,
U.S.A.
c. 1935-1940

THE MULTI-CENTERED
BUILDING: RECESSED CENTER

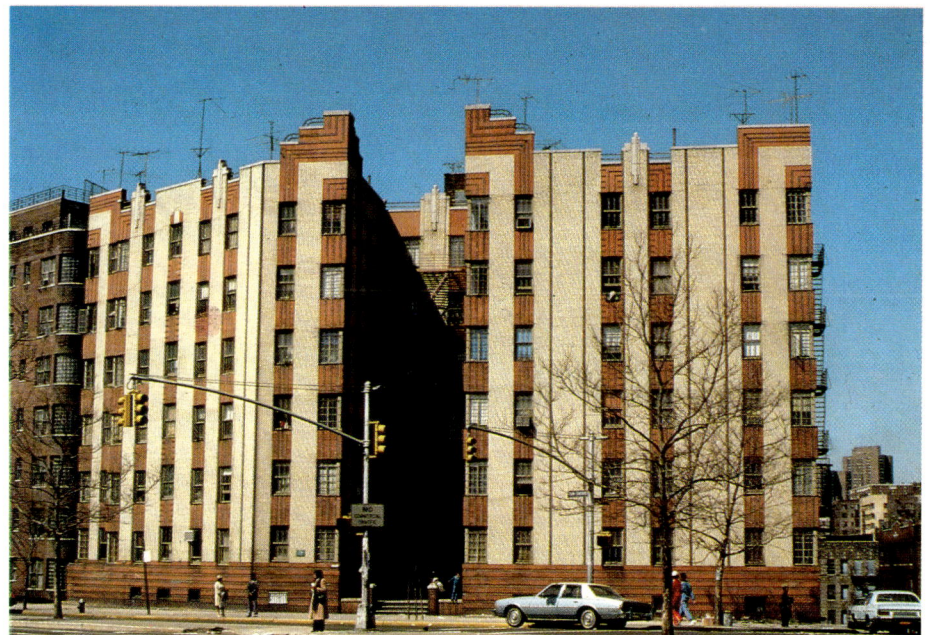

52b
Maison no. 14
in Louis-Ambroise Dubut, *Architecture civile...*,
1803, pl. 30
Louis-Ambroise Dubut (1769-1846)

52c
Apartment building
1791 Grand Concourse, Bronx, New York,
U.S.A.
1936 (Sullivan)
Edward Franklin

53a
Crest Hotel (left) & Chatham Apartments (right)
James St., Miami Beach, Fla., U.S.A.
1941 (MDPL)
Edward A. Noland

53b
Apartment building
Via Tasso 193, Naples, Italy
1934-1935
Giulio Rossi (1912)

BUILDING AS GARDEN
(BALCONIES, TRELLISES)

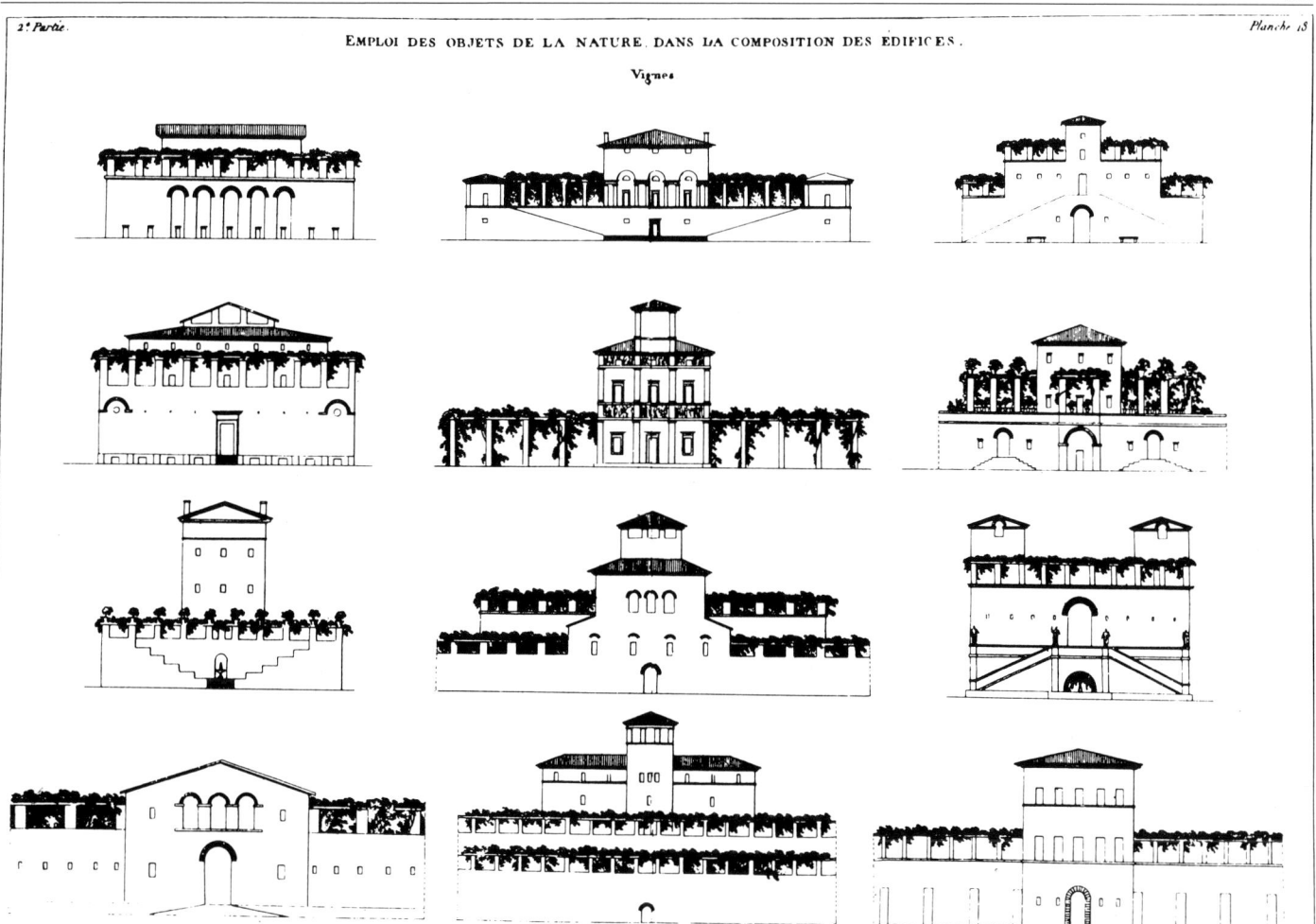

53c
Emploi des objects de la nature dans la composition des edifices. Vignes
in JEAN-NICOLAS-LOUIS DURAND, *Précis...*, 1823, pl. 18
Jean-Nicolas-Louis Durand (1760-1834)

RETURN TO ESSENTIALITY

54a-54b
Surfside Garden Apartments
Surfside, Miami Beach, Fla., U.S.A.

55a
Apartment building
Collins Avenue, Miami Beach, Fla., U.S.A.
c. 1935-1940

55b
Helen Marie Apartments
1050-1056 Jefferson Avenue, Miami Beach, Fla.,
U.S.A.
1948 (MDPL)
L. Murray Dixon (1901-1949)

56a
Euclid Place Apartments
1227-1231 Euclid Avenue, Miami Beach, Fla.,
U.S.A.
c. 1939
Henry Hohauser (1895 or 1896-1963)
(attributed)

THE PLAY OF VOLUMES

56b
Villa Schiozzi
Via Manzoni 36, Gorizia, Italy
1933
Umberto Cuzzi (1891-1973)

56c
Project for a National Theatre
c. 1800
Friedrich Gilly (1772-1800)
Technische Hochschule, Charlottenburg, Berlin,
B.D.R.

57a
Warsaw Ballroom (formerly Hoffman's Cafeteria)
Collins Avenue, Miami Beach, Fla., U.S.A.
1940 (MDPL)
Henry Hohauser (1895 or 1896-1963)

CAMING BACK TO THE BEGINNING

57b
Temple of Poseidon
Paestum, Italy
c. 460-450 B.C.

THEMATIC ESSAYS
WITH CATALOGUE ENTRIES

The thematic essays have been organized by J. Raspi Serra and N. Zanni.

CLASSICAL AND MODERN AS PURE CONTRAST
CLASSICAL AND MODERN AS COMPLEMENTARY
1a; 1b; 1c.

The essence of the Classical as a volumetric entity contains the principle of elementary geometric forms which imposes itself on the natural space. Classical is here opposed to modern, not as ancient opposed to new but as closed form against open form seen as the free insertion of volume in the environment. In this sense Classical and Modern come from Greek Revival and Picturesque architecture; both originate in the 18th century interpretative conquest of the individualistic architectural ideal: architecture as volume, architecture as movement. 20th century aesthetical theory ties Classical to static architectures conceived as an opposition to movement. «The Classical was concerned with the static build-up of absolute form, the Baroque with movement over the wholesurface of the composition». In the words used by Doig commenting Theo van Doesburg's *Classical-baroque-modern* (1920). The source of this opposition stems from Wöllflin's *Principle of Art History* (1915): «after great contrast between linear and painterly style corresponds to radically different interests in the world...»[1]. Classical and modern, as a principal of opposition and unity reveals its origin in the tension of the relationships that the new Greek «truth» established in the second half of the 18th century. It is known how, besides the pluralism of the 19th century, architecture renewed itself by finding in its past — the reasons for each form. The task is, now, to rediscover the underground path that, rooted in the «revolutionary» interpretations, reverberates in the modern vocabulary as remembrance or invention: everyday architecture proposes an interpretation of the main examples, sometimes reconstructing it in a synthesis, sometimes breaking it up in constituent elements.

J.R.S.

[1] See: Doig, 1986, p. 20 also for the quotation from Wöllflin.

1a - Counter-constructive analysis of a Maison particulière
1923
Theo van Doesburg (1883-1931)
Van Doesburg Collection, Rijksdienst Beeldende Kunst (AB 5122), The Hague, Holland
Bibl.: Doig, 1986, fig. 60, pp. 156-157

«Van Doesburg's new conception of architecture was the ultimate conclusion of his fight against stylistic historicism. The previous acceptance by architects of styles as *a priori* formulae prompted van Doesburg to call his conception of a new architecture "astylar" and formless. "The coloured planes of a painting which delimit each other and hold each other in strict, right-angled, determinate proportionality, remove once and for all the idea of form. The same applied to architecture in terms of strict, determined and compositionally balanced bodies in space» (Th. van Doesburg, 1921)[1].

[1] See Doig, 1986, pp. 156, 132, 157, 161; also for the quotations from Th. van Doesburg («De beteekenis der mechanische esthetick voor de architectuur en de andere vakken», *Bouwkundig Weekblad,* XLII, n. 28 (9 July 1921), 183 and «L'Evolution de l'architecture moderne en Hollande», L'Architecture vivante», III, n. 9 (Autumn and Winter, 1925), 14-20).

1b - Temple of Poseidon
460-450 B.C.
Paestum, Italy

1c - Apartment building
1211 Pennsylvania Ave., Miami Beach, Fla., U.S.A.
1939 (MDPL)
Henry Hohauser (1895 or 1896-1963)
Gravity and anti-gravity: classical and modern as complementary. A modern cube (horizontal bands, balconies, and eroded upper corners) protected by a classical (Doric) portico[1].

T.K.

[1] See: «The Temple and the Aeroplane» by *F.A.B.*

Fig. 1

PERSISTENCE OF THE CLASSICAL IN MODERN ARCHITECTURE
2a; 2b.

Starting in the first decade of the 19th century,[1] the most up-to-date architectural interests are oriented toward the image of the Doric temple which assumes an emblematic meaning for an epoch in the making: memory and first source of imitation.
The return to the Doric and to Paestum, valued for their evocative qualities and for their structural validity, is translated by Schinkel in the Greek image of his public works[2] and in the constructive essentiality[3] of his ordinary buildings according to the new code of 19th century architecture: different styles for different buildings. Hence the debate initiated by Soane is resolved formally by transforming the memory of the rough Paestum Doric into images of force[4] and essentiality, alternating exaltation of the temple form with reduction to its own «natural» characteristics — tree, hut... —[5].
The «noble simplicity» and the «quiet greatness», recognized by Winckelmann in the eternal values of Greece, show themselves in monumental expression and in constructive functionality, resulting everywhere in the most diverse interpretations. The ancient form of the Doric temple gains favor over time and enters the 20th century, once more as absolute image and primary essentiality.

J.R.S.

[1] Refer to the Cat. *La fortuna di Paestum e la memoria moderna del dorico,* vols. I and II, 1986, for the images of Doric architecture up to about 1830.
It is to be noted that only some examples providing an interpretation of the «moments» in the thematic discourse will be given — without any intention of providing an exhaustive study-.
In the course of the thematic essays the photo-

graphic citations include works referred to in the chronology.
[2] Neue Wache, Berlin, 1815-1818, K. F. Schinkel (*Fig. 2*).
[3] Bauschule, Berlin, 1832-1836, K.F. Schinkel (*Fig. 38*).
[4] Bank of England, vestibule on Prince Street, London, 1804-1805, J. Soane (*Fig. 1*).
[5] Moggerhanger House, Bedfordshire, 1809-1811, J. Soane (*Fig. 3*).

2a - Bronx County Building
Grand Concourse, Bronx, New York, U.S.A.
design 1931 or 1932, built 1933 (cornerstone) - 1934 (Stern)
Freedlander (1870-1943) & Hausle

The Doric order (simplified) supporting an entablature (simplified) with dematerialized corners.

2b - Villa
31 rue de la Haye, Casablanca, Morocco
c. 1930-1940.

The Doric order (drastically simplified): modern architecture as an assemblage of pure forms (cubes) but adding a rudimentary abacus/cornice. «It is revealing to examine the distortions the modern repertoire underwent in this process of transcription [«to a bloodless classicism»]... Imitators... were concerned not to let the wall surface lose its physical consistency... this explained the widespread use of covering slabs»[1].

T.K.

[1] Leonardo Benevolo in «Political compromise and the struggle with authoritarian regimes», p. 548 in *History of Modern Architecture,* vol. II, 1980, M.I.T. Press.

Fig. 2

Fig. 3

VARIATIONS ON THE THEME OF THE COLONNADE

3a; 3b.

The facade of the temple is a well known architectural symbol. In the Doric revival of the first part of the 19th century, the image is often used for the front of ordinary buildings: the domestic constructions, also, appropriate it as a memory of the orders[1].
In modern architecture the separation of the temple image from its symbolic meaning recovers the 19th century use, almost an indelible imprint, in the various examples that recall it in ordinary buildings[2] or distort it in «other» frontal solutions[3].
In other cases the revived symbol appears as a quotation[4] or as formal organization[5].

J.R.S.

[1] Apartment house, Paris, Rue de Penthièvre, 1806, J.-B.-Ph. Harou le Romain (*Fig. 4*).
[2] The abattoir of La Mouche, Lyons, 1906, T. Garnier; AEG Turbine Factory, Berlin, 1909, P. Behrens; Model factory, German Exhibition, Cologne, 1914, W. Gropius and A. Meyer (*Figg. 79, 86, 102*); Stockholm Cotton Mill, Stockholm, 1916, C. Johansson (*Fig. 5*); Covered swimming pool, Wembley, London, 1934, O Williams (*Fig. 6*).
[3] Front elevation of Basel Station, Basel, 1903, J.M. Olbrich (*Fig. 76*).
[4] Design for a theatre, Berlin, 1913, H. Scharoun (see F. Neumeyer, 1984).
[5] State Telephone building, Naples, c. 1943 (*Fig. 7*); Ministry of Foreign Affairs building (model of the front), Rome, 1938, G. Moretti (*Fig. 8*).

3a - Project (facade) for the competition for the pavilion of the U.S.S.R. at the Exposition des Arts decoratifs et industriels modernes, Paris 1925
1924
Ivan Aleksandrovič Fomin (1872-1936)
Gnima, Moscow, U.S.S.R.
Bibl.: Cat. *Architettura nel paese Soviet*, 1983, p. 206.

Fomin was among those Russian architects who after an initial adhesion to the new modernistic currents fell back on a language nearer academic classicism. In this project the unusual development of the temple theme, which unifies the tympanum with the columnar pronaos, has great emotional impact, strengthened by the insertion of fragments of writings and of human figures.
This composition, so condensed and so filled with discordant elements creates another element of movement and rhythm by repeating the decomposition of the theme along the front of the tympanum.
The relation between the mixture of the languages of the avant-garde in the preceding decade and the substantial academicism of the composition creates a tension which is not completely resolved formally.

P.M.M.

Fig. 4

Fig. 5

Fig. 6

3b - School of Rhythmic Gymnastics (Dalcroze Institut)
Hellerau, Dresden, D.D.R.
1910-1911
Heinrich Tessenow (1876-1950)
Bibl.: WANGERIN - WEISS, 1976, pp. 65-66; TAFURI - DAL CO, 1979, p. 88.

The Institute, founded by Wolf Dohrn, was meant to be a model school in the recently constructed garden city of Hellerau near Dresden. The project was only partially realized.
The central «temple» body protrudes in the quadrangular court, which contained classrooms, rooms for performances, dressing-rooms, etc., dividing it into two areas.
In this building the recovery of essential forms and the composition by distinct functional elements, typical of the design method of Tessenow, allies the constructive module with the primary forms of the Doric temple. Here the transformation consists of the reduction of the formal elements, which connote the parts of the building — the tympanum, the pronaos — to geometric forms (or light and shade) of solids and voids. Also significant is the use of square pilasters in the pronaos.

P.M.M.

Fig. 7

Fig. 8

THE TEMPLE
4a; 4b.

4a Maritime Terminal
Trieste, Italy
1926-1928
Umberto Nordio (1891-1971)
Bibl.: E.N.R., *Rassegna d'architettura*, 1932, pp. 154-159; CONTESSI, 1981, pp. 78-80.

The building that rises in the official quarter of the city, establishes a dialogue with the neo-classical mansions of the sea-front. In the temple facade, marked by thin strip pilasters framing the great windows, there is the memory of that simplified classicism that Wagner and Hoffmann had instilled in the language of the Viennese Secession, recovering the essentiality introduced by John Soane and, after him, by Karl Friedrich Schinkel. The tympanum, sustained by two stylized figures (by the sculptor Franco Asco), reintroduces the use of the flat and reduced tympana of «Greek» taste of so many of Soane's buildings (Dulwich Art Gallery, Moggerhanger House) (*Fig.* 3).
In 1932, two years after the inauguration of the Terminal, Rogers noted the «pure harmony between [its] structure and aesthetic expression… a model of modernity». Rogers does not fail to underline the elementary planimetry and the chromatic accentuation of the details of the interiors, which correspond perfectly to its function «the rhythm of the solids and voids find in the color accent almost a melodic accompaniment. The play of the complementaries, green and red, which compete for the domination of the senses, appearing and disappearing among the large windows of the two great halls, is extremely suggestive and almost rouses the visitor from his marine isolation». Today, on the exterior, the whiteness of the plaster emphasizes the essentiality of the structure, both of the front and the long lateral porticoes, once painted in brick red.
N.Z.

4b - Bus Kiosk
Porte de la Villette, Paris, France

THE PORTICO
4c; 4d.

4c - Unexecuted project for the New Theater of Udine
Udine, Italy
1934
Cesare Pascoletti (1898-1986).
Bibl.: C.E., *La panarie,* 1934 (the project was lost; there remains only the reproduction which appeared in *La panarie*); DAMIANI, vol. II, 1982, pp. 254-263.

«It looks like a gigantic organ with its pipes stretched out to the open sky»; this was the judgment of a contemporary (1934) on a complex work destined to resolve a problem that had dragged on for years at Udine.
Pascoletti, who had to reckon with a pre-existing building begun before the war and then abandoned, chose the solution of great blocks with a portico with square pillars which recall the projects of Piacentini (with whom Pascoletti was an active collaborator) for the Palais des Nations in Geneva (1927). It was in line, therefore, with the «simple monumentality» invoked during those years by Pagano in the magazine *Casabella* for buildings of a certain importance. In fact, Pascoletti does not hesitate to be assertive in this building that by its very function should have become a reference point in an expanding urban environment, recovering, in the choice of the monumental Doric, the language of the orders, in the typical mode of the «new architecture» which in the second half of the 18th century preferred the Doric order for its theatres
N.Z.

4d - Project for a pavilion for the exhibition «Extensiors»
Iª Esposizione Italiana di Architettura Razionale
Rome, Italy
1928
Adalberto Libera (1903-1963)
Bibl.: PIACENTINI, *Architettura e Arti Decorative*, 1928; CENNAMO, 1973 *passim*; Cat. *Il Razionalismo…*, 1976, p. 78; QUILICI, 1981, p. 33.

The design was presented at the 1st Italian Exhibition of Rational Architecture, held at the Palazzo delle Esposizioni in Rome during March and April of 1928, and organized by Libera and Gaetano Minnucci.
Libera, already a member of «Gruppo 7» since 1926, in which he had taken the place of Castagnoli, enunciates in this project numerous formal themes common to Italian «Rationalism», and applies a sort of «syncretism» to the «modernizing»

tendencies. This syncretism, which had been theorized by individual writings as well as by the Group, takes its distance as much from the Avantgarde of the preceding decade as from the classicism of those years.
Within a poetic of typification, this pavilion shows the aggregation of many of the new linguistic elements: composition by simple volumes, lightening of the corners, overhang eyebrows, and lettering. But it is particularly the relationship between the long, glass parallelepiped and the portico realized with vertical fins that identifies the pavilion and gives the measure of the «new spirit» of this reinterpretation of the classical language.

P.M.M.

THE PIER WALL
5a; 5b.

[1] Pfeilerhalle, Technische Hochschule, Charlottenburg, Berlin, end of 19th c., F. Gilly (*Fig.* 9).
[2] Grange Park, Hampshire, 1809, W. Wilkins (*Fig.* 10).
[3] Project for New York University, Washington Square, New York 1832, A. Jackson Davis (*Fig.* 11).
[4] A Technical School, Leningrad, 1936-37, L. Galeprin and A. Knyawev (*Fig.* 12); monumental entrance to the Città Universitaria, Rome, 1935, A. Foschini (*Fig.* 13); Casa dei Mutilati e Invalidi di Guerra, Naples, 1940, C. Guerra (here the pillar is cut in half by a deep groove, offering a variation on the theme that reinforces the effect of light and shadow) (*Fig.* 14).

The use of the four-sided pillar as a column in the porticoed solutions of the modern lexicon goes back to Gilly[1]. Present in Wilkins[2], it acquires with Davis[3] the autonomous formulation of many solutions of the 20th century[4]. Nevertheless the element is often converted into a strip pilaster defining itself as a rhythmic division of a large facade. Lexically Soane[5] had already realized this new feature, which became frequent in the language of Schinkel[6] and Davis[7]. The use of typical Soane's strip-pilaster reappears also in some modern buildings[8].

N.Z.

Fig. 9

Fig. 10

Fig. 11

Fig. 12

Fig. 13

Fig. 14

Fig. 15

Fig. 17

[5] Houses and shops for John Robins, Regent Street, London, 1820-21, J. Soane (*Fig.* 15) (for the use in architecture before Soane, see, for example, the facade of the Kensington Palace, Kings Gallery, London, 1765, N. Hawksmoor).
[6] Military Prison and Barracks, Lindenstrasse, Berlin, 1817, K.F. Schinkel (*Fig.* 16).
[7] Project for Commercial Exchange, 1862, A. Jackson Davis (*Fig.* 17).
[8] Project for an extension to the School of Arts and Crafts, Vienna, 1906, J. Hoffmann (*Fig.* 82); model factory, German Werkbund Exhibition, Cologne, 1914, W. Gropius and A. Meyer (*Fig.* 102).

5a - Post Office Madison Square Branch
East 23rd St., New York, U.S.A.
1935 (cornerstone) - 1937 (Stern)
Lorimer Rich

The «back» of this post office, on 24th St., is more modern in style, reflecting the normal status modern architecture had achieved by 1935 and thus demonstrating the honorific intention of the front. This building was admired by Hamlin (Stern), author of *Greek Revival Architecture in America*, the first words of which seem written for this catalogue and exhibition: «This book is but an Introduction to a great subject — the architecture of an entire country in its eager and searching adolescence». — except one would substitute «modern world» for «country»[1].

[1] T. HAMLIN, *Greek Revival Architecture in America*, 1944, Oxford University Press, p. VII.

T.K.

5b - Project for the V.I. Lenin Working People's House competition
Ivanovo - Voznesensk
1924
Vladimir Fedorovič Krinskij (1890-1971)
Gnima, Moscow, U.S.S.R.
Bibl.: Cat. *Architettura nel Paese dei Soviet*, p. 209.

This project is characterized by the solemn volumetry of the robust pillars, which emerge free at the top, with a greater dynamism than the more common versions of Behrensian or classical derivation. This is a variation that is often found in current buildings of some formal importance, accentuating the vertical tension and the effect of light and shadow. Here vertical tension is obtained by inserting the row of pillars between the two glazed pure volumes, but above all by the overlapping on the crown of a recessed second order, which carries the letters.

P.M.M.

THE FREESTANDING COLONNADE
6a; 6b.

Since the beginning of the 19th century, the theme of the colonnade in British Doric architecture had assumed a strong emphasis making it prevail in the organization of the architectonic lexicon of facades, qualifying itself as an exponent of that quest for «more picturesqueness» exalted by Thomas Hope[1]. Undoubtedly, the autonomous role of the column takes on value in the 20th century with the example of Loos for the Chicago Tribune Competition in 1922, which instills in the monument-column recovered from Doric culture[2] a lyrical meaning of monumental gigantism, a totemic exaltation of the symbol. The varied and autonomous organization of the freestanding colonnade[3] may be related to Loos interpretation of classicism.

N.Z.

[1] St. Bernard Crescent, Edinburgh, 1825, J. Milne; Carlton House Terrace, The Mall, London, 1827-1857, J. Nash (*Fig.* 18); National Gallery of Scotland, Edinburgh, 1850-1857, W.H. Playfair. Hope recommended that the porticos at Downing be made as deep as possible so as to give «to the entire facade more motion, more picturesqueness, and more dignity» (WATKIN, 1968, p. 83).
[2] Cf. RASPI SERRA, Cat. *La fortuna di Paestum...*, 1986, vol. I, pp. 12-14.
[3] Cultural center of the city of Ube, Ube, Yamaguchi, Japan, 1937, T. Murano (*Fig.* 19).

6a - Town Hall
Villeurbanne (Lyon), France
competition 1930, built 1931-34
Robert Giroud (1890-?)

6b - Padiglione della Stampa
V Triennale di Milano, Milan, Italy
1933
Luciano Baldessari (1896-1982)
Bibl.: *Padiglione della stampa,* 1933; «Padiglione della Stampa», *Casabella,* 1933; VERONESI, 1957, *passim*; Cat. *Il razionalismo...*, 1976, p. 87; LUCIANO BALDESSARI, 1978; MANTERO, 1984, p. 100; Cat. *Luciano Baldessari,* 1985.

Baldessarri, like Libera, had been active among the Italian rationalists. This project spread far and wide in the Italian architectural journals because of its volumetric and functional organization, and especially because of the relationship between the parallelepiped body and the colonnade. The latter, in free standing elements, assumes a scenographic and monumental character recalling the heroic value of the Doric column.
This theme is underlined in the exhibition catalogue of the 5th Triennial: «On the flank of the pavilion, five very tall columns bring about a classical rhythm translated with lively modernity: ancient elements recalled in honor to express with masculine vigor the new Latin monumentality».

P.M.M.

Fig. 18

Fig. 19

THE CENTERED FACADE WITH PORTICO
7.

The recovery of geometric forms characterizes the «new architecture» of the second half of the 18th century with a predilection for cubic shapes as shown in the work of Ledoux. Gilly had often proposed in his projects the lightening of the cubic structure with horizontal delineation.
This solution is modified and renewed in 20th century everyday architecture by the influence of modern culture. It is necessary, however, to mention some examples which recall classical forms[1].

J.R.S.

[1] For instance, see the Pavilion of the Austrian Institute of Culture, Rome, 1937, K. Holey (*Fig.* 20).

THE PAVILION
7a; 7b; 7c.

7a - Building for the Comunità Autonome Artigiane
Esposizione del Valentino, Turin, Italy
1928
Alberto Sartoris (1901)
See *ultra* the interview to A. Sartoris
See *supra* "The Temple and the Aeroplane" by F.A.B.

7b - Design for a gateway to a city
c. 1800
Staatliche Schlösser, Sans-Souci (Inv. no. 899)
Potsdam, D.D.R.
Friedrich Gilly (1772-1800)
Bibl.: REELFS, Cat. *Friedrich Gilly*, 1984, no. 63, pp. 144-145.

Gilly in this, as well as in other works created on his return from the journey to France, conveys to us, through his ingenious intuition, the known theoretical and cultural presuppositions, addressing the new architectonic conscience which required elementary geometric volumes.

J.R.S.

7c - Villa Lazienkowskiego
Warsaw, Poland
1784
Bibl.: Cat. *La fortuna di Paestum...*, 1986, vol. II, K 59.

Of particular interest is the facade where the portico is hollowed out of the volume of the villa. The porch thus creates an area of shade denoted by the Doric columns, which are in line with the lateral bodies marked by a slight rustication. The attic is interrupted in the center above the portico by a balustrade (an element of 16th century origin, frequent in 18th century European culture), alternating here with very simplified piers and in agreement with a taste of «noble simplicity».

N.Z.

THE CENTERED FACADE
8a; 8b.

In the recall of themes of antiquity there was a prevailing interest in the great arcade and the rhythm of the colonnade, recovering the semicircle and the line. Exacerbated by the force of the «visionary» French architects[1] and also by the most avant-garde scholars of the past, these linguistic accents become, in the culture of 20th century builders structural and contribute to the emblematic expression of the building's function[2] as everyday architecture points out.

N.Z.

[1] Project for a theater and for the public baths at Lille, Musée des Beaux-Arts, Lille, 1794, F. Verly (*Fig.* 21).
[2] Main Station, Helsinki, 1904-1914, E. Saarinen; Railway station, Stuttgart, 1911-1914, P. Bonatz, F.E. Scholer (*Fig.* 96).

8a - Union Railroad Terminal
Cincinnati, Ohio, U.S.A.
1929-1933 (Wilson)
Fellheimer & Wagner

8b - The Cisternone
Livorno, Italy
1829-1842
Pasquale Poccianti (1774-1858)
Bibl.: Cat. *The age of neoclassicism*, 1972, p. 991.

Among the most remarkable and original works of Poccianti, the «Cisternone» (large cistern), linked to the acqueduct of Colognola, furnishes the city of Livorno a part of its water supply.
The massive simplicity of its forms, memories of Boullée and of Ledoux, is reinforced by the appropriate use of a Doric colonnade sustaining the rising arch of the facade, producing a strong, monumental effect.

N.Z.

Fig. 20

Fig. 21

VARIATIONS ON THE ISSUE OF SYMMETRY: THE URBAN FACADE	THE CENTERED FACADE WITH WINGS 9a; 9b; 9c.	THE CURVED FACADE 10a; 10b; 10c; 11a; 11b; 12a; 12b.

Is it «truly» regrettable, as Kaufmann noted, that Soane did not reach the future goals of architecture implicit in his inventive multiplicity or isn't his unequivocal mark already a definite message which only subsequent generations could stamp as definitive?

The baroque tradition of unity of the building block is broken in the Dulwich Gallery project, as already tried in the unexecuted project for Brasenose College, Oxford (1807)[1]. Here, according to Kaufmann, an element — the cornice — that was one of the strongest connecting factors of baroque building, is over. Materially the various building parts are coherent but no attempt at emphasizing their mutual dependence is made. The parts free themselves, as Kaufmann thinks, from the ancient dependence to the whole[2].

In the Dulwich Art Gallery (1811-1814) Soane entrusts the most modern aspects of his architectural experimentations to the substantial simplification of the decoration, achieved by the use of elementary, geometric forms (parallelepipeds, cubes) and by the relationship of the parts.

The work, because it is without style, becomes a model.[3]

J.R.S.

[1] Project for Brasenose College, Oxford, 1807, J. Soane (*Fig.* 22).
[2] Cf. Kaufmann, 1966, pp. 64-74.
[3] Among the numerous modern examples, the Project for the competition for the Palace of the Soviets, Moscow, 1932, O.H. Hamilton (*Fig.* 23).

9a - UOP Fragrances Factory (formerly Knickerbocker Laundry)
Dreyer Ave., Long Island city,
Queens, New York, U.S.A.
1931 (BDR) - 1932 (Stern)
Irving M. Fenichel

9b - Dulwich Art Gallery, second project, western perspective
London, England
1811 (July 12th)
John Soane (1753-1837)
Sir John Soane's Museum, London, England
Bibl.: *John Soane*, 1983, pp. 77-99

9c - Public Library
Grand Army Plaza,
Brooklyn, New York, U.S.A.
1937-1941 (Stern)
Alfred Githens, Francis Keally

Fig. 22

Fig. 23

«Le projet de cirque que je présente ici est conçu pour remplir des vues morales et politiques. Je me suis assuré que nul spectacle ne serait plus grand, plus magnifique, et j'ose dire, d'après les motifs qui m'ont guidé, que rien ne serait plus touchant et plus intéressant» (BOULLÉE, 1968 ed., p. 121).

Boullée discovers, by choosing a circular form remembered from antiquity, here the Colosseum — «Le Colisée, à Rome est un des plus beaux monuments de l'Italie» —, the ideal form, exalting its perfection by transforming the object enlarged in his imagination as though by a mental hyperbole.

It is well-known that he initiated the return to the antique as the sublime. «L'image du grand» is the new form of the «classical», imposing in its extreme monumentality, negative in its «colossal» form[1].

The distinction given by Boullée between great and gigantic — («en croyant... *faire grand*, il a fait *gigantesque*») — is stated precisely and clearly in the poetics of Heidegger, showing us the meaning of the modern world. «A sign of this process is founded on the fact that everywhere, in the most diverse forms and disguises, the gigantic comes forward... Instead the gigantic is that which, through the quantitative, constitutes itself in its own quality, becoming in such a manner an eminent way of the great... As soon as the gigantic of the planning... leads the quantitative to overturn in its own quality, the gigantic and what is apparently always calculable transform themselves... into the incalculable... To know that incalculable... is possible for man only in virtue of a creative interrogation...»[2].

In the memory of everyday masters[3], the underground recollection is allied with solutions suggested by the main architecture[4]. But even in these examples, the adaptation of the ancient formula of the curved facade to the modern style, pays tribute, perhaps, to the invention of Boullée[5].

J.R.S.

---

[1] For the quotations from Boullée, cf. BOULLÉE, 1968 ed., pp. 82, 84, 119.
[2] Cf. HEIDEGGER, (1950) 1968, pp. 100-101.
[3] The emphasis of the curve is present in 20th century architectural forms: the classical world revisited in the monumental returns in the Colosseum, 435 Riverside Drive in Manhattan, 1910, Schwartz and Gross (*Fig.* 24).
[4] Schocken Department Store, Chemnitz, 1928-1929, E. Mendelsohn (*Fig.* 144).
[5] The language of everyday architecture often corrupts the pure geometric movement of the curve with rectangular blocks at the ends. We can find these solutions already used in the 18th century: e.g. in the project of Château-Neuf, Saint-Germain-en-Laye (1777) by Bélanger (*Fig.* 26). This solution comes back in the Gorkij Palace of Culture, Leiningrad, 1925-1927, by A.I Gegello and D.L. Kričevskij (*Fig.* 25).

10a-10b - Central Post Office
Naples, Italy
1929-1935
Giuseppe Vaccaro (1896-1971), Gino Franzi (1898-1973)
Bibl.: Cat. *Il razionalismo...*, 1976, p. 209; MANTERO, 1984, pp. 75-77.

The great curved facade that characterized this building is also present in many other projects entered in the competition of 1928 (Canino, Limongelli), but with heavy and backward linguistic solutions.
The project of Vaccaro and Franzi, on the contrary, plays on the purity of the volumes and the sharpness of the one great curved wall. The obvious reference is to the Schocken Department Store in Chemnitz by Mendelsohn (1928-1929), but here in Naples the strong central access prevails, creating an axis of symmetry. The rhythm of the windows and the contrast in color and material between the glazed band of the base and the white marble surface underlines the importance of the axis, while the sequences of the attic openings recompose the overall unity and give unity to the curved volume.
For these analogies one should remember the project of Visontai, Ortensi, and Villa for the competition for the theater of Kharkov[1].

P.M.M.

[1] Cf. GODOLI, 1983, p. 75.

10c - «Les Tilleuls» (La Rotonde)
11-19 rue Charles Giron, Geneva, Switzerland
1928-1929
Maurice Braillard (1879-1965)
Bibl.: «Unterbrochene Stadt...», *werk archithese*, 1978, p. 58, fig. 25; BRULHART, FREY, 1986.

In the domain of the curved facade the example of La Rotonde, punctuated by a rhythm of columnar volumes, constitutes the opposite pole to the smoothness of the facade. This is a solution that seeks a dynamic and monumental effect, obtaining it with the verticality of the cylindrical bodies that interrupt the continuity, as well as with the different rhythm between the various cylindrical volumes. The recalling of columns is not casual. It alludes to a tholos: it is this «out of scale» magnification that creates the monumental presence of this urban building.

P.M.M.

10d - Project for a Circus, plan of the second solution
Etienne-Louis Boullée (1728-1799)
Bibliothèque Nationale, Cabinet des Estampes, Ha 55, n. 22, Paris, France
Bibl.: PÉROUSE DE MONTCLOS, 1969, pp. 173, 245.

11a - Casa della Giovane Italiana
Gorizia, Italy
1934
Gino Miozzo (1898-1969), Francesco Mansutti (1899-1969)
Bibl.: «La casa della Giovane Italiana...», in *Edilizia moderna*, 1937.

The asymmetrical plan is quite remarkable, consisting of a rectangular body and a semicircular one, the latter underlined by strip windows which follow the curvilinear course. The building, plastered in red brick, is inserted in the urban context without causing traumatic discontinuity since it maintains, even in the novelty of the architectural form and in the volumetry, a measure well adapted to the surrounding buildings that form the historical *substratum* of a small city such as Gorizia.

N.Z.

11b - Palazzo delle Corporazioni
Cosenza, Italy
1936
Mario De Renzi (1897-1967), Giorgio Calza Bini (1909)
Bibl.: Cat. *Il razionalismo...*, 1976, p. 134.

This building has typical features of much public monumental constructions displayed as it is on a long curved facade that has as its fulcrum and axis of symmetry a robust «void» punctuated by the pillars of the balcony, a monumental element of Behrensian origin. The volumetric composition, plays on the relation between the curved facade and the end block asserting its «typicalness» by the use of other compositional elements, from the strip windows of the base to the windows in between fins

Fig. 24

Fig. 25

Fig. 26

in the center part, by the use of marble and by the bichromy that distinguishes the bands in the base from ones at the top.

P.M.M.

12a - Post Office in the Milvio Quarter
Viale Mazzini, Rome, Italy
1932
Armando Titta
Bibl.: SAPORITI, 1953, p. 88; CRESTI, 1986, pp. 175-176.

The 1932 competition for four post offices in Rome, later built, was an important moment for modern architecture in Italy; as evidenced by the presence in the jury of architects such as Calza Bini, Pagano, Del Debbio, Vaccaro, and Giovannoni.
In this project, the large central opening defines the principal axis of the curved facade. This centrality dissolves itself along the curved marble cladding which is set into the building's body. The top is punctuated by long, horizontal windows in a different rhythm, which already allude to horizontal bands.

P.M.M.

12b - Villa Jeanne Michele
Marrakesh, Morocco
c. 1930-1940.

THE MULTI-CENTERED FACADE OR BUILDING
THE BENT TEMPLE
13a; 13b; 13c.

The interest in focal plurality in the organization of architectonic masses begins with Soane. The Bank of England is a field of experimental work from which the English architect launches a series of new solutions.
This work was the most prestigious commission that Soane (still young) ever had and he kept it for almost all of his life (1792-1826).
This building (today largely replaced by Baker's work) represents a fine example of synthesis, typical of the architecture of Soane. It shows a very modern taste for simplicity of line, a careful study of the exigencies of function, an organization and relation of volumes, a correlation of various points of view for the utilization of the complex and its spatial

Fig. 27

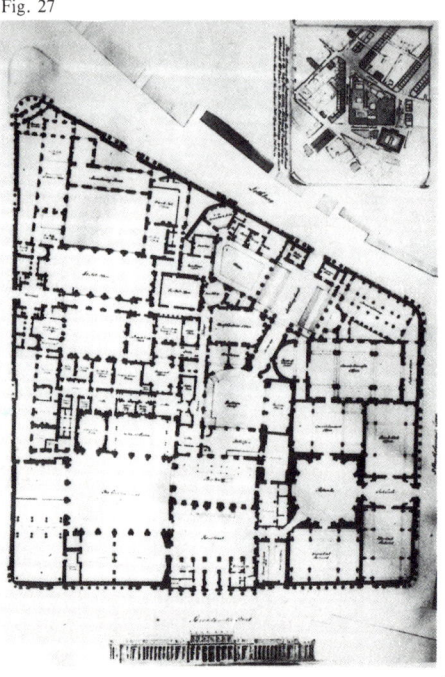

insertion, and the formal rigor of the classical citations (Tivoli Corner).
This explains, why this Bank became the model for subsequent constructions, for example in the United States (cf. the work of Benjamin Latrobe) and why Soane may be considered one of the precursors of 20th century architecture[1].

N.Z.

[1] Bank of England, plan, London, Sir John Soane's Museum (*Fig.* 27).
«Plan of the Bank of England as completed by Soane with the elevation to Threadneedle Street and an inset site plan. Soane's main halls, 1792-1794 and 1818 are grouped round the Rotunda on the right (east). As further property was acquired Soane introduced two new axes — a north-east axis through Lothbury Court, 1797-1798, and an east-west axis through the Princes Street entrance on the west, 1804» (*John Soane,* 1983, p. 63).

13a - Apartment building
Lungotevere Flaminio 78-80, Rome, Italy
c. 1936
Gra

The corner solution of this building has the connotation of a true facade, distinguished by the sequence of the hollows of the windows and by the continuation of the vertical band of the marble base. In this it recalls the other facade, that on the rectilinear side, which conversely is framed vertically by a double order of pilasters. The unity of the vigorous composition is recomposed by the upper band, where the alternation of the windows creates the effect of a Doric frieze, and by the crowning balustrades. The use of marble underlines the monumental tone that is given to this new urban building. The interest in marine taste is shown by the railings which recall sailors' ropes and knots.

P.M.M.

13b, 13c - Tunnel Garage
Broome St., New York, U.S.A.
1922 (facade)
Hector Hamilton (BDR)

A transitional building: stylistically conservative, in the manner of early twentieth-century American industrial architecture, but organized with a decided modern horizontality and with an axis of symmetry at the curved corner prefiguring the «*curved corner*» of innumerable *Moderne* buildings from the 1930s (for example entry **14a**). This curved corner has a complicated history including the corner tower of a Medieval castle, certain eighteenth-century French domestic buildings, e.g. the Pavillon de Hanovre, certain early nineteenth-century urban works of Soane and Nash (where the curved corner effects an urbanistic transition as along Regent St. and the block containing the Lowther Arcade) and finally innumerable later nineteenth-century urban commercial works like the Mappin building in London and Sullivan's Schlesinger and Mayer store in Chicago.
As a footnote one can note that Hamilton won one of the two first prizes in the competition for the Palace of the Soviets in 1932 (see *Fig.* 23).

T.K.

THE CURVED CORNER AS A CENTER
14a; 14b; 14c.

The curved corner as a center is the elegant invention that Soane adopts in the construction of the Bank of England to solve the corner that would have resulted from the intersection of the front walls. In all probability, Soane follows the idea used by George Dance in the project for the interior of St. Luke's Insane Asylum[1]. But the corner in Soane, underlined by the rich crown, assumes a dominant character, becoming a new center vying with the entrance for importance.

This new solution introduces new possibilities for town planning.

It appears in various forms in the 19th century: the classical frontality is now over[2].

Otto Wagner[3] adopts this solution which will be very frequent in both the high and the low architecture of the 20th century[4].

N.Z.

[1] St. Luke's Insane Asylum, interior, London, 1781, George Dance the Younger (*Fig.* 28).
[2] Building, Rue de la Raffinerie, Neuchâtel, 1868 (*Fig.* 29).
[3] Majolika-Haus Linke Wienzeile 38-40 and Kostlergasse 3, Vienna 1898-1899, O. Wagner (*Fig.* 74).
[4] See e.g.: «Berliner Tageblatt» Administration building, Berlin, 1921-1923, E. Mendelsohn (*Fig.* 117); Siedlung Kiefhock, Rotterdam, 1925-1929, J.J.P. Oud (*Fig.* 135); Apartment building, Via De' Rolandis 1 (angolo Via Zamboni) Bologna, 1933-35, Giuseppe Gualandi (*Fig.* 30); Everyday's building, Athens (*Fig.* 31).

14a - Hecht Warehouse
Washington D.C., U.S.A.
1937 (Greif)
Abbot, Merkt & Co.

14b - Bank of England, Lothbury front
London, England
1795
John Soane (1753-1837)
Sir John Soane's Museum (DR, Xii.1.1.), London, England
Bibl.: *John Soane,* 1983, p. 68.

Fig. 29

Fig. 30

14c - Covered Market
Via Carducci, Trieste, Italy
1935
Camillo Iona (1886-1974)
Bibl.: «Il primo mercato rionale coperto...», *Riv. mensile della Città di Trieste*, 1935; Crusvar, Cat. *Gli affreschi di Carlo Sbisà...*, 1980.

Among Iona's notes concerning the planning of the Covered Market there are quite a number of references to the new Soviet and English cooperatives directed at finding the best response to the numerous problems of the building program. The market is built in a triangular area and has a fingernail-shaped plan; inside, the two floors are occupied by a great hall — in the manner of Trajan's Market. The flat arches are a clear reference to the salons of the ship Victoria, an example of advanced design, which the Lloyd Triestino had launched in 1931. In the dining room the free arches evoke images of the old wood structures — the memory of great cross beams, a really nautical construction as contrasted with the more usual «historicizing» appointment of earlier ships.

The functionality, which dominates the interior space of the market, is also represented by the helicoidal ramp connecting the first and second storey which must have served for the circulation of carts for the supply of goods. This solution, which has historical roots in the ramps of Palace of Caprarola, had been «reinvented» by Mattè Trucco in the Fiat Lingotto in Turin (project: 1916) and subsequently seen in many garages in Europe and America (cf. Lenzi, 1928). The ramp is contained in a small tower, planned by Iona to resolve the problem of the sharp angle.

The strip windows (the frames had a «special» handwheel closure that ensured more adeguate ventilation) follow the rising lines of the turret until reaching the apex marked by a luminous clock. The solution making the corner the hinge of the building, (here one can recall the architectural forms of Mendelsohn) had already been used at the beginning of the 19th century by John Soane in the Bank of England.

N.Z.

Fig. 31

Fig. 28

THE CURVED CORNER
15a; 15b.

The architectural solution of the curved corner goes back to the medieval «tourelle» (turret). The remembrance of this image and of its rich and felicitous history, from the «picturesque» expressions of the second half of the 18th century[1] to the 19th century return to the Gothic, transforms the cities into fortified citadels[2].
In the modern reconquest of a past using volumetric juxtapositions and clarity of stylistic characteristics, the element assumes a deeper purpose of essential organization of parts[3]. In so doing it recovers the meaning of the stairway tower, as in the Fagus Shoe - Last Factory by Gropius[4] which opens the way to a compositional choice that emphasizes this element by using glass[5].
Everyday culture responds by not renouncing the traditional element of the corner hinge «tourelle», sometimes reinterpreting it in glass.[6]

J.R.S.

[1] Project for a State prison, Louis-Jean Desprez (*Fig.* 32).
[2] Larish Palace, Vienna, 1867-1868, E. von der Müll (*Fig.* 33); Apartment building, Neuchâtel (*Fig.* 35). Also to be cited: American Hôtel, Amsterdam, 1898-1902, W. Kromhout, which also expresses a message in the heraldic sense.
[3] Karma Villa, Rue St. Moritz, between Clarens and Vevey (Switzerland), 1904-1906, A. Loos (*Fig.* 77); Project for a house for Josephine Baker, Paris, 1928, A. Loos (*Fig.* 146).
[4] Fagus Shoe - Last Factory, Alfeld-an-der-Leine, 1910-1911, W. Gropius (*Fig.* 34).
[5] Novocomum, Como, 1926-1928, G. Terragni.
[6] Offices, Budapest, 1912, Málnai Béla (*Fig.* 36).

15a - Apartment building
1150 Grand Concourse, Bronx, New York, U.S.A.
1937 (Sullivan)
Hyman I. Feldman (1899-?)

15b - House of the Mchat
Brjusovskij Alley, Moscow, U.S.S.R.
1928
Aleksej Viktorovič Ščusev (1873-1949)
Gnima, Moscow, U.S.S.R.
Bibl.: Cat. *Architettura nel paese dei Soviet...*, 1983, p. 212.

The architecture of Ščusev, one of the major Russian modern architects, often utilizes linguistic elements very different from each other, from the more popular ones to those of the new academic tradition. However it is Constructivism that chiefly influences his work. Here such influence is evident in the volumetric play of the corner solution, an important element of the design.
The continuous curve is eroded laterally by the strip windows, while the insertion of the corner balconies blocks the vertical thrust of the corner at the same time as it creates a dynamic reverberation of its movement.
The result is to transform the curved corner into a corner column, even though it remains in the plane of the wall and has the great void of the entrance as its base.

P.M.M.

Fig. 32

Fig. 33

Fig. 34

Fig. 35

Fig. 36

THE CENTERED FACADE WITH DEMATERIALIZED CORNERS
16a; 16b.
THE CENTERED FACADE: VERTICAL CENTER / HORIZONTAL EDGES
17a; 17b: 18a; 18b.

CONTRAST OF VERTICAL (CLASSICAL) AND HORIZONTAL (MODERN)

Modern architecture offers a plurality of points of view: the new importance given to minor elements reduces the role of the facade as the screen of culture, as an indication of the norm or the expression of function. Now the building itself moves, following those who look at it, and articulating itself in the urban space as it is no longer obliged only to point.

The connections with modern culture cost the ordinary building the integrity and coherence of its own appearance. The interest in horizontality and the dematerialization of the corner by the use of glass wear away the unity of the building already compromised by the modern plurality of points of view. The memory of the antique remains in the use of verticality, a halberd passing through the mass (see **16a**). The antique and the modern meet in the vertical and horizontal.

J.R.S.

16a - Apartment building
Via Morghen 37, Naples, Italy
1937

The building is structured around a central axis underlined by the movement of the semicircular balconies, as drums of a column of giant order. This verticality is confirmed by the treatment of the exposed brick, devised as two giant strip pilasters fluted at the flanks of the row of balconies. The center is closed laterally by two *brise soleil*, common in many Italian buildings of this period. This gives impetus to the dematerialized wings which have semicircular balconies, with a solution by now «typical», further on eroded by the openings at the corner.

P.M.M.

16b - La Vigneronne Touraine (wine cooperative)
La tour d'Aigues, Vaucluse, France
1933 (owner)
Georges Salomon (1899-1976) D.E.S.A.

A temple fronted villa: modern horizontal banding (see 28b) weaving through classical vertical piers which support a pediment (simplified) with an inscription (oversized modern letters). The color suggests Pompeii and Rome[1].

T.K.

[1] See *supra*, «The Temple and the Aeroplane» by F.A.B.

17a - Apartment building
Viale Michelangelo 50, Naples, Italy
1939
Ferdinando Chiaromonte (1902-1985)

This large building with two entrances, built by one of the most active Neapolitan building contractor (Roberto Fernandes), is along one of the main streets in the new quarter of the Vomero, developed intensely since the 1930's.
Like many of the buildings in this area, it composes, with originality, the most recent architectural elements with decorative ones tied to tradition. Thus the great pilaster strips: the center one that divides symmetrically the composition of semicircular balconies, and the fluted ones separating them from the long balconies with curved corner.
This very frequent motif, originates in the architecture of the 1910's, in Naples specifically with that of Gino Avena, with whom Chiaromonte often collaborated. A Neapolitan example is given by the large building of Avena in Via Tasso (1914) in which the passage from the Doric pilaster strip to this treatment in stucco is clear.

P.M.M.

17b - Apartment building
Via Tasso 203, Naples, Italy
c. 1938
Tommaso Cotronei (1902-1984)

The building is located near Giulio Rossi's (see 53b) and is part of a group of buildings of the same period which are similar in their formal solutions. Here the symmetry, established by the vertical window openings and the entrance, is reaffirmed by the curved balconies that flank the axis.
The whole decorative and architectonic solution — from the modulated openings of the windows and the stucco bands, to the balconies with their tubular railings and the compositional organization that dematerializes the corners, receiving vigor from the treatment of the rough stucco — shows a continuous cross-pollination between the strong Neapolitan Jugendstyl tradition and the new international linguistic elements with interesting and original results.

P.M.M.

18a - Apartment building
1500 Grand Concourse, Bronx, New York, U.S.A.
1935 (Sullivan)
Jacob M. Felson (1866-1962)

Vertical (classical) and horizontal (modern) united. Compare with 16b: in both cases the horizontal corners represent cantilevering, an anti-static form of construction.

T.K.

18b - Botanical Institute
Città Universitaria, Rome, Italy
1932-1935
Giuseppe Capponi (1893-1936)
Bibl.: Cat. *Il razionalismo...*, 1976, p. 176.

The building by Giuseppe Capponi, one of the protagonists of the M.I.A.R., is part of the Città Universitaria of Rome, planned by Marcello Piacentini. It is characterized by two projecting, symmetrical glass volumes, centrally divided by a large red wall, which creates, with the reveal that separates them, a perspective effect. The use of glass which recalls the industrial architecture or futurist and constructivist solutions, not only serves to unveil the framework of the structure, but helps to define and to lighten the vertical mass of its fins, and to contrast them with the horizontal structure with its strip windows of the wings.

P.M.M.

THE URBAN FACADE
19a; 19b; 20a; 20b; 21a; 21b; 21c.

The reconquest of Greek «truth» with the «discovery» of Paestum and the return of Gothic «memory» with its recall of origins, annul, from the middle of the 19th century, the credibility of the Vitruvian norm in the composition of the facade. The possibility of different sources — the Greek and the Gothic — opens the way to a pluralistic combination of styles (proposed by Schinkel at the beginning of the 19th century) as well as to the free interpretation of the building's facade. Everything becomes possible. The free individualism expresses itself in the enlargement or in the reduction of the vocabulary, in the deformation of the elements and in their desecration. A that differently acts from the «Manner» which tormented the elements fixed in their place by «rule». The liberated imagination now freely conceives, plays with the past and creates a game that, in time, becomes history. The facade purifies itself, ruled only by the remembrance of the ancient theme, enriches itself in an orgy of disparate motifs or fortifies itself in symbols. The decorative elements are now independent of the volumes, expressing themselves in the use of materials, exalted themselves in the ancient emblem of the Order: the decoration favors focal multiplicity and contributes to the spatial dynamism of the building — an image of the new mechanical velocity. In the new compositional liberty, the everyday building is in line with the direction shown by the past, but it is also subjected to the influence of modern taste. Even in this historical recall, as in the more explicit image of the temple, the taste expressed by vernacular buildings joins and registers the reactions of main architecture.

J.R.S.

RETURN TO ESSENTIALITY
19a; 19b.

«Ornaments are to be cautiously introduced: those ought only to be used that are simple, applicable and characteristic of their situations; they must be designed with regularity and be perfectly distinct in their outlines; the Doric members must not be mixed with the Ionic, nor the Ionic with the Corinthian, but such ornaments should only be used, as tend to show the destination of the edifice, as assist in determining its character, and for the choice of which the architect can assign satisfactory reasons» (SOANE, *Plans, Elevations and Sections of Buildings...*, 1788, p. 8).

Decoration of a linear type, introduced by Soane and taken up by only a few architects contemporary with him[1], found its greatest diffusion with the architects of the first years of the 20th century, especially Hoffmann.

The strip pilaster decorated by fluting which ends in a geometric design, (like Deco), used more and more by Soane as an allusive and reductive representation of the order, reappears not only in Hoffmann, but also in Messel, Behrens, Littmann and up to Oud[2].

In an anti-tectonic reading of the order the accentuation of the linear decoration allows a dismantling of the classical structure, isolating its single elements that are simplified and re-utilized for their value as memory for an «economic» (minimum thickness) valorization of the facades.

N.Z.

[1] Design for a villa from Hints for Dwelling, 1804, D. Laing; House, 24 Hill Street, London, c. 1806, J. Leicester, Sir John Soane's Museum, London, 1812, J. Soane (*Fig.* 37); St. Andrew's Chapel, Plymouth, Devon, 1823, J. Foulston; Allgemeine Bauschule (Bauakademie), Berlin, 1832-1836, K.F. Schinkel (*Fig.* 38).

[2] Messrs. Wertheim's premises (main hall), Leipziger-Strasse, Berlin, 1904, A. Messel (*Fig.* 39); Theater, Munich, 1908, M. Littmann (*Fig.* 40); Joseph Feinhals House, Cologne, 1908-1909, J.M. Olbrich (*Fig.* 84); Crematorium, Hagen, 1906-1907, P. Behrens (*Fig.* 81); Austrian pavilion, Sala Klimt, Rome 1911, J. Hoffmann (*Fig.* 92); Skywa - Primavesi House, Vienna, 1913, J. Hoffmann (*Fig.* 99); Austria pavilion, Exhibition of the German Werkbund, Cologne, 1914, J. Hoffmann; Standardized workers' houses (plan), 1918, J.J.P. Oud (*Fig.* 112); Page Warehouse, Tulsa, 1927, B. Goff.

19a - Warehouse (destroyed)
Gerard Ave., Bronx, New York, U.S.A.
after 1931
Irving M. Fenichel (attributed)

Fig. 37

Fig. 38

«The urban facade - a return to essentiality:
"... the golden temples of Paestum... their absolute, essential architectonic force...
"To trace their mark... is to follow the course of the Doric revival, encouraged implicitly by enlightened rationalism, whose values of essentiality, natural primitivism and formal restraint resulted in... re-evaluation of the order as a pragmatic formula in the new town planning.
"... the rigorous search for rational essentiality exalted Paestum and the Doric order encouraging a return... to extreme reduction of vocabulary, tending to simplify form to its structural essentiality - as in the work of Soane...» (Cat. RASPI SERRA, *Paestum and the Doric revival 1750-1830*, 1986, pp. 15-16).
The building to the right in the photo is by the Cory Brothers, architects of the Starrett Lehigh building (See **30a**).

T.K.

19b - Entrance Gateway
Tyringham Hall, Buckinghamshire, England
1793-1801
John Soane (1753-1837)
Bibl.: ZANNI, Cat. *La fortuna di Paestum...* vol. II, 1986, L. 28.

Incised lines emphasize the flat surface of the entrance block to the residence of William Pread, a Fleet Street banker who had hired Soane to rebuild the villa in 1792. The great arch in grey stone is flanked by two lodges in Doric style in its most simplified version, which thus contrasts with the more noble Ionic order of the «colonnaded bow» of the villa, where surfaces — compact and barely animated by «Greek» decoration — prevail.

N.Z.

Fig. 39

Fig. 40

MODERN COMBINATIONS
20a; 20b.

20a - Women's Prison
Würzburg, Germany
1809
Peter Speeth (1777-1831)
Bibl.: VOGT, Cat. *La fortuna di Paestum...*, 1986, II,. I 59.

The decorative pluralism of the facade of the prison of Speeth creates a lively interaction of elements freeing the whole from its gloomy finality. On the other hand, the memory of the building's purpose — the prison — is entrusted to the details the Doric rustication, the pediment, the portholes. One finds in this facade the thematic rigor of the «orders», charged with symbolic meaning — the temple front may be interpreted as a symbol of moral rebirth — and combined in a stylistic pluralism which liberates decoration giving it the freedom of the vernacular, rich in emerging memories of the antique.

20b - Tiffany & Co. Store
57th St. & Fifth Ave., New York, U.S.A.
1939-1940 (Stern)
Cross & Cross

THE FACADE AS A CITY WALL WITH TOWERS
21a; 21b; 21c.

21a - Project for «Intérieur de ville de guerre»
Etienne-Louis Boullée (1728-1799)
Bibliothèque Nationale, Cabinet des Estampes (Ha 55, pl. 31) Paris, France
Bibl.: PÉROUSE DE MONTCLOS, 1969, pp. 185, 247.

The exaltation of mass is accentuated by the smooth course of the masonry: two typical traits in the designs of Boullée that show in this interior of a fortified city, which recalls the might of the town-walls of antiquity. It demonstrates the value of the wall as symbol, enormous barrier between the inhabited reality and the external world. «C'est ainsi qu'en offrant des moyens multipliés de défense, je suis, je crois, parvenu non seulement à faire regarder la ville comme imprenable, mais encore à donner de la variété à mon sujet». (Boullée, 1968 ed., p. 144).
The memory of the fortified cities of the past shows in the closed, fortified *Siedlungen*[1], in the high walls which in the modern epoch surround the housing complexes: enclosed domains, chosen for the defense of groups in the moment in which the illusions of a new social formula of human habitation are proposed.

J.R.S.

[1] Miniature from Duke of Berry's Book of Hours; Air photograph of Berlin S.W., from BEHNE (1928) 1984, pl. 8 (*Fig. 41*).

21b - Karl Marx-Hof
Vienna, Austria
1927
Karl Ehn
Bibl.: TAFURI - DAL CO, 1979, pp. 159-164.

The construction of the new residential quarters in Vienna is, for the importance of the protagonists and for the variety of the solutions, one of the main episodes of the new architecture at the end of the 1920's. The Karl Marx-Hof by Karl Ehn, formed in the Wagnerschule, is for its ideological value and for its imposing undertaking, the most important of these urban works. The building blocks are treated, on both facades, as long walls modulated by towers. These, in the relationship between the semicircular opening and the flagpole, produce a vertical tension of epic tone. This tone is later confirmed by the orthogonal grid of the wing balconies and by the interpenetrations of the two volumes (the relief of the towers, and the flat facade which runs behind them), and is reinforced by the two-colors: brick-red and yellow-ochre. The linguistic

elements of the tradition of the new abound.
P.M.M.

21c - Building of the Gioventù Italiana del Littorio (G.I.L.)
Foro Italico, Rome, Italy
c. 1937
C. Costantini (?-1986)

THE ELEMENTS
HERALDIC ELEMENTS

22a; 22b;23a; 23b; 24a; 24b; 24c; 25a; 25b; 26a; 26b.

DEFINITION

Vertical member(s) attached to the body of a building, usually in the most forward and highest position: the remembered sign identifying it.
«Herald n.: 1. The bearer of significant news, an important message, etc. 2: A forerunner or portent of something to come; harbinger» (J.G. FERGUSON, *The Illustrated Contemporary Dictionary,* Encyclopedic Edition, 1978, Chicago, Ill.).

PROLOGUE

This piece is speculative, depending on a subjective reading of certain forms, or rather motifs, used frequently during the 1930s. These motifs, while entirely abstract, will be seen as figurative, that is as representing the human body. While there is no evidence to support this reading, there is ample precedent for abstract representation of the figure, or parts of the figure, in architecture (Building as Body). This figurative reading has two somewhat contradictory aspects: one, these motifs act as guardians, reinforcing the official, the public, aspect of the buildings, or at least of the public parts such as the entrance; two, when these elements are flagpoles, one of the most frequent instances, the flag itself transforms the guardians into dancers, into ecstatic figures, and the memory of this conditions our reading of the flagpoles when they are empty, as they often are. It is this dancing which is most speculative and therefore receives the most attention in what follows. The material supporting the idea of dancers is deliberately diverse. It has been assembled for consideration, without extended explanation. It consists of two parts: A) examples of drapery as representing action (Clark), and B) examples of explicit dancing figures in architecture (Louis XIV medal) and abstracted drapery as decoration (Loïe Fuller pavilion). Since these examples are familiar, or at least sources (Utrecht Psalter) for what later became ubiquitous and since the empathetic reading of architecture was given prominence just before the period we are examining (Scott), then one can conclude that this reading is effected unconsciously. Before beginning this study we had no consciousness of this ourselves, but repeated examination and reflection on our reactions have led to these conclusions. For us, now, these abstract motifs are as figurative, as alive, as the classical column was for the students of Vitruvius.

BUILDING AS BODY

«The Temple of Luxor is indisputably devoted to the Human Microcosm. This consideration is not merely a simple attribution: the entire temple becomes a book explaining the secret functions of the organs and nerve centers». (R.A. SCHWALLER DE LUBICZ, *The Temple in Man* (1949) 1977, Inner Traditions International, 24) (*Figg.* 42,43)[1]. «We consider that an Edifice is a Kind of Body...»

Fig. 41

Fig. 42

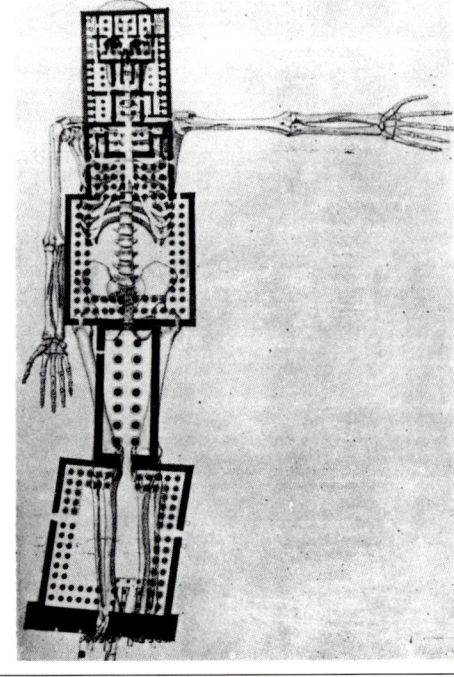

(LEON BATTISTA ALBERTI, *De re aedificatoria*, c. 1450 from E. HOLT, *A Documentary History of Art*, Vol. I, *Middle Ages an Renaissance*, 1957, Doubleday Anchor, 223). «The first thing they [the Ancients] observ'd, as to number, was that it was of two sorts, even and uneven... they never made the... Columns, Angles and the like, in uneven numbers; as you shall not find any Animal and the like that stands or moves upon an odd number of feet. On the contrary they made their Apertures always in uneven numbers, as Nature herself has done in some instances, for tho' in Animals she has placed an ear, an eye and a nostril on each side, yet the great Aperture, the Mouth, she has placed singly in the middle» (*Ibid*, 238) (*Fig. 44*)[2]. «He [Bernini] said that the beauty of everything in the world, as in architecture, consists in proportion; that you might say that it is a divine particle, since it is derived from the body of Adam, who was not only made by God's hand, but who was made in his image and likeness; that the variety of the orders of architecture proceeded from the difference between the bodies of man and woman». (PAUL FRÉART, *Diary*, c. 1665, from J. RYKWERT, *The first Moderns, The Architects of the Eighteenth Century*, 1983, M.I.T. Press, 6-7) (*Fig. 45*)[3]. «The center of that architecture was the human body; its method, to transcribe in stone the body's favourable states; and the moods of the spirit took visible shape along its borders, power and laughter, strength and terror and calm. To have chosen these nobly, and defined them clearly, are the two marks of classic style» (GEOFFREY SCOTT, *The Architecture of Humanism, A Study in the History of Taste*, (1914-1924) 1954, Doubleday Anchor, 177). «But the great flag-bearing insignia have got to be, I think, among the most moving of twentieth-century shapes, certainly among the most empathetically powerful. Fireplaces, chimneys, and balconies, not to mention Egyptian temples, Roman triumphal arches, and Gothic cathedral facades, are condensed into one body with outstretched arms to make the mother of all forms» (VINCENT SCULLY, «Frank Lloyd Wright and the Stuff of Dreams», *Perspecta* 16, 1980, 26: On the Karl Mark Hof. (1977)

These quotations and illustrations, a mere sampling, should be sufficient to demonstrate the role of the human figure as a basis for architecture throughout its history, not only within the specific classical tradition but elsewhere as well. The final quotation brings that long tradition within the scope of the present (**21b**).

In the quotations above Scott and Scully emphasize the empathetic response to architecture, that is our imagining our bodies as participating in the support of loads and looking out from facades. It is in this way, perhaps, that we are responsive to the heraldic devices, the projecting flagpoles and half-round bays, found so frequently in the EVERYDAY MASTERPIECES we are studying. This empathetic response engages us actively in the building's activity. These heraldic elements provide one of the principal means for mediating between the novelty of seemingly weightless buildings (the modern style) and our familiarity with traditional mass architecture (the classical style) where we feel satisfaction if the weight seems to rest comfortably on the earth. Because we are familiar with the use of specific figurative elements in buildings, with the vertical as ourselves standing erect, and with drapery as a symbol of activity, then these heraldic motifs of the '30s as warriors offer protection and as dancers, exhileration.

DANCERS AND WARRIORS

«In the colonnade in front of St. Peter's, the enormous columns bear no weight; Bernini aligned them four by four, like figures in a procession. Perrault, in the facade of the Louvre, aligned the

Fig. 43

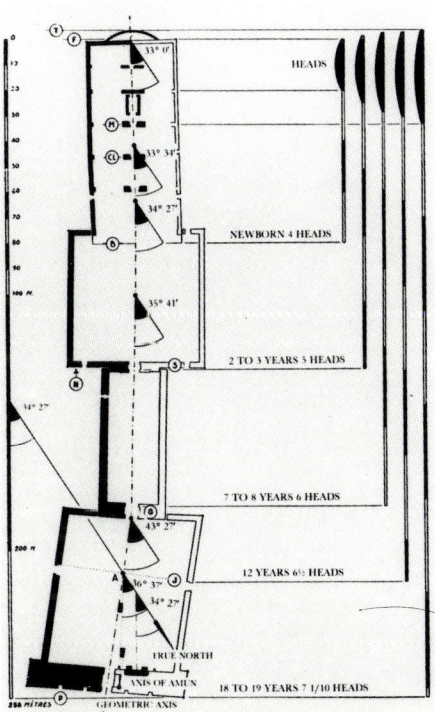

Fig. 44

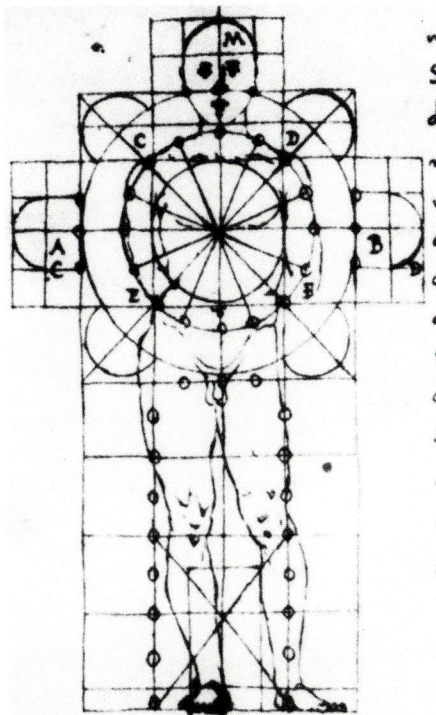

Fig. 45

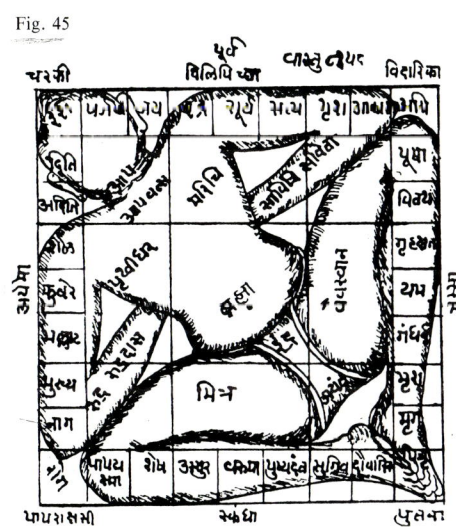

columns like a bodyguard of soldiers presenting arms. Rainaldi, in Santa Maria in Campitelli, hoisted them up to the second story of the facade like banners on flag-poles, repeating them like the hosannas of a hymn» (GIULIO CARLO ARGAN, *The Europe of the Capitals, 1600-1700*, 1964, Skira, 105). In a sense, one of these heraldic figures, one of these forward-thrusting elements, whether flagpole or half-round bay, used everywhere during the 1930s, can tell us all we need to know of architecture during this period. They embody the conflict between the retrograde classicism and *avant garde* modernism, between a lingering figuration and an advanced abstraction, combining both in a synthesis, in a mastery, at which the present-day architect can only marvel. We can begin two places at once: with the dancing figures of the *Utrecht Psalter* — those nervously written drawings which reintroduced the classical tradition to the court of Charlemagne — and with Louis XIV's first military review before his palace upon the parapet of which the heirs of these Carolingian figures dance: «18,000 men, 'one of the most spectacular actions of the reign', which was supposed to have 'kept all Europe in disquiet'. Several years later, a medal was struck to commemorate the event... On the right, the king, right foot forward, commands the exercise itself with a stick. On the left, they have raised their right arms to shoulder height and are holding their rifles exactly vertical, their right legs slightly forward and their left feet turned outwards. On the ground lines intersect at right angles, to form, beneath the soldier's feet, broad rectangles that serve as references for different phases and positions of the exercise. In the background is a piece of classical architecture. The columns of the palace extend those formed by the ranks of men and their erect rifles, just as the paving no doubt extends the lines of the exercise. But above the balustrade that crowns the building are statues representing dancing figures: sinuous lines, rounded gestures, draperies... The order of architecture, which frees at its summit the figures of the dance, imposes its rules and its geometry on the disciplined men on the ground». (MICHEL FOUCAULT, *Discipline & Punish*, The Birth of the Prison, (1975) 1979, Vintage Books, p. 188) (*Fig.* 46)[4].

All of this is far afield from the heraldic gestures placed atop buildings during the 1930s, but it is perhaps useful to review these gestures within a larger perspective and to note the combination of the ecstatic and the military. We say note because we will attempt no explanation for this combination of the joyful and the sinister, the promise of fullness and threat of repression which modernity has offered mankind. While on the one hand the weight-defying lifting which knowledge has made easily attainable seems an offer of ecstatic freedom, on the other that same knowledge has put us in a «society... of surveillance»*.

---

* A few years after Bentham, Julius gave this society its birth certificates (Julius, 384-6). Speaking of the panoptic principle, he said that there was much more there than architectural ingenuity: it was an event in the 'history of the human mind'. In appearance, it is merely the solution of a technical problem; but, through it, a whole type of society emerges. Antiquity had been a civilization of spectacle. 'To render accessible to a multitude of men the inspection of a small number of objects': this was the problem to which the architecture of temples, theatres and circuses responded. With spectacle, there was a predominance of public life, the intensity of festivals, sensual proximity. In these rituals in which blood flowed, society found new vigour and formed for a moment a single great body. The modern age poses the opposite problem: 'To procure for a small number, or even for a single individual, the instantaneous view of a great multitude'. In a society in which the principal elements are no longer the community and public life, but, on the one hand, private individuals and, on the other, the state, relations can be regulated only in a form that is the exact reverse of the spectacle: 'It was to the modern age, to the ever-growing influence of the state, to its ever more profound intervention in all the details and all the relations of social life, that was reserved the task of increasing and perfecting its guarantees, by using and directing towards that great aim the building and distribution of buildings intended to observe a great multitude of men at the same time'.

Julius saw as a fulfilled historical process that which Bentham had described as a technical programme. Our society is one not of spectacle, but of surveillance; under the surface of images, one invests bodies in depth; behind the great abstraction of exchange, there continues the meticulous, concrete training of useful forces; the circuits of communication are the supports of an accumulation and a centralization of knowledge; the play of signs defines the anchorages of power; it is not that the beautiful totality of the individual is amputated, repressed, altered by our social order, it is rather that the individual is carefully fabricated in it, according to a whole technique of forces and bodies. We are much less Greeks than we believe. We are neither in the amphitheatre, nor on the stage, but in the panoptic machine, invested by its effects of power, which we bring to ourselves since we are part of its mechanism.

(*Ibid.*, 216-17).

The *Utrecht Psalter* (*Fig.* 47)[5] was one of the radical innovations of the Carolingian period. It blew away the abstract figures of the Celtic masterpieces. If the scribes who drew these dancing warriors were from the East, fleeing the Byzantine Iconoclasm, then the line to Greece would be direct. Behind these figures, and all the subsequent dancers in the manuscripts (*Fig.* 49)[7] and on the jambs of Romanesque and Gothic churches, would lie the ecstatic, energy releasing Dionysiac Greek works, such as the famous Nike of Samothrace still proclaiming victory from her position on the Louvre stair (*Fig.* 48)[6]. All are blessed beings, powerless to contain their joy — optimism in the face of events. During our period, 1920-50, these figures were abstracted, distilled to the forward thrusting, vertically held flagpoles (like the representation of the soldiers' arms in the Louis XIV medal illustrated above) with their characteristic methods of attachment. The flag itself is the dancer represented as drapery: memory of Greece. «In the rigorous nudity of the male athlete Myron and his successors had deprived themselves of the chief aid to the representation of movement that art had to offer: the rhythmic line of drapery. Clinging drapery, following a plane or contour, emphasizes the stretch or twist of the body; floating drapery

Fig. 46

makes visible the line of movement through which it has just passed. Thus the aesthetic limitation of the nude body in action, that it is enclosed within an immediate present, is overcome. Drapery, by suggesting lines of force, indicates for each action a past and possible future» (KENNETH CLARK, *A Study in Ideal Form, The Nude*, 1959, Doubleday Anchor, 245). And, «Here for the first time... we see the defiance of gravity transferred from water to air. The dream of buoyance, with all it implies of liberation, becomes more rapturous and more invigorating. As with the first embodiments of ecstasy, the suspension of our reason is achieved by the intricate rhythms of the drapery that sweep and flow irresistibly around the nude figures. Their bodies, by an endlless intricacy of embrace, sustain the current of movement, which finally flickers down their legs and is dispersed like an electric charge». (*Ibid.*, 381-82). Thus Kenneth Clark describes how drapery, or in our case a billowing flag, can suggest the active figure. A late literal use of drapery in architecture was the pavilion by Henri Sauvage at the Paris fair of 1900 for the dancer Loie Fuller (*Figg.* 50, 51)[8]. It represented her. At its ends the drapery is thrust upward in a climatic gesture: a forerunner of the more abstract heraldic motifs of our period (*Figg.* 52, 53)[9].

Fig. 47

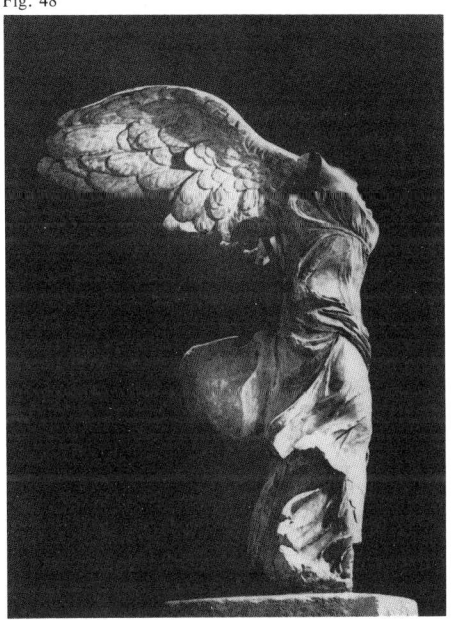

Fig. 48

Fig. 49

Fig. 50

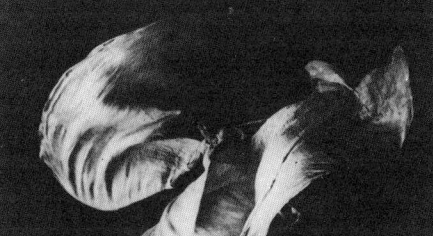

Fig. 51

That abstract motif had an ancient model: the pylons of the New Kingdom temples in Egypt. Except that the Egyptian flagpoles were supported directly on the ground, their method of attachment matches that used during our period (*Fig.* 54)[10]. Formally, symmetrically mounted flagpoles reinforce the centrality of the facade. Symbolically, they give the building a public character, which depends, of course, on the long-establi-

Fig. 52

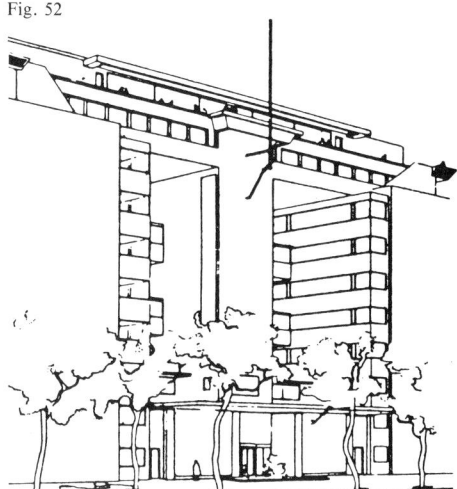

Fig. 53

shed tradition of the flag/banner as the emblem of authority. In as much as the new repertoire of methods of holding the flagpoles was easily identifiable as new, the buildings to which they were attached were immediately understood as modern. At the same time the flag itself reinforced the official character of the building.

The canonic accounts of Modern Architecture during the period 1920-40 by Hitchcock and Johnson, Giedion, Pevsner, J.M. Richards, *et al.* — even up to those written around 1960 by Benevolo and the Smithsons (*The Heroic Period*) — are significantly devoid of works displaying conspicuous heraldic motifs. While the major figures, Le Corbusier, Mies van der Rohe, Aalto, *et al.*, began their careers working in a stripped neo-classical mode, the canonic accounts avoid discussing this work except as examples from before the 'great leap forward' made after 1920 when overt classical references were avoided. The radical break, without any retrospection, was the basis of the story: the heroism of the Heroic Period. As the International Style spread, as it became popularized, it became contaminated with classical references, which were condemned by the spokesmen defending the style's orthodoxy (the commentary in Hitchcock's and Johnson's *The International Style* of 1932 is a case in point). Among the contaminations were heraldic motifs: flagpoles, either singly or in rows, and projecting half-round bays. These heraldic motifs are among the most interesting, most provocative, of these contaminations for being specifically architectural and usually not recognizable as derived from the classical vocabulary. Nevertheless, they are anthropomorphic — like the column itself. Their use was frequent and widespread, as if this gesture released the building from the too austere, too doctrinaire, quality of orthodox Modernism. These heraldic motifs permitted architecture to be totally modern, yet popularly acceptable.

Within the catalogue which follows is a section devoted to «Heraldic Elements», **22** through **26**, as well as **21b** and **38a & b**. Scanning the catalogue will reveal others, depending upon how one makes his definition. Unquestionably one would include **31a & b**, **45b**, **47a**, and **53a**, but what of the two vertical piers in **4b**, the projecting columns of **6a & b**, the roof top fins of **7a**, the clock with its two piers in **8a**, the corner tower of **14a** and sign of **13b**, the keystone of **27b**, the tall frontispiece of **34b**, the face-like motif of **35a**, the glass tower of **40b**, and even the vertical void of **52c**? Our everyday masters were skillful at devising motifs. Most of these buildings were confined within tight budgets, conventional construction and ordinary sites, but by their inventiveness within a narrow stylistic range, they suggested that their buildings were worth our attention. This exhibition celebrates their extraordinary ordinary talents.

T.K.

[1] Projection of the plan of the Temple of Luxor on a human skeleton (*Fig.* 42); Diagram of the Temple of Luxor showing the ages of man (*Fig.* 43): R.A. Schwaller De Lubicz, *op. cit.*, p. 23 & p. 122.
[2] Francesco di Giorgio, Drawing from Cod. Magliab., Bibl. Naz., Florence (*Fig.* 44): R. Wittkower, *Architectural Principles in the Age of Humanism*, 1971, Norton, pl. 1a.
[3] Indian mandala the *vastu-purusha*; from an old Indian manual of architecture (*Fig.* 45): S. Kostof, *A History of Architecture Setting and Rituals*, 1985, Oxford University Press, p. 228.
[4] Medal commemorating Louis XIV's first military revue in 1668 (B.N. Cabinet des médailles) (*Fig.* 46): M. Foucault, *op. cit.*, p. 76.
[5] 39 Psalm 26 from the Utrecht Psalter (fol. 15 recto), Reims; about 820 (*Fig.* 47): J. Beckwith, *Early Medieval Art Carolingian, Ottonian, Romanesque*, 1974, Oxford University Press, p. 49 top.
[6] Nike of Samothrace, c. 190 B.C. (*Fig.* 48): H. Read, *The Art of Sculture*, 1961, Bollinger Foundation, New York, pl. 181.
[7] King David, Abbot Salomon's *Psalterium Aureum*, St. Gall, 890-920 (*Fig.* 49): J. Beckwith, *op. cit.*, p. 76.

[8] Loïe Fuller (1862-1928) with her "butterfly veils" (*Fig.* 50); Théâtre de la Loïe Fuller, Exposition Universelle de 1900, Paris (*Fig.* 51): *Henri Sauvage 1873-1932*, 1976, Editions: Archives d'Architecture Moderne, p. 117.
[9] Immeubles Villas 1922, Le Corbusier (*Fig.* 52): *Le Corbusier et Pierre Jeanneret, Oeuvre Complète de 1910-1929*, 1956, Girsberger, p. 41; Théâtre de la Loïe Fuller, detail (*Fig.* 53): *Henri Sauvage*, cit.
[10] A pylon, after a New Kingdom relief (*Fig.* 54): J.L. De Cenival, *Living Architecture: Egyptian*, 1964, Grosset & Dunlap, p. 89.

22a - Garage Citroën
Latina, Italy
Oriolo Frezzotti (1888-?)
Bibl.: Zardini, *Casabella*, 1984.

The corner position of the building, in an area being reorganized by James Stirling, is such that the rectilinear front of the short side appears as a real facade. Here a large overhang, as in Oud's architecture, recomposes the unity of the various fronts, but the part at the front preserves its own volumetric autonomy. This is shown by the contrast between the lower part with the large opening of the entrance and the upper blind part, which contains the lettering. The effect is confirmed and emphasized by the two flagpoles on its curved ends, which, with the crowning balustrade, create a vertical thrust, attenuating the neatness of the volume.

P.M.M.

22b - The Oath of the Horatii
1782
Jacques-Louis David (1748-1825)
Musée des Beaux-Arts, Lille, France
Bibl.: Scottez, Cat. *Autour de David...*, 1984, n. 15, pp. 47-48.

The drawing is a study for the famous painting done by David during his second Roman sojourn (1784-1785) for the Count d'Angivillier. The focus of the composition is the upraised swords, a point of iconological convergence: symbol of heroism debated in the drama of the scene, a declaration of virile force, underlined by the Doric architectural structure, the fruit of the «annotations made 'by David' during his visits to the Roman palaces»

J.R.S.

23a - Greystone Hotel
Collins Ave., Miami Beach, Fla., U.S.A.
1939 (MDPL)
Henry Hohauser (1895 or 1896-1963)

23b - «Vue d'un Rocher élevé dans le centre du Camp de Fédération... Lyon le 30 Mai 1790...»
1790
Claude Cochet le Jeune (1715-1790)
Musée Carnavalet, Pc Hist. 11B, Paris, France
Bibl.: Mosser, Cat. *La fortuna di Paestum...*, vol. II, 1986, H 1.

«The theme of the 'Rocher' is transformed into the symbol of liberty and political unity. Nature, source of all prosperity and model of all virtue, becomes — with its escarpments and its rocks — the «speaking» ornament of the effort brought to an end. Only Doric columns with smooth and massive shafts can suit this association between the natural rock and Republican virtues — here Concord. Perhaps in this precise moment the symbolic use of the 'order' of Paestum reaches its greatest value» (Mosser).

Fig. 54

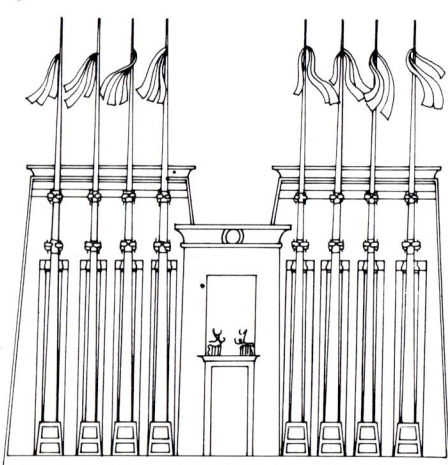

24a - Essex House Hotel
Collins Ave., Miami Beach, Fla., U.S.A.
1938 (MDPL)
Henry Hohauser (1895 or 1896-1963)

24b - Kirchgemeindehaus Wipkingen mit Post und Wohnungen
Rosengartenstrasse 1, Zürich, Switzerland
1930-1932
Vogelsanger, Maurer
Bibl.: «Unterbrochene Stadt...», *werk archithese*, 1978, p. 63, fig. 40.

The corner position and the slimness of the cylinder body create a point of view rich in emotional power for the observer: an epic tone which refers to the staff of a flag, formed by the wrap around balconies and by the emerging of the cylinder at the top and finally, perhaps by chance, by the relation with the circular clock. This is a particularly original variant of a formal motif frequent in central European and Dutch architecture, from De Klerk (Eigen Haard housing estate, 1917, Amsterdam) to Mendelsohn (Cohen-Epstein Stores, Duisburg, 1926-1927).
P.M.M.

24c - Nelson's Pillar
1818
Francis Johnston (1761-1829)
Murray Collection, National Library of Ireland, (A.D. 2088), Dublin, Ireland.
Bibl.: MCCARTHY, Cat. *La fortuna di Paestum...*, vol. II, 1986, H 16.

The first Doric column in honor of Nelson was erected in Dublin (destroyed by a bomb in 1966). The proposal by Johnston for a flagpole crowning the column was presumably made in response to the criticism of the trireme that Wilkins had placed on the summit in a preceding project (1807). In the version realized, the column was surmounted by the statue of a naval hero, a banal response to the more «modern» commemorative intent expressed by Johnston.

25a - Pan Pacific Auditorium
7600 Beverly Blvd., Los Angeles, Calif., U.S.A.
1935-1938 (Gebhard)
Wurdeman & Becket

25b - Villa
Avenue Mohammed V, Safi, Morocco
c. 1930-1940

26a - Project for a pavilion of building materials
I Esposizione Italiana di Architettura Razionale
Rome, Italy
1928
Guido Frette (1901-1986)
Bibl.: PIACENTINI, *Architettura e Arti Decorative*, 1928; CENNAMO, 1973, *passim*.

In addition to the usual assemblage of pure volumes and to linguistic elements such as the strip window or large glass window, this project is characterized by an anomalous element, the mast with half round balconies, which will become typical in the 1930's in the use of superimposed balconies and which, transposed and emphasized in a variety of forms, can be related to the studies of Mendelsohn of 1917 and, more generally, to the new forms that the aesthetics of the machine was defining.
P.M.M.

26b - Ferdinand Buisson High School
Boulogne, Seine, France
1932 (cornerstone)
Cauvet & Ogé (cornerstone)

RUSTICATION
27a; 27b; 27c; 27d.
28a; 28b; 28c; 28d.
LETTERING AS RUSTICATION
29a; 29b.
THE STRIP WINDOW AS RUSTICATION
30a; 30b; 31a; 31b.

Rustication is an element that the new architectural culture of the 18th century made its own, since the *opus rusticum* was connected to the rediscovery of the Doric as a symbol of force and nature.
Rustication characterizes the facing of the Doric facade since, as Serlio had indicated, it could have be used with this 'primitive' order. Giulio Romano gave to this «licentious» variation of the order an expressive efficacy that no one had attained before him. He created a true «transgressive» system, going from the smoothest facings, almost incisions in the plaster, to the heavy rough blocks — as if they had just left the quarry —. He adopted the ''banded'', ''ringed'' columns, the ''block columns'' (where the vertical shaft is interrupted by refined square drums) and he used the keystones out of scale[1].
The rich and very sophisticated repertoire elaborated by him undoubtedly inspired the 18th century culture of a Dance or a Ledoux and, through these, also the main and ordinary architecture of the 20th century.
The visual effects produced by rustication are of two kinds: on one hand, contrast between light and shadow, rendering the element with expressionistic exageration while retaining a decorative value[2]; on the other hand, the accentuation of horizontal coursing that re-emerges in the use of «strip windows as rustication»[3].
Even lettering, according to a «licentious» invention, brings the theme of publicity into the mainstream of the tradition. «Advertising architecture must act as the call of the sirens» (VONDER MÜHLL, 1931, p. 241).
N.Z.

Medieval return, linguistic identity, and expressionistic freedom are fused in the vernacular recovery of exposed brick, beyond the disputes on materials, on artisan values, on the relation of material and form that have gone on since the end of the 19th century.
The memory passes over the examples of industrial architecture of the first few decades of the 1900's and once again the lexical transformation carried out and transmitted by Soane returns. The transfusion of ancient ways — here Roman and Romanesque — appears in modern use: in the dwellings, in the apartment houses and in the utilitarian buildings. At that moment in which the use of marble begins to increase, the brick gives new possibilities for relating function and structure. «Gratitude is due to him [Soane] who strikes out a new path and aspires to perfection...» (Sir J. REYNOLDS).
The way is opened to the industrial interpretation of T. Telford and of P. Hardwick or to the utilitarian buildings of Schinkel[4].
Then tradition and modernity are blended: the vernacular lexicon flows, diffusing the memory of the past in a new formula of the moment[5].
J.R.S.

[1] Church of St. George-in-the-East (door to the gallery Staircase), London, 1714-1729, N. Hawksmoor; State Paper Office, St. James's Park, London, 1829-1833, J. Soane.
[2] Chilehaus (detail), Hamburg, 1922-1923, G. Höger (*Fig.* 55).
[3] It seems useless to dwell on the well-known motif of strip windows, one of the most affirmed in modern architectural culture on all levels. For the suggestion put forward by Wright on European culture, see V. SCULLY, 1986, p. 16, and also note 7 of «The picturesque composition», *infra*.

Fig. 55

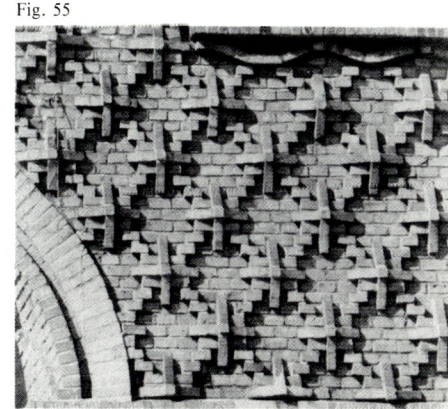

[4] Dulwich Mausoleum, London, 1811, J. Soane; Sketch by a pupil of Soane during the progress of work, 1812 (see *John Soane,* 1983, p. 96, n. 47) (*Fig.* 56); Military Prison and Barracks, Lindenstrasse, Berlin, 1817, K.F. Schinkel; St. Katherine's Docks, London, 1827-1828, T. Telford and P. Hardwick (*Fig.* 57).

[5] Stock Exchange, Amsterdam, 1898-1903, H.P. Berlage; Chemical factory, Luban, 1911-1912, H. Poelzig; Farben Office Building, Höchst (Frankfurt-am-Main), 1921-1925, P. Behrens.

27a - Rose Court Apartments
Bennet Ave., New York, U.S.A.
1936 (BDR)

Fig. 56

Fig. 57

Horace Ginsbern (1900-1969) (BDR) with Marvin Fine (1904-1981)

An abstract two-story rusticated portal with keystone: a linear abstraction of massive construction (see article by Anthony Robins).

T.K.

27b - Apartment building
1791 Grand Concourse, Bronx, New York, U.S.A.
1936 (Sullivan)
Edward Franklin

Glass block representing structure, seeming to support a massive crown representing both rustication with a keystone and a simplified giant triglyph (for a view of the entire building see **52c**).

T.K.

27c - Barrière des Ministres
1785-1789
Claude-Nicolas Ledoux (1736-1806)
Bibl.: KAUFMANN, (1952) 1982, p. 254

A double purpose, giving movement to the composition and exhibiting the quality of materials, guides the majority of projects for the barrières of Paris, an assignment that was entrusted to Ledoux in 1784 by the Ferme Générale for the enclosure walls of the capital. Even in the general uniformity each Customs-House presents an autonomous typification. The Barrière des Ministres, for example, evokes the solemnity of the Greek temple but, in the tympanum, a massive keystone is inserted as Vanbrugh and Hawksmoor had already done to render doors and windows expressive.

N.Z.

27d - Entrance to an arsenal (model)
1785
Carl August Ehrensvärd (1745-1800)
Marin Museum, Karlskrona, Sweden
Bibl.: VOGT, Cat. *La fortuna di Paestum...*, Vol. II, 1986, I 53.

28a - Montezemolo Barracks
Via A. Baiamonti, Rome, Italy
c. 1938
Vittorio Cafiero (1901-1981)

The traditional use of exposed brickwork on facades, which had important plastic application in Dutch architecture of the 1910's and the 1920's, finds in horizontally banded structures a further application, recalling, in the rustic effect and in the compositional cadence, the facade with horizontal rustication. This is how in this building, according to a new compositional tradition, the entire facade is treated with a sober, monumental effect, reinforced by the tight rhythm of the strip windows and by the compactness of the volume, where the curving of the front introduces a slight movement.

P.M.M.

28b - Newgate Gaol (demolished in 1902)
London, England
1769
George Dance the Younger (1741-1825)
Bibl.: SUMMERSON, 1986, pp. 137-138.

George Dance the Younger, architect of the City of London, recalling the *Carceri* by Piranesi, employed rustication and festoons of iron chains upon the entrance to give gravity and a bit of horror. All this shows the purpose of the building as a fortified place of punishment, an example of «architecture parlante».

N.Z.

28c - Hôtel des Monnaies (lateral facade)
Rue Guénégaud, Paris, France
1768-1775
Jacques-Denis Antoine (1773-1801)
Bibl.: BRAHAM, 1982, p. 119.

The architect Antoine reveals himself in 1766 with the commission for the construction of the new building for the «Monnaie royale» (1768-1775). Apart from the typological innovations introduced in the main facade, Antoine underlines in this lateral facade the function of the building, using the Doric rustication, therefore coming to an understanding of the typological tradition that Sansovino had reserved for the Mint.
Here Antoine, in a decorative exaltation, emphasizes the meaning of the building: a compact block like a safe.

J.R.S.

28d - Butler Brothers Warehouse
Jersey City, N.J., U.S.A.
c. 1905
Jarvis Hunt (C. Wyatt)
Bibl.: HITCHCOCK and JOHNSON, (1932), 1966, p. 67.

The horizontal brick banding is remarkable given the early date of this building (it is one of three similar contemporary warehouses by Jarvis Hunt, the nephew of Richard Morris Hunt, the others in Chicago and Minneapolis). Clearly more research is needed, but this building antedates by 26 years Hitchcock's and Johnson's complaint:
«One of the chief vices of contemporary architecture, which has superseded in Europe the emulation of the verticality of the American skyscraper, is what may be called «fake banding», a purely decorative scheme of tying windows together in a horizontal row».

T.K.

29a - Project for a building in Piazza San Babila
Milan, Italy
1934
Aldo Andreani (1887-1971)
Bibl.: SOMARÈ, 1937, *passim;* Cat. *Il razionalismo...,* 1976, pp. 65, 122, 126-127; Cat. *Ricostruzione Futurista...,* 1980, p. 280; GODOLI, 1983, pp. 151-153.

The new arrangement of Piazza San Babila is included among the episodes of town-planning of the 1930's in Italy. In addition to the project by Andreani, one by Baldessari in 1936 must also be mentioned. This building shows many different elements which recompose themselves in a «picturesque» way, from the classicist colonnade of the central body to the strip windows, and to the dynamism of the lateral bodies. At the top the lettering has antecedents in the typographic architecture of Prampolini («Futurismo» pavilion, Turin exhibition, 1928), although here, as in several other instances it is reduced to a pure graphic sign, turning into a new fundamental element of the urban landscape.

P.M.M.

29b - Design for the Campari Pavilion
1931

Fortunato Depero (1892-1960)
Bibl.: DEPERO, 1940, pp. 224-225; Cat. *Il razionalismo...*, 1976, p. 96; Cat. *Ricostruzione Futurista...*, 1980, pp. 279, 387-399; GODOLI, 1983, pp. 151-153.

The interest of Depero for the typographic composition of architecture is already manifested in 1927 with the pavilion of the Bottega del Libro at the 3rd Biennial of Monza.
We can see many examples in which the facade is organized by lettering. What distinguishes the Campari pavilion is the plasticity of the type. The effect of light on the out of scale letters gives them the importance of rustication.

P.M.M.

30a - Starrett-Lehigh Building, Warehouse
W. 26th to W.27th St., Eleventh to Twelvth Aves.
New York, U.S.A.
c. 1930-1931 (Stern)
R.G. & William Cory with Y. Matsui

30b-30c - Apartment building
127-129, Avenue Moulay Hassan I, Casablanca, Morocco
1934 (cornerstone)
J. Balois & P. Perrotte (cornerstone).

31a - Fiat Garage
Ave. Lalla Yaquote & Mustapha El Maani
Casablanca, Morocco

31b - Ibex House
42 Minories, EC3.
London, England
1937
Fuller, Hall and Foulsham (Jones & Woodward)
Bibl.: TAFURI - DAL CO, 1979, p. 224.

The alternation of horizontal void and solid bands, used in 20th century buildings, gives a new effect of relief which has strong connections to classical rusticated facades. There are many examples of this technique of facade weaving, which develop the use of the strip window.
The plain banding is here interrupted by a glass cylinder, as a giant column, which is the axis of the building.

P.M.M.

THE TUSCAN / RUSTIC ORDER
32a; 32b.

It was Giulio Romano who created a true organic system in which all the possible variations of the «tuscan rustic order» appear[1]. Applied in antiquity to utilitarian buildings to underline their rudeness, it expands widely after Giulio in the mannerist period. The column formed by polished cubical drums appears for the first time in the drawing for his house in «Macello de' Corbi» in Rome.
This example spread by the plates of the Trattati (from Serlio to Palladio to Inigo Jones) gets through to Ledoux, who widely uses it in the project for the «Salt Works» at Chaux. Here he enphasizes the prototype: the modern approach of altering the scale is evident.

N.Z.

[1] This definition is used by JAMES ACKERMAN, 1983.

32a - Spear & Company Store
22 West 34th St., New York, U.S.A.
1933-1934 (Stern)
De Young & Moscowitz

32b - House of the Director, detail of the portico
Salt Works
Chaux, Arcs, et Senans, France
1775-1790
Claude-Nicolas Ledoux (1736-1806)
Bibl.: Cat. *La fortuna di Paestum...*, 1986, vol. II, p. 272.

Ledoux, interested as he is in the variations of the *opus rusticum* (codified in the Manneristic age) applies it here after the interpretation of Giulio Romano to enliven and give an effect of light and shadow to the temple facade with structural elements that assume ornamental character.

N.Z.

THE GIANT ORDER
33a; 33b; 34a; 34b;
35a; 35b; 36a; 36b.

The giant order is the order in which the columns ascend through more than a single story. The expedient of confining two stories within a single order, introduced by Michelangelo in the Capitoline Palaces, provided a useful heritage.
The structural possibilities and the formal suggestions offered by this element are widely exploited in the architectural culture of the 20th century and, of course, felt in the vernacular lexicon[1].

N.Z.

[1] The giant order is so widely used in the 20th century architecture that it is superfluous to give here examples.

33a - Apartment building
Via Barnaba Oriani 91, Rome, Italy
1936
Bianchini
Bibl.: DE GUTTRY, 1978, p. 55; GODOLI, 1983, pp. 21-29.

This building, located in an area developed between the 1920's and the 1940's, shows a variation on the motif of cylindrical facade blocks used as columns of a giant order. This motif was already found in Italy, in a «cultured» manner, in Mario Chiattone's studies of apartment houses done in the middle of the 1910's.
Here the two columns free at the top and fluted by the openings, are interrupted by balconies.

P.M.M.

33b - Villa
Via Aniello Falcone, Naples, Italy
1938
Tommaso Cotronei (1902-1984)

34a - Daché Building (destroyed)
East 56th St., New York, U.S.A.
1936 (BDR) - 1937 (Stern)
Shreve, Lamb & Harmon (BDR)

By the architects of the Empire State building.

34b - J. Kurtz & Sons Department Store
162 Jamaica Ave., Queens, New York, U.S.A.
Built 1931
Allmendinger & Schlendorf (LPC)

35a - Cinema
Amiens, France

35b - Colonia Marittima «Villa Rosa Maltoni Mussolini»
Calambrone, Tirrenia, Italy
1925-1933
Angiolo Mazzoni (1894-1979)
Bibl.: Forti, 1978, p. 40; Godoli, 1983, pp. 218-219; Cat. *Angiolo Mazzoni*, 1985, pp. 118-123.

During its construction the seaside colony of Calambrone received enthusiastic comments in the press and in the Italian architectural community. The buildings, as a whole articulate a complex interplay realized through the simplified volumes (cubes, cylinders, porticoes), the chromatism of the reddish-orange colors, and the contrast between the transparancy of the windows and the mass of the buildings. It is a game of combination which creates an array of solutions.
P.M.M.

36a - Apartment building
Cairo, Egypt
c. 1930-1940
R. Antonius, architect/engineer (cornerstone)

36b - Apartment building
Heliopolis, Egypt

THE HALF ROUND BAY
36c; 37a; 37b; 38a; 38b.

In the second half of the 18th century, the new «revolutionary» architecture, ruled by the principle of independence, annuls the «exclusive and hierarchical baroque» scheme, generating a series of new solutions for planimetric relationships. Among the numerous schemes singled out by Emil Kaufmann, «interpenetration», is exemplified in the plans of the two dairies of Soane.
«Interpenetration, which under the revolutionary (individualistic) system means that one feature seems to intrude into another, or even to tear it apart (The term "interpenetration" has often been used to indicate the intermingling or coalescing of features in the Baroque, and has also been applied where one part seemed to grow out from another, like a protuberance). The pattern of interpenetration (in the revolutionary sense) can be visualized either by the crossing of masses, or by volume (space) intruding into mass. Interpenetration was almost exclusively a spatial pattern. It played an important part in the nineteenth century, and like the other patterns of antithesis it plays a still greater role in our time»[1].
J.R.S.

[1] Kaufmann, 1955, p. 189.

36c - Villa
Rabat, Morocco
c. 1930-1940

37a-37b - Hammels Park dairy, Hertfordshire, plan
1783
John Soane (1753-1837)
Sir John Soane's Museum (Al Designs for various Buildings by John Soane Architect, 1789-1794, Item 6 and 7), London, England.

Rustic dairy, two alternatives
1781
John Soane (1753-1837)
Victoria and Albert Museum (3306, 161) London, England

37c - Perrigny-Poste 1, Railroad Switching Station
Dijon, France

38a - Traffic Tower project
Berlin, Germany
1924 (Schulze)
Ludwig Mies van der Rohe

38b - Ristorante Cora
Fiera Campionaria di Bari
Bari, Italy
Nicolaj Diulgheroff (1901-1982)
Bibl.: Cat. *Il razionalismo...*, 1976, p. 96; Pinottini, 1979, pp. 73-77; Godoli, 1983, pp. 116, 189.

Often the development of architecture is linked to «ephemeral» works such as pavilions for exhibitions. So it is with this pavilion, which in the variety of its architectural motifs and the freedom of their composition, from the strip windows to the emphasis on the lettering, and the terrace on pilotis matches a new planning «tradition», that had grown around the MIAR since 1928.
The center of the composition, accented by the flag is the large semicylindrical volume supported on pilotis the only closed element of a space prevalently open and perforated by the glass entrance, which continues under the jutting volume. The complexity of the design mitigates the vigor of the half round bay.
P.M.M.

"ARCHITECTURE PARLANTE"

Eighteenth-century man, discovering an emotional tension in himself and in material objects, transformed this tension into artistic creation — into a medium for reaching out to the surrounding world and drawing it into the realm of sentiment. Buildings of the later eighteenth century, animated by an emotional tension of this kind, became pieces of 'speaking architecture'. This term, coined at a late stage as a pejorative characterisation of the works of Ledoux, has in fact come to assume a rather different role, that of defining the new emphasis on the content of works of architecture — as opposed to their purely formal qualities — which began to make its appearance from the middle of the century onwards, but which in reality only Boullée and Ledoux were able to express in terms of *sensibilité*.

The concern with giving architecture a 'speaking' quality went beyond a mere emphasis on the functional, finding expression not in the employment of a particular range of forms but, rather, in an attempt to apply an analysis of the conceptual roots of feeling to the process of architectural design. The resulting buildings could be defined either as works serving to rouse creative emotion or as focal points of interest.

An architectural enterprise expresses itself, then, in the manifestation of its 'character'; in other words, it should «employer avec justesse tous les moyens propres à ne nous faire éprouver d'autres sensations que celles qui doivent résulter du sujet» (BOULLÉE, 1968 ed., p. 73)[1].

«Architecture inspires emotions in man. The task of the architect is therefore to state precisely the emotion... The Palace of Justice must appear to the secret vice as a threat...»[2] In 1910 Loos is looking for the same "character" exalted by Boullée and Ledoux. The architectonic idea is finalized by stressing the meaning of functional character. «J'ai traité ce sujet le plus en grand qu'il m'a été possible parce que le lieu où réside le trône de la justice doit être très imposant. Si j'avais rempli le but que je me suis proposé en cherchant à donner à ce monument le caractère qui lui est propre, j'aurais rempli une tâche difficile». (apropos of the Palais de Justice, BOULLÉE, 1968 ed., p. 114)

In the epoch that lives under the sign of the machine, «*the house is a machine for living in*»[3]. Now the transmission of the message entrusted to architecture no longer concerns, as in Loos, the function of the single building but characterizes the meaning of an epoch. The structures move; become boats, machines; animate themselves with marine and aerodynamic decorations[4]. Buildings and manufactured objects have now a close association: they adopt a style now referred to as «streamline moderne»[5]. In the *machine age* the new characters assume the ancient value of symbols.

J.R.S.

[1] RASPI SERRA, Cat. *Paestum and the Doric revival...*, p. 104.
[2] LOOS, 1986, p. 255.
[3] LE CORBUSIER, (1923) 1952, p. 100.
[4] Triple Hydroplane Caproni, from LE CORBUSIER, (1923) 1952, p. 131 (*Fig. 58*).
[5] *American architecture...*, 1986, p. 47.

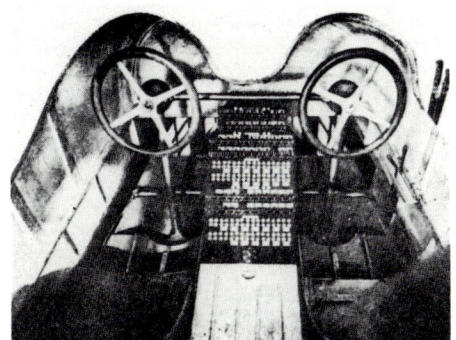

Fig. 58

MODERN DISPERSION: BUILDINGS AS VEHICLES
39a; 39b; 39c.

«... Therefore the work may have the same claim to consideration as a 'work of art' as an ocean liner, a locomotive or a battleship»[1].

[1] WRIGHT (1910) 1963, pl. 39.

39a - Motorboating Association A.M.I.La. Club
Tremezzo, Italy
1926-1927
Pietro Lingeri (1894-1968)
Bibl.: PAGANO, *La Casa Bella*, 1930; «Un club sul lago di Como...», *La Casa Bella*, 1931; «Due opere di Pietro Lingeri», *Domus*, 1931.

The Club of the Associazione Motonautica Italiana del Lario, built on the banks of the Lake of Como, «fits into the landscape with the frankness of the outboard motor... logical and naked like the bridge of a ship; exquisitely plastic in space like the lines of naval construction» (*La Casa Bella*, 1931).
Lingeri drew his inspiration from marine architecture for the color as well: «white plaster of cementite, deep azure of the parapets and the railings, resplendent orange of the doors» (*Domus*, 1931).

N.Z.

39b - Maison destinée aux Surveillants de la Source de la Loue, vue perspective
in CLAUDE-NICOLAS LEDOUX, *L'architecture...*, 1804, pl. 6.
Claude-Nicolas Ledoux (1736-1806)
Bibl.: KAUFMANN, (1952) 1982, pp. 329-330

This project is an example of *architecture parlante*. An «avant-garde» water installation that seems to represent the aspiration for technological progress in the epoch in which the problem began to be felt. The hand of man competes with the liberty of nature. Ledoux makes the river pass through the building in such a way that the powerful barrel vault makes a bridge over the waters that flow into the concave portion. The hollow of the tunnel, which contrasts with the fullness of the geometrical solids, becomes the focus of the design and the paradigmatic symbol of the aqueduct.

N.Z.

39c - Heliotherapeutic Colony
Cattolica, Italy
1933

Clemente Busiri-Vici (1877-1965)
Bibl.: Godoli, 1983, pp. 165-168; Mantero, 1984, p. 18.

This design belongs to the architecture explicitly imitating the forms of ships and trains (a theme already present in the debates of the 1910's and 1920's). Among these, the forms inspired by trains, the least frequent usually echo the culture of the second Italian futurism: an immediate antecedent is the complex of workers' houses and of lodging and huts for farmers presented in the manifesto, «Architettura Futurista Poggi», of January 3rd, 1933.

P.M.M.

DYNAMIC COMPOSITION: THE BUILDING AS A SHIP

40a; 40b; 40c; 41a; 41b; 42a; 42b; 42c.

The idea of the new nautical[1] architecture passes everywhere, to various clubs[2], maritime stations, airports... emblematic images of an epoch that imperiously assumed by now as its own the themes of naval architecture[3]. They had already been adopted, as functional suggestions, in the typology of office buildings since the time of Root[4].

J.R.S.

[1] Club at San Sebastiano (Spain), 1929 (La Bayen

Fig. 59

Fig. 60

and Aizpierna), from H.R. Hitchcock and P. Johnson, (1932, 1966) 1982, pp. 172-173 (*Fig.* 61).
[2] Club, Lungotevere Thaon de Revel, Rome (*Fig.* 62).
[3] L'Aquitania, Cunard Line, Le Corbusier, (1923) 1952, p. 94 (*Fig.* 59). Modern Architecture: S. S. Australia (from B. Taut, 1928) (*Fig.* 60).
[4] Mumford (1931) 1977, p. 104.

40a - Fort Hommel und Fort sur l'Isle Pelee
1797
Friedrich Gilly (1772-1800)
Destroyed, formerly in the Technische Hochschule, Charlottenburg
Berlin (B.D.R.)
Bibl.: Neumeyer, Cat. *Friedrich Gilly*, 1987, pp. 64, and esp. p. 49.

The «visionary» anticipation of Gilly's project is expressed in this drawing where the object is rendered by lines and surfaces, geometrically similar to the machine», hinting at, as Fritz Neumeyer points out, «the heroic phase of the modern during the 1920's».

J.R.S.

40b - «G. Nicelli» Airport
Venice, Lido, Italy
1932

The airport ressembles an anchored ship on the waters of Venice. It presents decorative and constructive details of a typical modernity: the design of the helicoid ramps (having become by then a common theme) animates the composition, which culminates in the glass control tower.
In the latter, there is a specific recall of naval forms, especially of those of submarine turrets, already used by Mendelsohn, transformed by him into elements of current use.
The strip windows in the horizontal block (in lieu of the expected portholes) guarantee good illumination and at the same time underline the shape.

N.Z.

Fig. 61

Fig. 62

40c - Castello d'acqua decorated by a public fountain
1780
August Cheval de St. Hubert (1755-1798)
Accademia di Belle Arti, Parma, Italy
Bibl.: ADORNI, Cat. *L'arte a Parma dai Farnese ai Borbone*, 1979, no. 446.

The project which won the first prize at the competition of 1780 proclaimed by the Accademia of Parma, was praised by the jury for, among other things, the «facaded of the Building of Doric Order... strewn with virile beauties in the forms and in the proportions, and the Temple, being isolated between two great walls, which join to the Fountain the other buildings demanded by us, acquires a character of tranquillity that is very pleasant for a sojourn and for the icy recesses of the river...»

41a - Apartment building
1360 Montgomery St., San Francisco, Calif., U.S.A.
1937 (Gebhard)
J.S. Malloch, developer / contractor

41b - Maritime Museum
San Francisco, Calif., U.S.A.
1936 (?)-1939 (Gebhard)
William Mooser & son

42a - Italian Pavilion at the Chicago World's Fair
1933
Adalberto Libera (1903-1963), Mario De Renzi (1897-1967)
Bibl.: Cat. *Il razionalismo...*, 1976, p. 93; CRESTI, 1986, p. 318.

In this pavilion the *littorio* symbol, at the back abstracted through the interpenetration of two vertical blocks, the hollow in the solid, seems like a rudder in a composition which plays strongly on the hydrodynamic form of the main block. The natural connotation of this architecture is a direct consequence of the expressive potential of the forms and of their composition, particularly the relationship of the half round bay and the main volume. This volume is repeated laterally with a deliberate nautical form, going as far as having portholes but which, compositionally, is not a repetition but an elision.

P.M.M.

42b - Coca Cola Bottling Co.
Los Angeles, Calif., U.S.A.
1936-1937 (Gebhard)
Robert V. Derrah

42c - «Un renfoncement rond comme l'oeil de boeuf»
in JEAN-JACQUES LEQUEU, *Architecture civile*, pl. 21, 59.
Jean-Jacques Lequeu (1756-1825)
Bibliothèque Nationale, Cabinet des Estampes (Ha 80, pl. 21, 59, Paris, France)
Bibl.: KAUFMANN, (1952) 1982, pp. 350-351.

An architectural detail in which the didactic attention, always pursued by Lequeu, is united to a reinterpretation of the particular classical structure that transforms it into a leading element, isolating it and removing it from its original context.

J.R.S.

THE PORTHOLE

Present everywhere, the porthole dates the buildings[1] and the villas of the 18th century, giving equal historical recognition to the modest provincial constructions and to the more innovative creations[2].
The porthole is a fortunate case of the persistence of a motif in the architectural lexicon due to its formal and structural simplicity: it passes safely through the course of centuries from the utilitarian Roman structures — e.g., the bridges[3] — to the most lively modernism of the 1920's. Reaffirmed by the Renaissance, it has with Palladio[4] its happiest European journey[5]. Renaissance and Classical are recalled in many 18th and 19th century examples[6].

J.R.S.

[1] Apartment house, rear facade, Athens 1933, S. Papadaki (*Fig.* 63).

Fig. 63

Fig. 64

Fig. 65

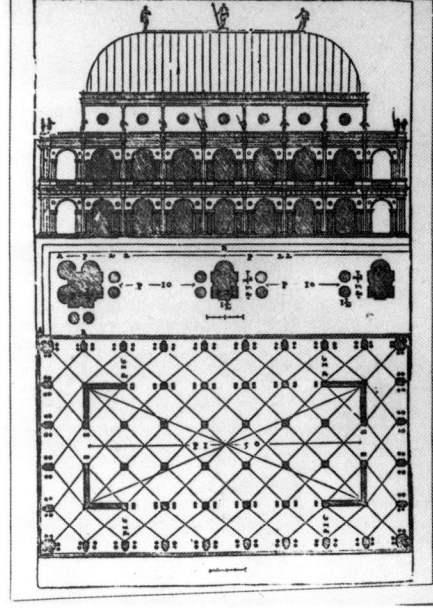

Fig. 66

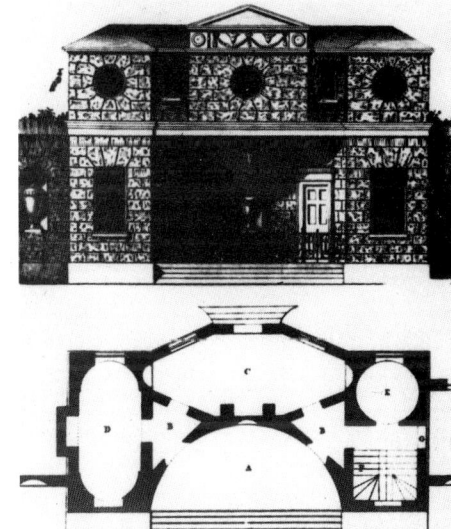

[2] Citrohan houses, second project, 1922, Le Corbusier (*Fig.* 120).
[3] Stone bridge, Roman age, Verona (*Fig.* 64).
[4] The Basilica of Vicenza, from A. PALLADIO «I quattro libri», Venice, 1570, III, p.42 (*Fig.* 65).
[5] Hunting Lodge, perspective and plan, in *The Builder's Magazine*, London, 1774-1778, plate LXVIII, J. Carter (*Fig.* 66).
[6] Garden pavilion, Kleinheubach, 1817, François Verly (*Fig.* 67); The Orangery after restorations, Villa Borghese, Rome, end of 18th century, A. and M. Asprucci (*Fig.* 68).

«THREE LINES»

The horizontal pipe railings of the great ocean liners of the first decades of the 20th century, for example the Bremen (1927), influenced everyday architecture in the accentuation of the horizontal bands[1]. The «three parallel lines» elevated to symbol of modernity and of aerodynamics become an applied decoration even on objects of design, appliances, typewriters, gasoline pumps[2,3]. This motif recovers at a decorative level the architectonic cornices that, beginning with Soane, undergo a reduction to a pure graphic sign and a simple emphasis on the division of buildings. Reused with the same value by Hoffmann, Mallet Stevens and Dudok[4], in Mendelsohn[5] they tend to produce dynamic effects and, in the trasposition of the machine, definitively assume the value of allusion to velocity and to movement.

N.Z.

[1] Building, Via A. De Gasperi, Naples c. 1940 (*Fig.* 72).
[2] Chrysler Airflow automobile, 1934 (*Fig.* 69).
[3] Locomotive train engine Raymon Loewy, 1938 (*Fig.* 70).
[4] Rob Mallet Stevens, Design for the entrance hall of an Embassy, 1925 (*Fig.* 71); W. M. Dudok, Hoek van Hogendorpsplein - Schiedamsche Singel, 1930.
[5] Weichmann silk factory, Gleiwitz, 1922, E. Mendelsohn (*Fig.* 124).

Fig. 71

Fig. 67

Fig. 69

Fig. 72

Fig. 68

Fig. 70

THE PICTURESQUE
COMPOSITION

43a; 43b; 43c;
44a; 44b; 45a; 45b;
46a; 46b; 47a; 47b.

With the theory of the «Picturesque» Price[1] inaugurates an aesthetic category which is part of beauty: «that sort of beauty called picturesque». The picturesque is a new relationship between man and nature, free, not geometricized by the classicist culture. The picturesque, exalting the individualism, is the negation of the classical. The picturesque is not a canon, but a freedom, a «non system» for buildings and planning.

Freed from rule, selectively linguistic, the counter-rule can only be that of irregularity.

«Houses should be irregular...» and therefore alive, gay. «I do not know a more melancholy object than classical houses of strict symmetry in the countryside»[2]. For Payne-Knight «asymmetry» is entrusted with the union of «houses in the country, that is, houses as part of landscape».

A new reality in the environment seeks truth in building and its relationship with the landscape: freedom in the choice and of the choice, freedom of projecting the house outside and inside, freedom of the house in its own natural environment and, therefore, truth. The sentimental emotion which arises from the stylistic irregularity, from directional duplicity, is definitively transformed for Payne-Knight[3] in the natural irregularity in which the building is realised, among the suggestions of various styles. «As regularity and proportion are fundamental ideas of absolute beauty, the Picturesque will be found always to depend upon the opposite conditions of matter-irregularity, and a partial want of proportion and symmetry. Thus, the purest Greek architecture, or the finest examples of Palladio, are at once highly symmetrical and beautiful; the varied Italian villa, or the ruder Swiss chalet, highly irregular and picturesque». In the middle of the 19th century, Downing, author of texts, that mark the future of architecture in the American environment, ties «the picturesque to the 'True' in architecture»[4].

Undoubtedly, the connection of forms and of styles, often bound to the most generic exteriority, will expire in a vain eclecticism or in a ridiculous, urban «ruralism»[5], degenerating into an «exterior falsity...» «...Whoever needs attitudes at all is *false*... Beware of all picturesque men!» (F. NIETZSCHE, *Ecce Homo*, p. 67).

But the profound meaning of "democratic" freedom of space and of volume in relation to the environment — source of happy emotion and hence of well-being — is the return to origins, to the primary, natural truth, «picturesque» combination-contraposition of elementary cubical and horizontal («the horizontal line is the line of domesticity») masses and of natural verticality, trees, mountainous heights («every tree [becomes] a tower above the great calm plains»)[6], presented by Wright to the Europe of 1910[7].

In the volumetric language of the 20th century the picturesque will retain its value in the contraposition and in the dynamism of opposites, will mark more and more the compositive expressions of everyday architecture, now far from picturesque emotion as «sort of beauty» and from a noly freedom in the dwelling.

J.R.S.

[1] Sir U. PRICE, *on the Picturesque: with an essay on the origin of taste and much original matter, by Sir Thomas Dick Lauder, Bart.,* (1794), Edinburgh-London, 1842. Cf. the study by U. Scoppeta on this subject.
[2] R. PAYNE-KNIGHT, *An Analytical Enquiry into the Principles of taste*, London 1806, 3rd ed. pp. 157, 222; PEVSNER, *Art Bulletin*, 1969. See Pevsner for the quotations.
[3] RASPI SERRA, Cat. *La fortuna di Paestum...*, 1986, vol. II, p. 14.
[4] A.J. DOWNING, *The Architecture of Country Houses...*, New York 1850, pp. 10, 20, 28-29, cited by SCULLY, 1971, pp. XLIII, LIX and *passim*. Cf. this fundamental text by Scully for a deeper understanding of the problem.
[5] Loos, (1914) 1986, p. 279: «The national artists try to apply rural architecture in the city».
[6] WRIHT, 1963, not paginated.
[7] Cf. SCULLY, 1986, p. 16: «Wright got rid of the shingles and the gable, adopted stucco, horizontal stripping, and the lowest possible hipped roof, and the resultant forms, as published in Germany by Wasmuth in 1910 and 1911, clearly helped to create the International Style».

43a - Pavilion of Bellevue
«Le Rendez-vous de Bellevue est à la pointe du Rocher».
Jean-Jacques Lequeu (1756-1825)
Bibliothèque Nationale, Cabinet des Estampes, Fonds Lequeu (Ha 80 fol, p. 55), Paris, France
Bibl.: MOSSER, Cat. *La fortuna di Paestum...*, 1986, vol. II, L 16.

«Since Kaufmann 'rediscovered' Lequeu, one of the most extraordinary creations of the architect has been seen in this design: a sort of emblematic image of his way of working. Numerous authors have attempted to analyze the manner in which, beginning from a kind of repertoire that is simply encyclopedic, Lequeu amuses himself by combining disparate elements according to the principles of juxtaposition and of 'collage'. Two points are particularly remarkable in his familiar themes: on one hand, the formal syncretism based on the recurrence of Greek, Egyptian and Renaissance styles, and, on the other hand, the insistence on the 'motif' of the rustic house, huts and vernacular decorum. The 'Rendez-vous de Bellevue' puts together a crenellated tower with an Italian house. Everything contributes to an indirect irregularity: anti-symmetry, extreme variety of the openings, disposition of contrasting masses. The Doric without basis, as 'citation', appears in the central body, in the entrance portico and in the principal staircase, and also in the Palladian opening of the gable. It seems that Lequeu utilizes it here as a formal element entrusted with a supplementary function of extraneousness. It has often been noted that the sapient dissonance of this composition could appear as a precursor of the eclecticism dear to the 'bâtisseurs de banlieues' at the end of the 19th century» (MOSSER).

43b - Project for the competition for the Central Telegraph and Broadcast Station
Tverskaja Street (now Gor'kij Street)
1925
Aleksej Viktorovič Ščusev (1873-1949)
Gnima, Moscow, U.S.S.R.
Bibl.: Cat. *Architettura nel paese dei Soviet...*, 1983, p. 212.

The compositional interest of this building depends upon the dynamic and «picturesque» relationship between the horizontal tensions, determined by the clean lines of the strip windows of the upper floors and the vertical movement of the ground floor and the vertical block at the corner which assumes a complex articulation uniting the foliated sequence at the crown with the horizontal division of the upper floor and the void of the entrance.

P.M.M.

44a - Casa del Combattente
Piazza Oberdan, Trieste, Italy
1929-1934
Umberto Nordio (1891-1971)
Bibl.: «La casa del Combattente...», *Architettura*, 1934; CONTESSI, 1981, pp. 102-103.

The Casa del Combattente (House of the Veteran), was the result of the town-planning scheme of 1933 that planned, together with other massive interventions in the city, the layout of the so-called Foro Ulpiano. It is exactly in the area of the modern Piazza Oberdan that the new town-planning design finds its most coherent achievement.
The bell tower, memory of the ancient medieval Broletti, is thus situated in an asymmetrical position and creates a «picturesque» composition. The use of materials is refined. The freestanding colonnades and the arches of white stone on the first floor stand out from the texture of the brick wall, whose design may evoke ancient Byzantine works. The horizontal banding that marks the building in white stone is placed in a way not common to the classical language, which is evoked however by the arches and by the Serlian windows of the connecting screen, mindful of the great Palladian arch of the Ca' Brütta by Muzio (1923), a fellow student of Nordios' at the Politecnico of Milan.
The result is thus a composition that combines the medieval and classical recall to «picturesque» effects, recovering the culture of the materials from the Dutch works of Dudock.

N.Z.

44b - Harmonious scale of buildings, unified with reflected structures: union of dynamic and static forms
1927-1928
Jakov Georgievič Černichov (1899-1951)
Černichov Family, Moscow, U.S.S.R.
Bibl.: Cat. *Architettura nel paese dei Soviet...*, 1983, p. 205.

The character of this project depends upon the title itself becoming a study in composition and a research on the dynamic possibilities of volumetric aggregation.
Here the visual center of the composition is the tall composite tower, rich in technological linguistic elements. Fins and volumes, as well as materials — iron and glass — intersect one another continuously without ever quite fusing, yet opposing each other dialectically. A «machine operator's» will, that utilizes single industrial elements and aggregates them within an aesthetics of «picturesque» construction, is evident here.

P.M.M.

45a - Union of single elements of a structure in a harmonious building. Visual characteristic of simplified structures with soft tonalities.
1932
Jakov Georgievič Černichov (1899-1951)
Černichov Family, Moscow, U.S.S.R.
Bibl.: Cat. *Architettura nel paese dei Soviet...*, 1983, p. 205.

This project of Černichov is also a study on the possibilities of constructive aggregations of architectural elements. As in the preceding example, the elements are deduced from the machines and industrial production, materials like iron and glass are arranged freely. Yet here the rhythm is more rapid and the volumetric organization more compact, without a visual fulcrum, but playing on the relationship between the two imposing building masses, both excavated and tormented in the play of the volumes and of the horizontal rhythm of solid-hollow. This relationship is built from the lower central body, that unifies the two masses and that breaks, in the crown divided by the glass volumes, its own sharpness given by the simple horizontal division of the strip windows.

P.M.M.

45b - Miroiterie (mirror shop)
Rabat, Morocco
c. 1930-1940.

46a - Building of the Opera Nazionale Balilla (O.N.B.)
Gorizia, Italy
1928
Umberto Cuzzi (1891-1973)
Bibl.: «O.N.B. Gorizia...», *Rassegna di architettura,* 1930; Pozzetto, 1974, p. 19; Damiani, 1982, pp. 196-197.

The work is commented on as follows in the pages of the journal *Rassegna di Architettura*, which had published their plans the year before (1929): «... the pursuit of horizontality remains the general expression, the combination of contrasting volumes, the effort at obtaining large uninterrupted planes; one sees that the typical Dudokian architecture is known to the author... The decorative effect is obtained by the use of economical materials and by different colors in flat tones».
The composition may be defined as «picturesque» for its asymmetrical design of classical volumes. Cuzzi learned the simplified classicism of Wagner and Loos, during his formative years at the Polytechnic of Vienna.

N.Z.

46b - Project for the competition of the Lenin Working People's House
Ivanovo-Voznesensk
1924
Il'ja Aleksandrovič Golosov (1883-1945)
Gnima, Moscow, U.S.S.R.
Bibl.: Cat. *Architettura nel paese dei Soviet...*, 1983, p. 207.

Golosov, member of S.A.S.S. from 1925 to 1932, was one of the major exponents of the Russian «Formalism». In this project the volumetric composition takes place through the ordered sequence of the different elements, each one typically well defined. Thus, the erection of the two «temples» against the background building, beside the three vertical blocks, each varying from the others, up to the projecting curved piece, assumes a balanced rhythm, like a detail of urban landscape.

P.M.M.

47a - Warsaw Ballroom (formerly Hoffman's Cafeteria)
Collins Ave., Miami Beach, Fla., U.S.A.
1940 (MDPL)
Henry Hohauser (1895 or 1896-1963)

47b - Casa della Gioventù in Trastevere
Rome, Italy
1933-1937
Luigi Moretti (1907-1973)
Bibl.: Cat. *Il razionalismo...*, 1976, p. 132; Rossi, 1984, p. 25; Santuccio, 1986, pp. 24-28.

Among the architects who were trained during the 1930's Moretti is one of the Roman figures most linked both to the Greek tradition and to monumentalism.
The youth hostel in Trastevere — as some «littorio» architectures — resolves the connection between the typological and volumetric elements through the emotional relationship that their reciprocal isolation determines. It is a compositive process, which is the opposite to that of reciprocal interference, but however using the same motifs. Here the transparent volume of the half round wing collides with the neat parallepiped, geometically defined by the continuous vertical glass and by the entrance porch. Yet the lower central portico gives unity to the volumetric articulation, softening the metaphysical tones and creating dynamic tension.

P.M.M.

THE NEW "QUARTIER"

«The wall of the club building that faced the road was white and blank, with no entrance door, no windows on the lower floor. The number was small but bright in violet-colored neon. 8777. Nothing else. To the side, under rows of hooded, downward-shining lights, were even rows of cars, set out in the white lined slots on the smooth black asphalt. Attendants in crisp clean uniforms moved in the lights.

The road went around to the back. A deep concrete porch there, with an overhanging canopy of glass and chromium, but very dim lights. I got out of the car and received a check with the license number on it, carried it over to a small desk where a uniformed man sat and dumped it in front of him.

"Philip Marlow", I said. "Visitor".

"Thank you, Mr. Marlow". He wrote the name and number down, handed me back my check and picked up a telephone.

A Negro in a white linen doublebreasted guards uniform, gold epaulettes, a cap with a broad gold band, opened the door for me.

The lobby looked like a high budget musical. A lot of light and glitter, a lot of scenery, a lot of clothes, a lot of sound, an allstar cast, and a plot with all the originality and drive of a split fingernail. Under the beautiful soft indirect lighting the walls seemed to go up forever and be lost in soft lascivious stars that really twinkled. You could just manage to walk on the carpet without waders. At the back was a free-arched stairway with a chromium and white enamel gangway going up in wide shallow carpeted steps. At the entrance to the dining room a chubby captain of waiters stood negligently with a two-inch satin stripe on his pants and a bunch of goldplated menus under his arm...» RAYMOND CHANDLER, *The High Window*, (1942) 1976, Vintage Books Edition, New York, pp. 103-4.

This is Raymond Chandler describing Los Angeles, but it could as easily be Miami Beach or Casablanca, or any of the other fashionable *quartiers moderne* of that period (1925-1940). Without the glitter of easy money it could be an *habitation à bon marché*.

The image, the ideal, was the same: modernity. The poverty and ugliness associated with the rapid and uncontrolled growth of cities resulting from the onset of the industrial revolution would be ameliorated by planning and the application of technology.

Society would take itself in hand.

In 1898 Howard published his *Tomorrow: Peaceful Path to Real Reform* wherein the Garden City was proposed and described. At almost the same moment Tony Garnier was beginning his *Cité Industrielle*.

With the disaster of the first world war the credibility of traditional society was shattered. If society in the past had done so badly, then hope lay in the future. The next disaster, the depression of 1929, confirmed this. During this same period a series of fairs, excluding traditional styles, announced the brighter world of tomorrow as would be created by technology.

While it is difficult today to recover this optimism, the dark years of the second world war were illuminated by this hope. Even the worst denizen of Chandler's underworld sought out the bright spots of the new style, the style proposed by Garnier for his *Cité Industrielle*. Prost's new *quartiers* in Morocco and Miami Beach, both erected between 1915 and 1940, embody it.

The most striking physical change during the past two centuries has been the enormous increase in population with its concomitant icrease in the size of cities. In 1800 London, Paris, New York, Milan, Vienna, Berlin, Tokyo, etc. were still at the scale of pedestrians, still consisted of a few *quartiers*. Now they are vast agglomerations, the parts linked, first by rail, and now by high-speed highways. Whatever one's opinion of Modern Architecture, the most prominent fact is its necessary quantity. That, more than new methods of building, is the basic condition of modern building.

Building the new *quartiers* provided the sites for the new style. These included both publically sponsored garden cities, as around Paris, and unplanned *laisser-faire* growth, as in Miami Beach.

The architects of these *quartiers* understood the value of tradition, of building according to the patterns of the traditional city. They tempered the ideology of the 'new', with its demands for uprooting streets.

We have included here a chart tracing the development of the new *quartiers* since around 1900.

Examples:

The houses in Elmhurst, Queens (**48c**) were built by G.X. Mathews Co. between 1931-40. Mathews had come to The United States from Germany in 1886 when he was 16 years old. In 1909 he founded his company to build «several hundred buildings... known as Mathews' Model Flats and Homes», including the group shown here. (*New York Times* 23 Sept. 1958 (obituary) of G.X. Mathews). Both this name and the character of the houses suggest that Mathews intended his work to be more than a mere profit making enterprise, that is we can see these houses as part of the idealistic community building following the new city proposals of around 1900. Furthermore in the style of the houses themselves we see evidence that Mathews kept informed about new housing in Europe. The group seems indebted to Bruno Taut, especially the outer facade of his horseshoe at Berlin Britz. But Mathews has done more than ape European social housing. His use of color is more than decoration.

The elevation admits of two contradictory readings, one traditional, the other modern. Taking the traditional first, we see the row as a series of separate houses with a brick chimney at the center. The dark brick is the house, the light brick, the sky. For the buyers, undoubtedly conservative lower middle class people, this image was likely reassuring. The modern reading is the reverse: the void is the center, which is the point of entrance. In certain of the houses (not shown here) this void is divided by an abstract vertical black line. Furthermore, the pattern of light vs. dark has an abstract character whose modernity is emphasized in the photograph here by the corner window. For the buyers these modern aspects represented the better world of the future.

The modern *quartiers* in Morocco were built after the French occupation in 1912 **(2b, 12b, 25b, 30b, 31a, 36c, 45b)**. The additions to these Islamic cities show many of the aspects of the various projects (Garnier, Mallet-Stevens) for *cités modernes* post 1900. The French governor, le Marechal Lyautey, brought Henri Prost to Morocco to plan the new districts. Prost had been a fellow student of Garnier at the Academy in Rome. While the new buildings in Morocco were not part of industrial development, the planning and the style of the new buildings show a relationship to Garnier's plates in the *Cité Industrielle* which was published in its final form just when Prost was preparing his master plans (BRIAN BRACE TAYLOR, «Planned discontinuity, Modern colonial cities in Morocco», *Lotus* 26, pp. 53-66).

The buildings we are showing were built in the 1930s by architects from France, working in the new *moderne* style of «*L'Exposition Internationale des Arts Decoratifs et Industriels Modernes*» at Paris in 1925.

Miami Beach was built at the same time **(48b, 49a b, 50b, 51a, 52a, 53a, 54, 55, 56a, 57a)**. It also is the *Cité Industrielle*: row after row of modern apartments — even the 50 foot lot matches Garnier's 15 meter grid. The atmosphere is redolent of the Mediterranean, as if a piece had broken loose and drifted across the Atlantic to refresh America. The resemblance to early 20th century utopian planning is fortuitous: no planning, in the European sense, was involved. It was a free enterprise effort, but like apartment building elsewhere the social ideals promulgated to overcome the effects of the depression had affected real estate activities. Private developers were meeting market expectations. Undoubtedly there was stylistic influence from the Century of Progress Exposition in Chicago of 1933-34.

Beyond stylistic characteristics the typological development must also be noted. Typically **(49b, 50b & 54)** two blocks will be built with an access court between them. Being narrow these courts are shaded and thus cooler than the area outside. Now that these buildings are used by retired people with abundant leisure, the social aspects of the planning be-

THE MODERN CITY: TIME CHART

La Cité Industrielle	Maroc	Miami/Miami Beach	Other
Tony Garnier 1869-1948 at *Ecole des Beaux-Arts* 1889-99 won *Prix de Rome* 1899, at French Academy - Villa Medici 1899-1904. 1st study of 'Cité' sent back to *Ecole* - 1901 - refused. 1904 exhibited 'Cité' and reconstruction of Tusculum. 1905 returned to Lyon. *Abattoirs de la Mouche* 1908-24 3 villas near Lyon 1909-11 hospital of Grange-Blanche 1911-27 Lyon stadium 1913-18	Leon-Henri Prost 1874-1959 Won *Prix de Rome* 1902 reconstruction of Constantinople *envoi* of 1905 1912 Morocco becomes French protectorate under Maréchal Lyautey, capital moved to Rabat. Prost to Morocco - Dec. 1913 'zoning codes' April 1914 master plan of Casablanca 1915, of Rabat 1915, of Marrakesh ca. 1916 'according to principles of the garden city'*	Flagler railroad to Palm Beach 1894, to Miami 1896 Wooden bridge to Miami Beach finished ca. 1913 at instigation of John S. Collins. 1st hotel shortly after; «houses were built; streets, parks, and by 1915, Miami Beach's population had grown enough to permit the incorporation of the city»*. Carl Fisher cut Lincoln Road through mangroves with circus elephants in 1915.	*Tomorrow: Peaceful Path to Real Reform:* Ebenezer Howard 1898 Letchworth Garden City 1902-3 Parker & Unwin Plan of Chicago 1909 D.H. Burnham Plan of Canberra 1911-13 W.B. Griffin Plan of New Delhi begun 1911 - Edwin Lutyens
La Cité Industrielle published 1917 'Etats-Unis' housing 1920 - 35* Townhall Boulogne-Billancourt* 1931-35	'Cité des Habous', Casablanca 1917-30 by Laprade, Brion and Cadet.	Land boom - 1920-23 1925 - 21 new hotels, 101 new apartments.** Hurricane 1926 and depression 1929 were end of 1st boom. ca. 1925 Espanola built up. 1940 - 41 new hotels, 166 new apartments.**	Amsterdam, *Zuid* district 1902-17 H.P. Berlage Henri Sellier, mayor of Suresnes, *Office Public d'Habitations à Bon Marché* for over 20 years after 1916. Cité jardin de Suresnes begun before 1926, A. Maistrasse, architect Cité jardin de Chatenay begun 1931, Bassompierre, de Rutté & Sirvin.*
* DORA WIEBENSON, *Tony Garnier: The Cité Industrielle*, 1969, George Braziller, New York.	* JEAN ALAZARD, «L'Urbanisme à Rabat», *Beaux-Arts Revue*, January 1930, pp. 22-23.	* *Miami Beach Comprehensive Plan*, City of Miami Beach Planning Division, 1980. ** *Architectural Forum*, December 1940, p. 10.	*JAMES READ, «The French Connection», *Architectural Review*, June 1978, pp. 343-352.

comes apparent. These courts, as well as tree shaded spaces in front, are the scenes of gathering and conversation. They are protected semi-private social spaces. There are fully public social spaces, most notably along Ocean Drive where hotels are lined up facing the beach.

The Bronx, a borough of New York City, like Miami Beach was built up during the period between the two world wars (**15a, 18a, 27b, 52c**). It contains an equally extensive district of *Moderne* apartments (DONALD SULLIVAN & BRIAN DANFORTH, *Bronx Art Deco Architecture*, 1976, Hunter College Graduate Program in Urban Planning). There are many similarities with Miami Beach, both stylistically and typologically. 1791 on the Grand Concourse, the major boulevard in the Bronx, illustrates these: it has a recessed center, the point of entry, creating a small semi-private space belonging to the building (the district is denser than Miami Beach — the buildings are taller, typically six stories, and the spaces are smaller) and color is used to enliven the street and to weave together the horizontal and vertical themes. The photograph of the entrance to 1500 Grand Concourse (**18a**) exhibits the same elements of design, the same modest grandeur befitting a middle class community.

Our last group of houses is from the inner suburbs of Cincinnati (**51b**), which was built following the second world war. If it is compared with the photograph from Miami Beach which faces it, the similarities are striking. Except that the buildings in Miami Beach are no entered in the center, the houses are nearly identical, but the differences are also instructive. In Cincinnati there is no hint of vacation. This is bare bones workers' housing, literally, the *Cité Industrielle*, but in a northern brick mode like those in Queens and the Bronx. Idealism is at a minimum. Nevertheless the stylistic devices give dignity to these simple apartments. Their frontality, establishing a hierarchical relation to the street, to each other and within the individual buildings, creates a coherent ensemble, understandable to everyone. They dignify their occupants: everyday palaces for ordinary people. So even these, one might say meager, houses have their idealism.

48a - Le Village de Maupertuis, vue perspective
c. 1800
Claude-Nicolas Ledoux (1736-1806)
Archives de Seine-et-Marne, Paris, France
Bibl.: SIMONCINI, Cat. *La fortuna di Paestum...*, 1986, vol. II, L 73.

48b - Bernstein Apartments
530-550 15th St., Miami Beach. Fla., U.S.A.
1938 (MDPL)
Henry Hohauser (1895 or 1896-1963)

48c - Townhouse Development
Elmhurst, Queens, New York, U.S.A.
1931-1940 (BDR)
George X. Mathews, developer/contractor

49a - Dade Boulevard Fire Station
Miami Beach, Fla., U.S.A.
c. 1939
R.L. Weed & E.T. Reeder

49b - Propylées de Paris, «vue perspective»
in CLAUDE-NICOLAS LEDOUX, *L'architecture...*, 1847, pl. 157 (I, 32)
Claude-Nicolas Ledoux (1736-1806)
Bibl.: KAUFMANN, (1952) 1982, p. 322.

The realization of simple Customs-Houses, an assignment that Ledoux received in 1784 from the Ferme Générale of Paris, was transformed by him into an occasion to provide the capital with monumental entrances, called by him «Propylaea».
Together they reveal the greatest formal variety. Here Ledoux assembles, in a very original way, independent elements: the «geometric» house surmounted by a rostral column rises on a fortress with angular projections. The traditional use of the column as mark and unequivocal point of reference in a scenographic urban design is reproposed.
N.Z.

49c - Don-Bar Apartments
1571-1573 Pennsylvania Ave., Miami Beach, Fla., U.S.A.
1937 (MDPL)
Albert Anis (1889-1964)

49d - Maison de campagne, «vue perspective»
in CLAUDE-NICOLAS LEDOUX, *L'architecture...*, 1804, pl. 29
Claude-Nicolas Ledoux (1736-1806)
Bibl.: ZANNI, *Arte in Friuli, arte a Trieste*, 1988, pp. 83-90.

The country house is one of the projects for residential buildings for the ideal city of Chaux illustrated in *L'architecture* but never carried out. Ledoux, interested in volumetric compositions more than in the treatment of surfaces, organizes these double houses by means of the juxtaposition of elementary geometrical forms.
The building devoid of decorations (in harmony with the Ledouxian ideals) uses a simplified Palladian language mindful of the turrets of the Nilotic buildings represented in the mosaics of Palestrina. These simplified forms of Ledoux, through their divulgation and typification by Durand shall appear in the masters of the 20th century: from Loos (Karma Villa, 1904-1906) to Wright (Bank of Mason City, Iowa, 1909) to Gropius (Model factory, Cologne, 1914).
N.Z.

50a - Townhouse
East 74th St., New York, U.S.A.

50b - Kesandra & South Shore Apartments
1525-1531 & 1535-1539 Pennsylvania Ave., Miami Beach, Fla., U.S.A.
1935 (MDPL)
Roy France (1888-1972)

51a - Apartment building
1425 Meridian (left) & 735 14th Place (right), Miami Beach, Fla., U.S.A.
1425 Meridian 1936 (?) (MDPL)
Henry Hohauser (1895 or 1896-1963).

51b - Apartment building
7159 and 7163 Eastlawn St., Cincinnati, Ohio, U.S.A.
c. 1945-1950.

51c - «Maison Bélanger», Paris
in J. - CH. KRAFFT - N. RANSONNETTE, *Plans...*, n.d., pl. 4
1787
François-Joseph Bélanger (1744-1818)
Paris, France
Bibl.: PAUPE, Cat. *La fortuna di Paestum...*, 1986, vol. II, K 9.

«The most elaborate palace constucted by Bélanger is located near the Monastery of Brongniart and still stands today despite various alterations... The facade freely unites Palladian themes: openings in 'terminal apse', central loggia, small and rustic pavilion that surmounts the pediment that Bélanger utilized even in his picturesque gardens...» (PAUPE).

52a - Claire Apartments
1350-1354 Euclid Ave., Miami Beach, Fla., U.S.A.
c. 1935-1940

52b - Maison no. 14
in LOUIS-AMBROISE DUBUT, *Architecture civile...*, 1803, pl. 30
Louis-Ambroise Dubut (1769-1846)
Bibl.: KAUFMANN, (1955) 1966, p. 255.

According to Kaufmann «the elements of Dubut are the simple solids», as is manifested by this project (undoubtedly similar to the country house of his master, Ledoux) in the compositional realization of volumetric blocks. Yet Dubut differs in his interpretation of the reassumed past, without rigor, in lexical form far distant from the interpretive example of Ledoux.
J.R.S.

52c - Apartment building
1791 Grand Concourse, Bronx, New York, U.S.A.
1936 (Sullivan)
Edward Franklin

53a - Crest Hotel (left) & Chatham Apartments (right)
James St., Miami Beach, Fla., U.S.A.
1941 (MDPL)
Edward A. Noland

53b - Apartment building
Via Tasso 193, Naples, Italy

1934-1935
Giulio Rossi (1912)

53c - Emploi des objects de la nature dans la compositon des edifices. Vignes
in Jean-Nicolas-Louis Durand, *Précis...*, 1823, pl. 18
Jean-Nicolas-Louis Durand (1760-1834)
Bibl.: Szambien, 1984, pp. 34, 229.

Durand diffuses the accentuated verticality of the «Italian house» with hanging gardens and flor-wered terraces, which integrate the building in the environment.
This typology, already noticeable in the French architectural culture, becomes typical in the 19th century, found success in France until 1920 (Szambien) and also in other spheres. The form is well-known, moreover, in the designs of Schinkel (cf., for example, the Gardener's House, Charlottenburg, (1829-1831), in Hitchcock, 1971, p. 58).
J.R.S.

54a, 54b - Surfside Garden Apartments
Surfside, Miami Beach, Fla., U.S.A.

55a - Apartment building
Collins Ave., Miami Beach, Fla., U.S.A.
c. 1935-1940

55b - Helen Marie Apartments
1050-1056 Jefferson Ave., Miami Beach, Fla., U.S.A.
1948 (MDPL)
L. Murray Dixon (1901-1949)

56a - Euclid Place Apartments
1227-1231 Euclid Ave., Miami Beach, Fla., U.S.A.
c. 1939
Henry Hohauser (1895 or 1896-1963) (attributed)

56b - Villa Schiozzi
Via Manzoni 36, Gorizia, Italy
1933
Umberto Cuzzi (1891-1973)
Bibl.: «Una villa a Gorizia», *Domus*, 1934; Pozzetto, 1974, p. 29, Damiani, 1982, p. 200.

The villa is remarkable above all for the play of volumes: cylinders and cubes alternate in a lively, well balanced rhythm, underlined by the bichromy of the smooth green and the rough yellow plaster. The round porthole window, more than in marine architecture seems here to recall the use of the great round windows of some examples of Belgian *Art Nouveau* (Hankar, Horta), now however stripped of all decoration. This element is utilized here to reinforce the taste for uniting various «geometrical» forms in the composition. Such taste is common to much European architecture: for example, the electrophysics laboratory at Lefortovo, near Moscow (1927), cited by Hitchcock and Johnson in their *International Style* (p. 238).
N.Z.

56c - Project for a National Theatre
c. 1800
Friedrich Gilly (1772-1800)
Technische Hochschule, Charlottenburg
Berlin, B.D.R.
Bibl.: Vogt, Cat. *La fortuna di Paestum,* 1986, II, I 159.

57a - Warsaw Ballroom (formerly Hoffman's Cafeteria)
Collins Ave., Miami Beach, Fla., U.S.A.
1940 (MDPL)
Henry Hohauser (1895 or 1896-1963)

57b - Temple of Poseidon
Paestum, Italy
c. 460-450 B.C.

Abbreviations

(MDPL): *Portfolio*, 1979 and *Miami Beach Art Deco Guide,* 1987 of the Miami Design Preservation League;
(Stern): *New York 1930, Architecture and Urbanism Between the Two World Wars*, Robert A.M. Stern, Gregory Gilmartin and Thomas Mellins, Rizzoli 1987.
(Wilson): *The Machine Age in America 1918-1941* by Richard Guy Wilson and others, Abrams, 1986;
(BDR): Building Department Records;
(Greif): *Depression Modern* by Martin Greif, Universe Books, 1975;
(Sullivan): *Bronx Art Deco Architecture* by Donald Sullivan and others, Publishing Center for Cultural Resources, New York City, 1976;
(Gebhard): David Gebhard's guides, for Los Angeles: *Architecture in Los Angeles*, Peregrine Smith Books, 1985 and for San Francisco, *A Guide to Architecture in San Francisco & Northern California*, Peregrine Smith Books, 1976;
(NYLC): a report prepared by the New York Landmark Preservation Commission;
(Schulze): a letter to T.K. by the author of the biography on Mies van der Rohe.
(C. Wyatt): Charles Wyatt & Associates «The Warehouse District of Jersey City», Cultural Resource Survey, National Register Nomination, May 1984.
(LPC): NYC Landmarks Preservation Commission, November 24, 1981, Designation List 150, LP.1132.
(Jones & Woodward): *A Guide to the Architecture of London*, Edward Jones & Christopher Woodward, published by Van Nostrand Reinhold Co. 1982.

EUROPEAN MODERN ARCHITECTURE
A CHRONOLOGY 1896-1933

In this chronology we point out some events quoted from the writings of the architects, of their contemporaries and of the historians particularly important for the architectural background of the everyday architecture.
Photos of mentioned designs, projects or buildings are given here or in the thematic essays.

1896
Moderne architektur by O. Wagner published in Vienna.

C.R. Mackintosh wins the competition for the new building of the Glasgow School of Art, Glasgow.

1898
Pavilion of the exposition of the Secession, Vienna, J. Olbrich.

Stock Exchange, Amsterdam, 1898-1903, H. Berlage. (*Fig.* 73).

«His fundamental conviction seems obviously to have been based on the contention that construction and material, i.e., iron, stone, and wood were to remain thoroughly pure — that is to say they were to be left naked and unadorned... He was probably the first to place the horizontal and vertical surfaces of a building under one definite law, thus adhering most consistently to the new aesthetic claims, which exacted that the beauty of a building should not be judged by its outside appearance and individual parts, but only after having ascertained that the diposition of its apartments, walls and openings were entirely in accordance with the regulations definitely laid down for the whole... The construction of the Amsterdam Exchange in 1900 must be regarded as an epochal achievement, as the inception of a new art of construction. Its tower and its crystalline purity endure imperishably». [B. Taut, 1929, p. 70]

Majolika-Haus, Linke Wienzeile 38-40, and Kostlergasse 3, Vienna, 1898-1899, O. Wagner (*Fig.* 74).

«Otto Wagner possesses a quality that up to now I have had occasion of observing only in several English and American architects: he succeeds in getting out of his architect's skin to enter the skin of any artisan. He creates a glass — and so he thinks like a glassblower... He makes a brass bed — and he thinks, he feels like a brass-smith. All the rest, his profound knowledge and architectural ability, has been left in his old skin. Only one thing he always takes with himself: his artistic being». [A. Loos, (12 June 1898) 1986, p. 32]

«Neither the archaeologist, nor the decorator, nor the architect, nor the painter, nor the sculptor must decorate our apartment. And whoever then? Well, it's very simple: everyone must be the decorator of himself. In that case, however, we would no longer live in apartments «in style». But it is also true that this «style», style between quotation marks, is not at all indispensable». [A. Loos, (12 June 1898), 1986, p. 25]

«The fundamental condition so that an object can be called «beautiful» is that it may not be in contrast with practicality». [A. Loos, (19 June 1898) 1986, p. 33]

«Each material possesses a formal language that belongs to it and no material can ascribe to itself the forms that correspond to another material». [A. Loos, (4 September 1898) 1986, p. 80]

«Look at the velocipede! Does it not perhaps recall in its forms the spirit of Periclean Athens? If the Greeks had had to construct a velocipede, it would have been completely similar to ours. The bronze tripods of the Greeks — I am not referring to those destined for votive offerings but to those of common use — are they not perhaps completely similar to our iron constructions? [A. Loos, (1 October 1898) 1986, p. 118]

1899
I. M. Olbrich is invited by Ernst Ludwig von Essen to found an artist's colony in Darmstadt. For him Olbrich builds on the Mathildenhohe: the Ernst Ludwig Haus (the colony studio) (*Fig.* 75) houses for a number of artists, an entrance portal and ancillary structures.

Histoire de l'Architecture by A. Choisy published in Paris.

1903
Front elevation of Basel Station, Basel, J. M. Olbrich (*Fig.* 76).

Apartment house, 25 bis rue Franklin, Paris, A. Perret.

«This apartment house by no means embodies the pure forms of the Chicago office buildings, and it fails to match the strength of Frank Lloyd Wright's work of the same period. The familiar European restlessness is still present to a considerable degree. Nevertheless, it represents the first employment of ferro-concrete as a medium for architectonic expression, and many of its features were to prove seeds for future developments». [S. Giedion, (1941) 1967, pp. 328-330]

1904
Kultur und Kunst; gesammelte Aufsätze über Künstlerische Fragen der Gegenwart by H. Muthesius published in Jena and Leipzig.

Karma Villa, 352 rue St. Moritz between Clarens and Vevey, 1904-1905, A. Loos. (*Fig.* 77)

«[...] The flattering assignment had been entrusted to me of constructing at Montreaux [he refers to his works for Karma Villa]... a small house for custodians. On the banks there were many stones and

Fig. 73

Fig. 74

Fig. 75

Fig. 76
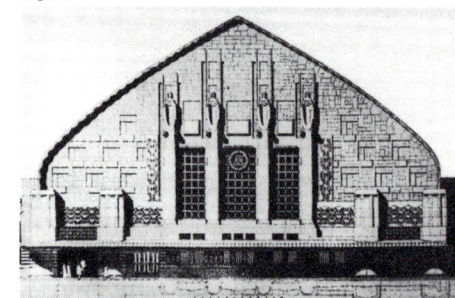
Fig. 77

since the early inhabitants of the place had constructed all their houses with these stones, I wanted to do it, too... The building was too simple. What had become of the ornaments? My timid objection that even the lake, when it is calm, is flat and without ornaments... was of no use». [A. Loos, (1910) 1986, pp. 231-232]

Main station, Helsinki, 1904-1914, E. Saarinen (*Fig.* 78).

One «of six buildings supposedly representative of what is happening in architecture on the continent of Europe». [H.R. Hitchcock Jr. - Ph. Johnson, 1932, p. 12]

1905

Palais Stoclet, Brussels, 1905-1911, J. Hoffmann. (*Fig.* 80).

«Beauty... is a consequence of centuries of caring and ordering... care includes the improvement of outer and inner man... The worker has no in kling of what enormous potential of cultural power he possesses through his work». [J. Hoffmann, undated ms. (Estate Ro), from Sekler, 1985, p. 232]

1906

The abattoir of La Mouche, Lyons (design: 1906-1909; execution: 1909-1924), T. Garnier (*Fig.* 79).

Crematorium, Hagen, 1906-1907, P. Behrens (*Fig.* 81).

Project for an extension to the School of Arts and Crafts, Vienna, J. Hoffmann (*Fig.* 82).

1907

German Werkbund, München meeting, October 5-6.

«Objective of the German Werkbund was to elevate the quality of the artisan and industrial production through close collaboration between handicraft, industry and artistic production...» [L. Hilberseimer, (1967) 1981, pp. 34-35]

«To understand the origins of the Werkbund, one must look beyond the events of October 1907... of the three individuals who can most justly be described as its founding fathers — Hermann Muthesius, Friedrich Naumann, and Henry van de Velde — only Naumann actually attended the Munich meeting. These three men, coming from very different backgrounds, agreed in their fundamental purposes, but each held distinctive views on matters of policy and organization. Their ideas and ideals deserve analysis because they helped to set the Werkbund on its course...

The man most frequently cited as *the* father of the Werkbund was Hermann Muthesius... Thus in 1907 Muthesius set forth a number of ideas that regularly reappeared in Werkbund propaganda... Because Muthesius knew that the controversy surrounding his person might jeopardize the new organization, he stayed away from the Munich meeting. But as soon as the Werkbund was established, he openly identified himself with it». [J. Campbell, 1978, pp. 11, 12, 15, 16]

«Hermann Muthesius, to whom we owe a series of instructive books on the English way of living and of dwelling, has illustrated the aims of the German Werkbund and has tried to justify its existence. The aims are good. But the German Werkbund will never achieve them.

The German Werkbund indeed. The members of this association are people trying to substitute our civilization with another. Why they do this, I don't know. But I know they will fail...

We have our civilization, our forms in which our life is mirrored and we have the manufactured objects which permit us to live this life. Men and associations have *not* created our furniture, our cigarette cases and our jewels. Time has created them». [A. Loos, (1908), 1986, p. 211]

1908

Adolf Loos writes *Ornament and Crime*

«We have conquered ornament, we have won through to lack of ornamentation. Look, the time is nigh, fulfilment awaits us. Soon the streets of the town will glisten like white walls. Like Zion, the holy city, the metropolis of heaven. Then we shall have fulfilment». [A. Loos (1908), 1986, p. 219]

Joseph Feinhals House, Cologne, 1908-1909, J. M. Olbrich (*Fig.* 84).

Cuno House, Hagen, 1908-1912, P. Behrens (*Fig.* 83).

1909

H. Tessenow discusses the typology of the house of small dimensions in «Der Wohnungsbaus» (Munich).

Ast House, Vienna, 1909-1911, J. Hoffmann (*Fig.* 85).

Fig. 78

Fig. 79

Fig. 80

Fig. 81

Fig. 82

Fig. 83

Fig. 84

«...Classicism in Behrens industrial buildings is related to their design not to their exterior decoration... Though Behrens buildings are different one from another, according to the different functions that they must carry out, they however present a common feature, which consists precisely in this classical spirit. The architectural conception of Behrens was nevertheless transformed with the passing of time, and gradually he also began to use «classical» compositive elements.
He built two sheds for AEG that attest to this transformation». [L. HILBERSEIMER, (1967) 1981, pp. 39-40]

AEG Turbine Factory, Berlin, 1909-1910, P. Behrens (*Fig.* 86).

1910

AEG Small Motors Factory, Berlin, P. Behrens (*Fig.* 87).

Adolf Loos writes *Architektur*, published in *Trotzdem*, Innsbruck, 1931.

«It is not by chance that the Romans were not capable of inventing a new order of columns, a new ornamentation. They were already too advanced to do this. They took all this from the Greeks and adapted it to their own ends...
... Since humanity has understood the greatness of classical antiquity, a single thought joins the great architects together. They think: just as I build, so the ancient Romans would have built. We know that they are wrong. Time, place, purpose, climate, and environment forbid this calculation.
But each time that architecture strays from its model with the minors, the «decorators», the great architect reappears who leads it back to antiquity.

Fischer von Erlach in the South, Schlüter in the North, were rightly the great masters of the 18th century. And at the beginning of the 19th century there was Schinkel. We have forgotten him. May the light of this extraordinary figure shine our future generation of architects». [A. LOOS, (1910), 1986, p. 256]

Artist's studios, project for a school of applied art: A certain number of studios with standard dimensions are grouped around a central teaching organization, Le Corbusier (*Fig.* 88).

Lecture *Über moderne Baukunst* by Berlage, November 26.

«In our western culture — Muthesius rightly declares — there have been two periods of splendor, above all in the arts: Greek antiquity and northern Middle Age. The first reached an artistic stature that man will be hard put to equal, the second represented the perfect artistic independence and the absolute national character, that represent the fundamental presupposition of an artistic age...
What is after all modern architecture? In what way

Fig. 85

Fig. 86

Fig. 87

Fig. 88

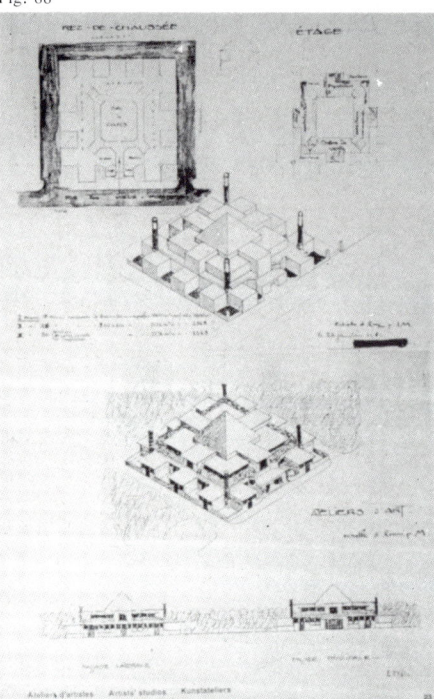

Fig. 89

Fig. 90

Fig. 91

does it yearn to express itself? I believe that I am able to answer: through the composition of volumes...

When architecture loses its way in the false tradition, objectivity disappears; each time objectivity springs up again, it is an indispensable condition for the manifestation of a great art. Consequence of objectivity is simplicity. Objective is synonymous with simple and with artistic...

Plaster, bricks, reinforced concrete are all very well; naturally, one must know their meaning and their structure». [*Zeitschrift des Oesterreichischen Ingenieur-und Architekten-Vereines*, Vienna, 1911, no. 21, pp. 321-326].

Adolf Loos writes two articles and one letter on the house of Michaelerplatz.

«I accuse our contemporary architects of consciously wishing to neglect a certain architectural feature...

«Viennese» is to close a building with a horizontal line...

And then we have plaster made with lime...

Plaster with lime is a skin. Stone is the structure... Plaster with lime has a closer kinship with leather, with tapestry, with materials for covering and with paints than with its cousin, limestone. When plaster with lime is shown honestly as the facing of a wall of bricks, it has as little to be ashamed of its simple origin as a Tyrolese with his leather pants in the 'Hofburg'». [A. Loos, (1910), 1986, pp. 235, 236, 237]

Looshaus, Michaelerplatz, Vienna, 1910-1911, A. Loos (*Fig. 89*).

«[...] And I found the most important thing: that is, that the style of 1900 is distinguished from that of 1800 only in the measure in which the tail-coat of 1900 is distinguished from the tail-coat of 1800. ... When it was finally my turn to build a house, I said to myself: the exterior of the house may be transformed at the most like the tail-coat. Therefore not much... The house does not have to strike the eye. Hadn't I once coined a motto: who shocks the eye, is dressed in the modern way... My house [he refers to the «Looshaus» in the Michaelerplatz, Vienna, which was built in the same year this article was written] stirred up a real scandal...» [A. Loos, (1910), 1986, pp. 251-252].

School of Gymnastic Rithmic, Hellerau (Dresden), 1910-1911, H. Tessenow.

Fagus Shoe-Last Factory, Alfeld-an-der-Leine, 1910-1911, W. Gropius in collaboration with A. Mayer (*Fig. 90*).

Exhibition of F. Ll. Wright buildings plans and designs at the Kunstgewerbemuseum, 1910-1911, Berlin.

«The works of Frank Lloyd Wright, which a short time afterwards were presented in the Kunstgewerbemuseum of Berlin constituted a surprise, but of a wholly other kind; it was a surprise that comforted us after the negative impression of the Embassy of Behrens [Editor's note. Hilberseimer, nevertheless, dates the work of Behrens to 1911-1912]. The buildings and designs of Wright represent one of the most important contributions to the new architecture and this exhibition was a great event». [L. HILBERSEIMER, (1967) 1981, p. 41].

F. L. Wright's *Ausgeführte Bauten und Entwürfe* is imprinted by Ernest Wasmuth of Berlin.

«What is style? Every flower has it; every animal has it; every individual worthy of the name has it in some degree, no matter how much sandpaper may have done for him. It is a free product — a by-product, the result of an organic working out of a project in character and in one state of feeling...
... One might swoop all the Gothic architecture of the world together in a single nation and mingle it with buildings treated horizontally as they were treated vertically or treated diagonally, buildings and towers with flat roofs, long, low buildings with square openings, mingled with tall buildings with pointed ones, in the bewildering variety of that marvelous architectural manifestation, and harmony in the general ensemble inevitably result: the common chord in all being sufficient to bring them unconsciously into harmonious relation.
I wish to say also — What is more to the point — that, ... in a structure conceived in the organic sense, thje ornamentation is conceived in the very ground plan, and of is the very constitution of the structure.
The horizontal line is the line of domesticity... To Europeans these buildings on paper seem uninhabitable; but they derive height and air by quite other means, and respect an ancient tradition, the only one here worthy of respect — the prairie. In considering the forms and types of these structures, the fact that they are nearly buildings for the prairie should be borne in mind; the gently rolling or level prairies of the Middle West; the great levels where every detail of elevation becomes exaggerated; every tree a tower above the great calm plains...» [F. Ll. WRIGHT, (1910), 1963, not paginated]

F.B. Henderson House, Elmhurst, Illinois (1901). Perspective and plans (*Fig. 91*).

«A plastered house with cement base and wooden trimmings of the open single room type, with alcoved ends, originated in the Warren Hickox house at Kankakee» [F. Ll. WRIGHT, (1910), 1963, pl. 18].

1911

Austrian pavilion at the International Art Exhibition in Rome, J. Hoffmann (*Fig. 92*).

One-family house, Heideweg 22, Hellerau, H. Tessenow (*Fig. 93*).

4th Annual Assembly of the Werkbund, Dresden.

«The potential dualism between quality and style became explicit in 1911 when Muthesius, addressing the Werkbund congress, asserted that the demands of form must take precedence over the requirements of function, material, or technique». [J. CAMPBELL, 1978, p. 71].

German Embassy, St. Petersburg, 1911-1912, P. Behrens (*Fig. 94*).

Fig. 92

Fig. 93

Fig. 94

Fig. 95

Fig. 96

«Behrens took the decisive step towards the strict «classicism» with the project for the building of the German Embassy in St. Petersburg (Leningrad). Here the piers that he used in Volta-strasse factory have become true columns, elongated and furnished with capitals; the architrave is crowned by a cornice; building's axis of symmetry is underlined not only by the balconies at the main floor, but also by a group of sculptures on the top» [Editor's note: AEG Small Motors Factory, Volta-strasse facade: see *Fig.* 87] [L. HILBERSEIMER, (1967), 1981, p. 41].

Chemical factory, Luban, 1911-1912, H. Poelzig (*Fig.* 95).

«Poelzig's factory at Luban had a «Gothic» character, not in form but in spirit; from this resulted an harmonious building, even if it is composed of parts contrasting from one another». [L. HILBERSEIMER, (1967) 1981, p. 39]

Railway station, Stuttgart, 1911-1914,

Fig. 97

Fig. 98

Fig. 100

P. Bonatz and F. Scholer (*Fig.* 96).

1912
Kröller-Müller House project, Wassenaar, Mies van der Rohe (*Fig.* 97).

«At the time of the Kröller project neoplasticism had not yet been borne. On the contrary, the works of Friedrich Schinkel, whom Mies admired very much, could have had an influence on him. In his project for the castle of Glienicke, as also in other projects of country houses, Schinkel — differently fom how he did with public themes, always rigidly symmetrical and monumental — almost always preferred a free disposition of volumes so as to show a typical, direct participation of the landscape in the architectural composition». [L. HILBERSEIMER, (1967) 1981, pp. 90-91]

1913
Gustav Scheu House, Vienna, A. Loos (*Fig.* 98).

Skywa-Primavesi House, Vienna, 1913-1915, J. Hoffmann (*Fig.* 99).

Design for a theater, Berlin, H. Scharoun (*Fig.* 100).

«The architecture of Berlin in the years preceding the first World War, was mostly rationalist and was founded on the use of materials and new methods of construction». [L. HILBERSEIMER, (1967), 1981, p. 54]

1914
German Werkbund-Exhibition, Cologne (*Fig.* 101).

Fig. 101

«The Cologne exhibition, now generally recognized as a milestone in the development of modern architecture, was originally intended primarily as a showcase for the products of the German art industries». [J. CAMPBELL, 1978, pp. 73-74]

«Yet the 1914 exhibition did bring all the association's problems

Fig. 99

Fig. 102a,b,c

into the open, particularly as they bore on the essential concept of the «new style»...

«... the Werkbund adopted the ideal of a «German style». Yet as its leading propagandists had to recognize, a style that mirrored the realities of contemporary industrial society was bound in some sense to be «international». To reconcile the two perspectives they appropriated the popular notion of a German cultural mission: Germany should aspire to lead the world both in terms of technology and quality, and through creation of a valid modern style». [J. CAMPBELL, 1978, pp. 76, 77]

Model factory, Cologne, W. Gropius and A. Meyer (*Fig.* 102 a b c).

«Why had Walter Gropius chosen as a theme for the Werkbund exhibition a machine room and an office block? «The bottom line of our time», he wrote, «is determined by commerce, by technique, and by systems of communication. Thus, he who designs, who sets about creating new forms, rather than keeping to the traditional building problems, is greatly attracted by giving new aesthetic solutions of the modern building problems presented by the department store, the factory, the office building, the machine rooms...» [L. HILBERSEIMER, (1967) 1981, p. 38-39]

Austria House, Cologne, J. Hoffmann (*Fig.* 103).

Glass pavilion, Cologne, B. Taut (*Fig.* 104).

«Bruno Taut had created a glass pavilion with a cement structure covered by a dome: this pavilion was dedicated to Paul Scheerbart... Around the drum some aphorisms by Scheerbart were reproduced, as for example this one...
We feel sorry for brick culture
Without a glass palace life becomes a burden». [L. HILBERSEIMER, (1967), 1981, p. 55]

Congress of the Werkbund, Cologne.

«The main moment of the Congress was the debate between Hermann Muthesius and Henry van de Velde; between a standardized production, or, on the contrary, the complete freedom in artistic creation». [L. HILBERSEIMER, (1967) 1981, p. 35]

The Domino Houses, Le Corbusier (*Fig.* 105).

«A structural system was conceived — a framework — completely independent of the floorplans of the house...» [W. BOESINGER, H. GIRSBERGER. 1967, p. 24]

Manifesto dell'Architettura Futurista, A. Sant'Elia.

«We have lost the sense of the monumentality, of the heaviness..., and we have enriched our sensibility with the TASTE OF THE LIGHT, OF THE PRACTICAL, OF THE EPHEMERAL AND OF

Fig. 103

Fig. 104

Fig. 105

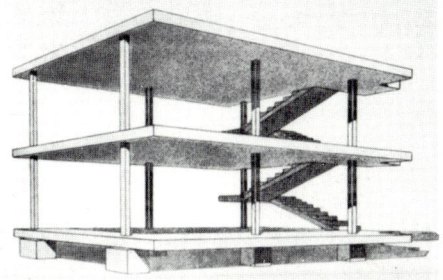

Fig. 106

Fig. 107

Fig. 108

Fig. 109

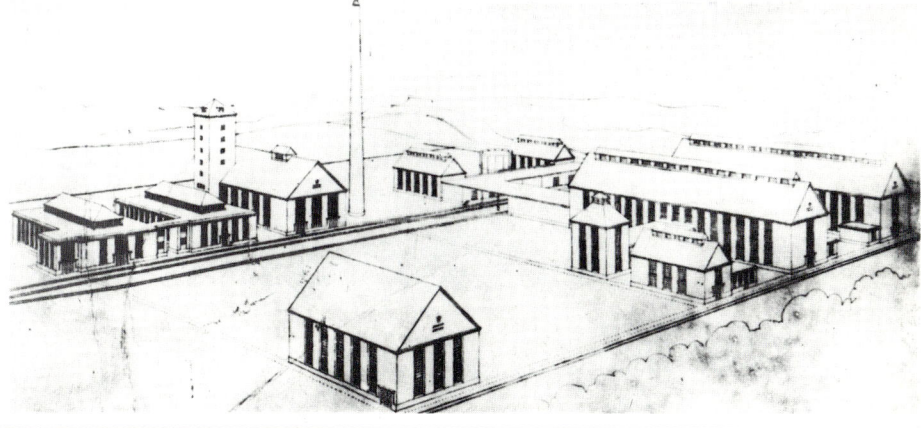

THE SPEEDY.
We feel that we are no longer the men of the cathedrals, of the palaces, of the assemblies, but the men, of the grand Hotel, of the huge streets, of the colossal harbours, of the covered markets, of the shining arcades, of the straight roads, or the necessary demolitions».

Design for a kiosk, A. Sant'Elia (*Fig.* 106).

Apartment building VII, M. Chiattone (*Fig.* 107).

1916

Hausbau und dergleichen published in Berlin by H. Tessenow.

«Sometimes one tends to identify simplicity with poverty; instead it is true that they have practically nothing in common. In fact, simplicity to which we aspire may represent the greatest wealth, just as the formal variety which we have may reveal itself as the greatest poverty». [H. TESSENOW, (1916), 1987, p. 112-113]

Alexander Wacker Company for electrochemical industry, Burghausen - am - Inn, Bavaria, J. Hoffmann (*Fig.* 108).

Sugar refinery, Rohrbach, 1916-1919, A. Loos (*Fig.* 109).

1917

Project for the Memorial for the Emperor Francis Joseph, Vienna, A. Loos (*Fig.* 110).

Eigen Haard housing estate, Amsterdam, M. de Klerk (*Fig.* 111).

A group of artists and architects is formed in Leiden and published a journal: *De Stijl*

Het Monumentale Stadsbeld by J.J.P. Oud published in *De Stijl*, no. 1, October, pp. 10-11.

«The concept of monumentality is of an inward and not an outward nature. It may be apparent both in the small and in the large. Material factors play no part in it at all...
[...] The modern street image will, therefore, sharply contrast with that of the past, with the houses that followed one another in an arbitrary fashion, and will be dominated by residential blocks in which dwellings will be set out according to a rhythmic play of surfaces and volumes.
The modern architect's major task is therefore the residential block. This task, for which the aid of public bodies is indispensable, calls for its own special solution, not yet to be found in the blocks that have been built to date, in which the influences of tradition are still strong».

1918

Kunst en machine by J. J. P. Oud published in *De Stijl*, no. 3, January, pp. 25-27.

«From our definition of *monumentality* as an organized and conscious relation of the subjective towards the objective, it follows that, at the highest level, this tendency will lead to a *monumental style*. A distinction must be made between the two direction in the tendency towards style.
The first direction, the *technical-industrial* one, definable as positive, strives to bring the products of the technical spirit to the level of aesthetic expression.
The second, which by comparison might be defined as negative (although it is equally *positive* in its *manifestations*!) is art, which tends by subtraction (abstraction) to arrive at «objectivity». The unity of both these trends forms the *essence of the new style*...
On the subject of the spirit on modern art, Severini writes: «La précision, le rythme, la brutalité des machines et leurs mouvements nous ont sans doute conduits vers un nouveau réalisme que nous pouvons exprimer sans peindre des locomotives».

Project for standardized workers' houses, J. J. P. Oud (*Fig.* 112).

Spangen housing estate, Rotterdam, 1918-1920, J. J. P. Oud (*Fig.* 113).

Architectonische beschouwing bij bijlage VIII, by J.J.P. Oud published in *De Stijl*, no 4 February, pp. 39-41.

«In the formative days of young Germany, as with the young Americans of today, there arose the tendency to link up the great technological and commercial developments with art and vice versa. This trend reveals itself in architecture in the search for the aesthetic solution of the modern building problems presented by the department store, the factory, the office building, machine rooms, etc. Especially Behrens and Olbrich (after Messel) achieved eminence in this field.
In this area, German art had the legacy of tradition

Fig. 110

Fig. 111

Fig. 112

Fig. 113

to bear, which, by a lack of critical discernment, worked counter to the achievement of a pure form of expression. Because of this obstacle, the movement began to crumble, and the struggle towards simplification and purification took the wrong path, in the direction of classicism. Examples of this were to be seen by the score at the Werkbund Exhibition in Cologne, held just at the outbreak of the war».

1919
In March, Gropius together with Meyer moved to Weimar to direct the Bauhaus.

«The first proclamation of the Bauhaus of April, 1919, named as an objective the understanding of every aspect of creative work and the developing of an idea of architecture that gathered the various

Fig. 114

Fig. 115

artistic research and put back the same «arts» in an adeguate reciprocal relationship». [L. HILBERSEIMER, (1967), 1981, p. 70-71]

Congress of the German Werkbund, Stuttgart: theme of the debate is the relationship between «Art, Industry, Crafts».

Alpine Architektur by B. Taut published in Hagen.

«Both Taut's Siedlungen and his alpine glass buildings, with their terraces and cascades, the arches of glass that surpass the snowy summits of the mountains, the gardens in glass decorated by flowers and leaves of crystal, are illumined by colored lights all during the night. Because also the dwellings of the Siedlungen should have shone with colored lights during the night as the stars». [L. HILBERSEIMER, (1967) 1981, p. 61]

Friedrichstrasse Office Building project (first scheme) competion entry (*Fig.* 114)

1920

Classique - baroque - moderne, by Th. van Doesburg, published in Paris.

«By the beginning of 1920, it became fashionable once more to stress the continuity of the postwar Werkbund with that of the founding years, and to deride the Expressionist movement as an aberration from accepted principles of sound art and design». [J. CAMPBELL, 1978, p. 146].

A GREAT EPOCH IS BEGINNING
No. 1, October, 1920.
Programme of *l'Esprit Nouveau*

«Nobody to-day can deny the aesthetic which is disengaging itself from the creations of modern industry. More and more buildings and machines are growing up, in which the proportions, the play of their masses and the materials used are of such a kind that many of them are real works of art, for they are based on «number», that is to say, on order. Now, the specialized persons who make up the world of industry and business and who live, therefore, in this virile atmosphere where indubitably lovely works are created, will tell themselves that they are far removed from any aesthetic activity.

Fig. 116

They are wrong, *for they are among the most active creators of contemporary aesthetics*. Neither artists nor business men take this into account. It is in general artistic production that the style of an epoch is found and not, as is too often supposed, in certain productions of an ornamental kind, mere superfluities which overload the system of thought which alone furnishes the elements of a style. Grot-

Fig. 117

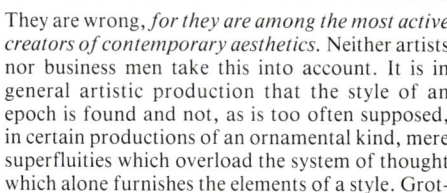

Fig. 118

to work does not make Louis Quinze, the lotus is not the Egyptian style, etc., etc.
From a tract issued by *L'Esprit Nouveau*». [LE CORBUSIER, 1952, p. 83]

First project for Citrohan house, Le Corbusier.

Einstein Tower, Observatory, Potsdam, 1920-1924, E. Mendelsohn (*Fig.* 115).
«Mendelsohn literally wrapped this astronomical «instrument» with a monumental covering, which had more features of a sculpture than those of an architecture. In fact, he was more a «creator of forms» than a researcher, that is, not a researcher of a precise, determined form. Even if the problem of the Einstein tower could have been resolved in a rational way, Mendelsohn had preferred to rely on his own romantic irrational vein». [L. HILBERSEIMER, (1967) 1981, p. 69]

1921

Dr. Bavinck School, Hilversum, W. M. Dudok.
Berliner Tageblatt Administration building, Berlin, 1921-1923, E. Mendelsohn (*Fig.* 117).
Farben office building, Höchst Frankfurt-am Main, 1921-1925, P. Behrens (*Fig.* 118).

1922

«First broached in the summer of 1919, the idea of cooperating with the *Deutsche Gewerbeschau*, planned for Munich in 1922, appealed particularly to members of the *Münchener Bund*.... The Werkbund accordingly decide in February 1920 to take part in the *Gewerbeschau*, despite opposition from the young radicals whose sentiments still carried

Fig. 119

Fig. 120

Fig. 121

Fig. 122

Fig. 123

Fig. 124

Fig. 125

considerable weight. Indeed, under radical pressure, the association had just withdrawn support from the Leipzig fair, Germany's largest and most important trade exhibition, on the grounds that its organizers lacked sympathy with the Werkbund program and merely sought to exploit Werkbund prestige for commercial ends...
The Werkbund's effort to reconcile the interests of art and industry through participation in the *Deutsche Gewerbeschau* was paralleled by an equally energetic attempt to cement the relationship between artists and craftsmen...» [J. CAMPBELL, 1978, pp. 150, 151, 157]

Project for the «Chicago Tribune Competition», A. Loos (*Fig.* 119).

«The great Greek column will be constructed if not in Chicago elsewhere.
If not for the Chicago Tribune for someone else.
If not by me by some other Architect». [A. Loos, in F.W., *Zeitschrift des Oesterreichischen — Ingenieur und Architekten — Vereines*, Vienna, 26 Jän. 1923, pp. 13-17]

Villa Besnos, Vaucresson, Le Corbusier (*Fig.* 121).

Citrohan houses, second project, Le Corbusier (*Fig.* 120).

«But the man who first made the world aware that

Fig. 126

Fig. 127

Fig. 128

a new style was being born was Le Corbusier...
The influence of Le Corbusier was the greater, the appearance of a new style the more remarked, because of the vehement propaganda which he contributed to the magazine *L'Esprit Nouveau*, 1920-1925...
When in 1922 he built at Vaucresson his first house in the new style, he failed to equal the purity of design and the boldness of construction of the *Citrohan* project». [H.R. HITCHCOCK, Jr., PH. JOHNSON, 1932, pp. 31-32]

Hochhaus Project für Banhof Friedrichstrasse in Berlin (FRÜHLICHT, 1, 1922, pp. 122-124) by Mies van der Rohe.

«I placed the glass walls at slight angles to each other to avoid the monotony of over-large glass surfaces. I discovered by working with actual glass models that the important thing is the play of reflections and not the effect of light and shadow as in ordinary buildings»» [(MIES VAN DER ROHE, 1922), from J. ZUKOWSKY, 1986, pp. 37, 53, n. 4].

Concrete Office Building project, Mies van der Rohe (first published in the inaugural issue of *G.* in the following year (*Fig.* 122).

«An event of great importance was the exhibition of Russian art at Berlin in 1922, which included the works of all those who had a clear influence on the artistic renewal in the Soviet Union». [L. HILBERSEIMER, (1967) 1981, p. 49]

Chilehaus, Hamburg, 1922-1923, F. Höger (*Fig.* 123).

Weichmann silk factory, Gleiwitz, E. Mendelsohn (*Fig.* 124).

Project for Apartments-Villas, Le Corbusier (*Fig.* 125).

1923

Vers une architecture by Le Corbusier published in Paris.

«Architecture has nothing to do with the various «styles».
Architecture is the masterly, correct and magnificent play of masses brought together in light. Our eyes are made to see forms in light; light and shade reveal these forms; cubes, cones, spheres, cylinders or pyramids are the great primary forms which light reveals to advantage; the image of these is distinct and tangible within us and without ambiguity. It is for that reason that these are *beautiful forms, the most beautiful forms...*
Not in pursuit of an architectural idea, but simply guided by the results of calculation (derived from the principles which govern our universe) and the conception of A LIVING ORGANISM, *the* ENGINEERS of to-day make use of the primary elements and, by co-ordinating them in accordance with the rules, provoke in us architectural emotions and thus make the work of man ring in unison with the universal order.
Thus we have the American grain elevators and factories, the magnificent FIRST-FRUITS of the new age. THE AMERICAN ENGINEERS OVERWHELM WITH THEIR CALCULATIONS OUR EXPIRING ARCHITECTURE (*Fig.* 126).

«If we forget for a moment that a steamship is a machine for transport and look at it with a fresh eye, we shall feel that we are facing an important manifestation of temerity, of discipline, of harmony, of a beauty that is calm, vital and strong.
A seriously-minded architect, looking at it as an architect (*i.e.* a creator of organisms), will find in a steamship his freedom from an age-long but contemptible enslavement to the past.
He will prefer respect for the forces of nature to a lazy respect for tradition; to the narrowness of commonplace conceptions he will prefer the majesty of solutions which spring from a problem that has been clearly stated — solutions needed by this age of mighty effort which has taken so gigantic a step forward.
The house of the earth-man is the expression of a circumscribed world. The steamship is the first stage in the realization of a world organized according to the new spirit.
«The Parthenon is a product of selection applied to an established standard. For a century the Greek temple had been standardized in all its parts. [LE CORBUSIER, 1952, pp. 27, 31, 33, 96-97, 123] (*Fig.* 127)

«After the first World War Germany was not only starved physically, but also spiritually. It was difficult to go abroad, to create new relations. One of my friends had the luck to be able to go to France, and brought back from Paris a copy of Le Corbusier book, *Vers une architecture*: for us it was an extraordinary event to possess this book, instead of only hearing about it». [L. HILBERSEIMER, (1967) 1981, p. 47]

Architectural Exhibition of the *De Stijl* Group in the Galerie Rosemberg, Paris (the models of the *Maison Particulière* and the *Maison d'Artiste* by Cornelis van Eesteren and Theo van Doesburg were

Fig. 129

Ist Biennial Exhibition of Decorative Arts, Monza.
Brick Country House project, 1923-1924, L. Mies van der Rohe (*Fig.* 128).

«The project for a brick country house that Mies van der Rohe drew up in 1923 is unusual from all points of view. This is the first expression of that new conception of space that will later become one of the principal characteristics of his projects. It might seem a paradox that Mies, a great admirer of the new technology, chose as the basic element for his project the brick wall instead of reinforced concrete or steel. But in what an extraordinary solution did he know how to apply this ancient material of construction». [L. HILBERSEIMER, (1967) 1981 p. 89]

1924
Housing estate Hoek van Holland, 1924-1927, J. J. P. Oud (*Fig.* 129).

Fig. 130

Fig. 131

Fig. 132
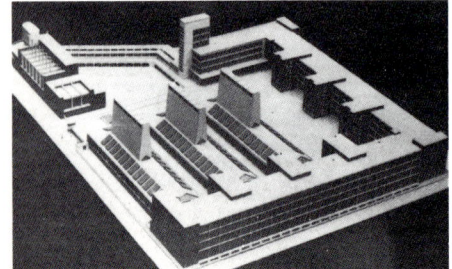

Fig. 133

Fig. 134

Fig. 135

Fig. 136

Fig. 137

Fig. 138

Klosehof, Vienna, J. Hoffmann (*Fig.* 130).

Siedlung, Schillerpark, Berlin-Wedding, 1924-1925, B. Taut (*Fig.* 131).

Fig. 139

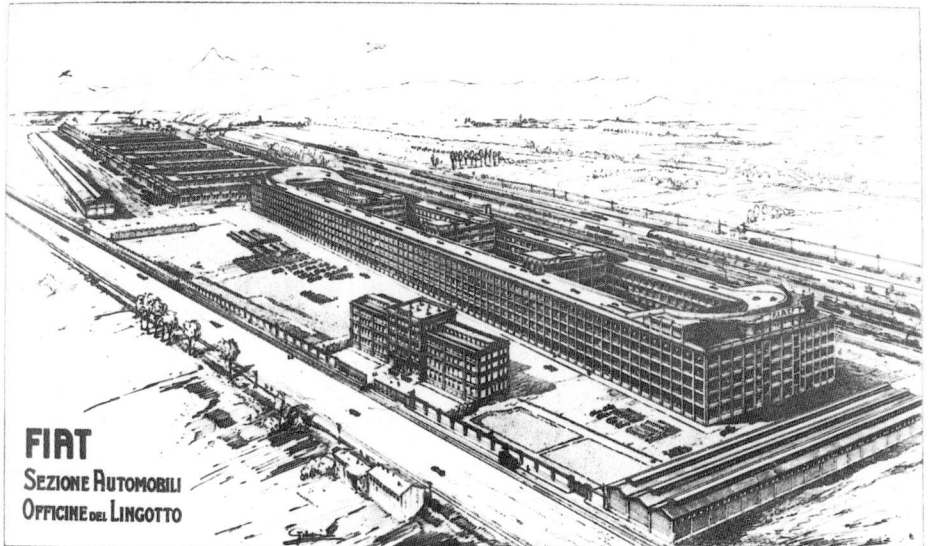
Fig. 140

Fig. 141

1925

Internationale Architektur published by W. Gropius in the first number of the *Bauhausbücher* (Munich).

Krasnoje Snamja textile factory, Leningrad, E. Mendelsohn (*Fig.* 132).

The Bauhaus moves to Dessau.

Schroeder House, Utrecht, G. Rietveld (*Fig.* 133).

International Exhibition of Decorative Arts, Paris: The Pavilion "Esprit-Nouveau", Le Corbusier (*Fig.* 134).

2nd Biennial Exhibition of the Decorative Arts, Monza.

Kiefhock housing estate, Rotterdam, 1925-1929, J. J. P. Oud (*Fig.* 135).

Fig. 142

1926

Architecture Internationale by A. Lurçat published in Paris.

Der Moderne Zwechbau by A. Behne (written in 1923) published in Munich.

«When the rationalist refers to the machine, he does so because he gathers its modern and elegant, concise beauty of the form.
On the contrary, the functionalist sees in it the mobile instrument, which better approaches the organic nature. The utilitarian appeals to the machine because he sees realized in it an economic principle: saving of labor, of energy and of time. The rationalist instead sees in it the representative and the promotor of uniformity and of standardization». [A. BEHNE, (1926), 1968, p. 52]

«[...] by 1926 its leaders [i.e., of the Werkbund], at least, identified themselves with the movement known as the *Neue Sachlichkeit*.
Variously translated as «Neo-functionalism» or «Neo-objectivity», the *Neue Sachlichkeit* dominated the modern movement in architecture (in German, *Neues Bauen*) at a time when architecture had become the Werkbund's prime concern». [J. CAMPBELL, 1978, p. 172]

Fig. 143

«When Mies was chosen to lead the Werkbund in 1926, he had only begun to prove himself as an architect...
Well-known in radical circles because of his role in organizing exhibitions for the *Novembergruppe*, Mies had been connected since 1923 with the «G» group that advocated novel principles of design diametrically opposed to those of the Expressionists». [J. Campbell, 1978, p. 181-182]

«Rational thinking, certainty of objectives, precision and economy characteristics up to now considered as belonging to the exclusive field of the engineers, must constitute from now on the basis of the new architecture. Each object must be fulfilled in itself, reduced to its essential form, organized in a sapient manner, carried to the greatest perfection possible». [L. Hilberseimer, «Grosstadtarchitektur», in *Der Sturm*, Berlin, 1924, from Hilberseimer, (1967) 1981, p. 83]

Project for Elektrobank building, Moscow, J. A. Golosov (*Fig.* 136).

Gruppo 7 (U. Castagnoli, L. Figini, G. Frette, S. Larco, G. Pollini, C. E. Rava, G. Terragni) is formed in Milan.

«The new generation seems to proclaim an architectural revolution: only an apparent revolution. A desire for truth, for logic, for order, a lucidity which tastes of Hellenism, here is the true character of the new spirit». [Gruppo 7, «Architettura, *Rassegna Italiana*, December 1926, p. 854]

Cohen-Epstein Department Store, Duisburg, 1926-1927, E. Mendelsohn (*Fig.* 137).

Novocomum, Como, 1926-1928, G. Terragni (*Fig.* 138).

Fiat automobile factory, Lingotto, Turin (project: 1916), 1926-1928, G. Mattè Trucco (*Fig.* 139).

Woga Buildings, Kurfürstendamm, Berlin, 1926-1928, E. Mendelsohn (*Fig.* 140).

Siedlungen Törten, Dessau, 1926-1928, W. Gropius (*Fig.* 141).

Internationale neue Baukunst by L. Hilberseimer published in Stuttgart.

1927
Weissenhof colony at Stuttgart (*Fig.* 142).

«[...] the 1927 Werkbund exhibition was an important event. With its associated displays, the Weissenhof attracted over half a million visitors. It established the reputation of Stuttgart as an exhibition center and of the Werkbund as a patron of the modern movement.
[...] While a section of this exhibition was to display modern home furnishings, the plan outlined by the Württemberg Werkbund group in addition called for construction of a permanent housing estate on land owned by the city of Stuttgart. Consisting of a group of dwellings designed by progressive architects from Germany and abroad, this «Weissenhof» settlement was intended as a model development incorporating the latest technical, hygienic, and aesthetic improvements in domestic architecture». [J. Campbell, 1978, pp. 188, 185]

«The architects who were called to collaborate in the planning of the «Weissenhof-Siedlung» at Stuttgart, agreed that the buildings should all be of the same color: white! Bruno Taut was the only one who used violent colors for his house, both inside and outside». [L. Hilberseimer, (1967) 1981, p. 49]

Siedlung Berlin-Prenzlauer Berg, 1927-1928, B. Taut (*Fig.* 143).

Die Baukunst der neusten Zeit by G.A. Platz published in Berlin.

Wie baut Amerika? by R. Neutra published in Stuttgart.

Competition for the Palace of League of Nations, 1927-1928, Geneva.

1928
1st CIAM (International Congress for Modern Architecture) (P. Artaria, H. P. Berlage. U. Bourgeois, P. Chareau, J. Frank, G. Guerekian, M. E. Haefeli, H.

Fig. 144

Fig. 146

Fig. 147

Fig. 148

Fig. 145

Fig. 149

Fig. 150

Fig. 151

Häring, A. Hoechel, H. Hoste, C. E. Jeanneret — Le Corbusier, P. Jeanneret, A. Lurçat, L. Maggioni, E. May, F. G. Marcadal, H. Meyer, W. Moser, G. T. Rietveld, A. Sartoris, H. Schmidt, M. Stam, R. Steiger, H. R. Von der Müll, J. Zavala, C. E. Rava by proxy).

«The International Congresses for Modern Architecture (Congrès Internationaux d'Architecture Moderne) (CIAM) were not founded to protect the rights of the profession — that is the task of the large official architectural organizations. The purpose of CIAM was to establish contemporary architecture's right to existence against the antagonistic forces of official architectural circles, who controlled the major building enterprises. The aim of CIAM was to deal with problems that could not be solved by the single individual. This was approximately the definition Le Corbusier gave of CIAM's purpose...

The reason that proved decisive was the need to provide for helplessly isolated architects in various countries an ideological basis and professional support that would enable them to tackle special problems and to defend their approach». [S. GIE-DION, (1941) 1967, p. 696-697]

Office building of Industria Sarmej Company, 1928-1929, Klausenbourg, J. Hoffmann.

Schocken Department Store, Chemnitz, 1928-1929, E. Mendelshon (*Fig.* 144).

Project for the competition for Lenin State Library, Moscow. P. A. Golosov (*Fig.* 145).

Project for a house for Josephine Baker, Paris, A. Loos (*Fig.* 146).

Competition entry for the redesign of the Alexanderplatz, Berlin (*Fig.* 147).

Exhibition in the Parco del Valentino, Turin.

Establishment of the MIAR (Movimento Italiano per l'Architettura Razionale) and the 1st Exhibition of Architecture, Rome.

«Therefore — solemn affirmation — we gather in Rome, in a first exhibition of Rational Architecture, a large part of attempts and of projects: executed or not.

We have decisively called it *rational*, although this word does not correspond perfectly to the concept, because one cannot define only rational a work that as the architectural one must be also art...

Rational architecture — as we mean it — finds again the harmonies, the rhythms, the symmetries in the new constructive schemes, the rhythms, the symmetries in the new constructiv schemes, in the characteristics of the materials and in the perfect correspondence to the requirements for which the building is intended». [A. LIBERA, G. MINNUCCI, *Introduzione all'esposizione*, Catalogue, from M. CENNAMO, 1973, pp. 103-105]

Università Cattolica, 1928-1938, Milan, G. Muzio (*Fig.* 148).

Tugendhat House, Brno, 1928-1930, Mies van der Rohe (*Fig.* 149).

Bauen in Frankreich — Eisen und Eisenbeton by S. Giedion published in Leipzig.

Eine Stunde Architektur by A. Behne published in Stuttgart.

1929

Naval Construction Depot, 1929-1930, Paris, A. Perret (*Fig.* 150).

Fig. 152

Fig. 153

Fig. 154

Fig. 155

Fig. 156

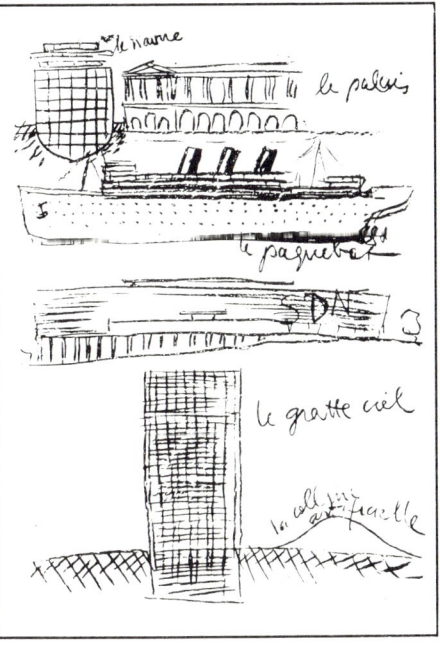

Fig. 157

Fig. 158

German Pavilion International Exposition, Barcelona, Mies van der Rohe (*Fig.* 151).
Project for the competition of the Palace of Culture in the Proletarskij district, Moscow, 1929-1930, I. I. Leonidov (*Fig.* 152).
Siedlung, Berlin Siemensstadt, 1928-1931, H. Häring (*Fig.* 153).
Villa Savoie, Poissy, Le Corbusier (*Fig.* 154).
«It is impossible to comprehend the Savoie house by a view from a single point; quite literally, it is a construction in spacetime. The body of the house has been hollowed out in every direction: from above and below, within and without. A cross section at any point shows inner and outer space penetrating each other inextricably». [S. GIEDION, (1941) 1967, p. 529]
2nd CIAM in Frankfurt; theme: Die Wohnung für das Existenzminimum.
Russland, Europa, Amerika. Ein Architektonischer Querschnitt by E. Mendelsohn published in Berlin.
«Architecture in everything, City planning in everything», lecture delivered by Le Corbusier to the Faculty of Exact Sciences, Buenos Aires, 8 October (*Figg.* 155-156).
«Les immenses problèmes contemporains de l'urbanisme et de l'architecture, apporteront à la Ville, en étendue et en hauter, des éléments d'une nouvelle échelle. L'unité sera dans le detail; la clameur sera dans l'ensemble». [LE CORBUSIER, 1930, pp. 83-84]
Centrosoyouz Building, Moscow, Le Corbusier (*Fig.* 157).

1930

House of Culture, Moscow, 1930-1933, Vesnin.
Luxenburgerstrassehof, Vienna, J. Hoffmann (*Fig.* 158).
3rd CIAM in Brussels; theme: Rationelle Bebauungs-weisen.

1931

Architektur als Symbol. Elemente deutschen neuen Bauens by J. Frank.
«We are thinking of adopting the flat roof, this very popular symbol of a clear Weltanschauung, not metaphysical, which distinguishes our epoch. Everyone understands that this symbol is less costly than the mystical one. But no one has understood well or dares to say why it is done, because one is ashamed to have a formal or indeed human sensibility, and therefore it is excluded». [J. FRANK, (1931) 1986, p. 38]
2nd Exhibition of Rational Italian Architecture.
Palace of the Soviets, Moscow, Le Corbusier.
«Costruzioni monumentali» by A. Sartoris published in *La nuova architettura*, Turin.
«In the future, the monumental character of architecture could assume the mission of being the rule of all art. And thus we will see architecture follow purpose that will not be uniquely the negation of the preceding generation, but the concentration of the new spirit of our epoch. Unification of all the elements of which the world is composed, monumental architecture, renouncing all the experiences in contradiction with the pre-eminence of the functional concept, will lead the art of building towards the lyricism and the pathetic which have characterized certain great periods, of ancient architecture». [A. SARTORIS, (1931), 1985, pp. 58-59]

1932

Gli elementi dell'architettura funzionale by A. Sartoris published in Milan.

1933

Adolf Loos dies.
«Without Loos, probably, our architecture would have remained only an ingenious and intelligent game, a speciality for artists, for abstract painting and plastic». [H. SCHMIDT, (1941, 1965) 1974, p. 123]
4th Congress of the CIAM. Theme: The Functional City. The delegates produced the well known document: The Athens Charter.
5th Triennial, Milan.

AMERICAN MODERN ARCHITECTURE A CRONOLOGY 1918-1933

"How did this change come about? In back of it stands a colossal man, Henry Hobson Richardson, an architect who almost single-handed created out of a confusion which was actually worse than a mere void the beginnings of a new architecture". (LEWIS MUMFORD, *The Brown Decades 1865-1895*, (1931), 1955, Dover Publications, New York, p. 114.)

BACKGROUND - 1878-1918

An American Modern Architecture can be seen to have begun with Richardson's (1838-86) breakthrough: the transformation of his architecture from the historicist Trinity Church in Boston (1873-77), to the non-historicist Sever Hall at Harvard (1878-80), followed by the Ames Gate Lodge, North Easton (1880-81), Crane Memorial Library, Quincy (1880-83), Bryant house, Cohasset (1880), Stoughton house, Cambridge (1882-83) and the Marshall Field Wholesale Store, Chicago (1885-87). From this beginning Modern Architecture developed, both a domestic and a monumental mode. This development manifested itself in three regional schools: Eastern (New York/Boston); Midwestern (Chicago/Prairie School); and Western (Los Angeles/Bay Area School).
Mention will be made of only Frank Lloyd Wright, who had a major impact in Europe (publication of his work by Wasmuth, 1910) and Irving Gill, whose «white cubes» of c. 1910-20 parallel the contemporary work of Loos in Austria.
Of these three regional schools, the Eastern turned toward a correct Roman/Renaissance vocabulary after c. 1890, while the Midwestern and Western were vital and active up to c. 1915, by which time the academic reaction initiated by McKim, Mead and White in New York had achieved nationwide ascendancy.
During the period between c. 1890 and c. 1915 there was a creative interaction between the Modernism initated by Richardson and the academic reaction which followed, but just when the academic reaction seemed dominant, as for example the triumph of Bertam Goodhue's Spanish Revival exposition in San Diego in 1915 over the local work of Irving Gill who was left with little work, Goodhue himself initiated a new Modernism, a pragmatic, evolutionary one which adhered to the composition based design of the academic revival but sought an architecture appropriate to the modern world.
«It is possible that we shall never again have a distinctive style, but what I hope and believe we shall someday possess is something akin to a style — so flexible that it can be made to meet every practical and constructive need, so beautiful and complete as to harmonize the hitherto discordant notes of Art and Science, and to challenge comparison with the wonders of past ages, yet malleable enough to be moulded at the designer's will, as readily toward the calm perfection of the Parthenon as toward the majesty and restless mystery of Chartres.» (B. GOODHUE, *The Craftsman 8*, June 1905).
This is interesting not only for predicting Goodhue's future direction but also for revealing discontent within the academic reaction.

The chronology which follows intertwines three streams: first, the continuation of Wright's work; second, imported European Modernism beginning with Schindler, who is a link between Wright and Europe; and third, a specific American stream of which the major product is the skyscraper. In the canonic histories of Modern Architecture this third stream was discredited because it was compromised by its ties with the hated *Ecole des Beaux-Arts*. While this discrediting has now itself been discredited, the winnowing out of what is Modern from the total has not been undertaken. The revisionist historians who have undertaken the rehabilitation of this native American style have been at pains to accept everything, thus in a sense continuing the view of the earlier historians of Modern Architecture, ie., instead of rejecting all, they have accepted all. The work included here is specifically chosen for its being Modern.

* Parallel to Richardson's innovation of 1878 is the rejected design for 44 Tite St., London of E.W. Godwing (1833-87) as well as the designs in silver of Christopher Dresser following his study trip to Japan in 1877 and, slightly later, Arthur Mackmurdo's «Brooklyn», c. 1883-87.

1918
Armistice in Europe

«State House — Characteristic Masses» from *The Meaning of Architecture*, Irving K. Pond (1857-1939), published Boston, 1918 (*Fig.* 159). The first (?) drawing of what was to become the typical New York skyscraper image.

«Hollyhock House», Aline Barnsdall house, Los Angeles, design 1918, built 1920, Frank Lloyd Wright.

1919
Horatio West Court, Santa Monica, Calif., 1919, Irving Gill.

1920
Nebraska State Capitol competition, 1920, won by Bertram Grosvenor Goodhue, built 1922-32.

«Goodhue, who wrought so beautifully in several traditional styles, has now thrown them all to the winds in order to create a new style...» («Prairie Architecture», *New York Times,* 25 July 1920).

«... it makes no pretense of belonging to any period of the past. Its authors have striven to present... a State Capitol of the Here and Now, and naught else». (B.G. Goodhue in the competition text).

James J. Fagan house, Woodside, Calif., 1920, Bernard Maybeck.

Free Public Library, Bergen Branch project, Jersey City, N.J., 1920, Rudolph M. Schindler (*Fig.* 160).

1921
Los Angeles Library, 1921-26, Bertram Goodhue (*Fig.* 161).

Convocation Building project, Madison Square, New York, 1921, B. Goodhue, rendering by Hugh Ferriss.

Liberty Memorial competition, Kansas City, Mo., 1921, won by H.V.B. Magonigle with Bliss & Faville built 1921-35, rendering by Hugh Ferriss.

Sand Block House project for the Mojave Desert, 1920-21, Frank Lloyd Wright.

Kings Road house, Hollywood, 1921-22, R.M. Schindler.

Glen Alpine Springs resort, El Dorado, Calif., 1921, Bernard Maybeck.

1922
Chicago Tribune competition, Chicago, won by Howells and Hood, second prize to Eliel Saarinen. 263 entries submitted including W.B. Griffin, W. Gropius, A. Loos, B.G. Goodhue, M. Taut.

Evolution of the step-back building, a study of the effects of New York's 1916 zoning law, commissioned by Helme and Corbett, drawings by H. Ferriss.

«Civic Architecture of the Immediate Future», with illustrations, by Hugh Ferriss published in *Arts and Decoration*, Nov. 1922.

The culture of the automobile: three projects.

Ford Glass Plant, Detroit, 1922, Albert Kahn.

Bronx River Parkway, Westchester County, N.Y., design begun 1919, substantial completion in 1923, staff of Westchester County Park Commission under Gilmore D. Clark.

Steamlined automobile, patent filed 1922, issued 1927, Paul Jaray (*Fig.* 162).

1923
Millard house, Pasadena, Calif., 1923, Frank Lloyd Wright.

Barclay-Vesey building, New York, designed 1922-23, finished 1926, McKensie, Voorhees & and Gmelin, Ralph Walker, designer.

Illustrated in *Towards a New Architec-*

Fig. 161

Fig. 159

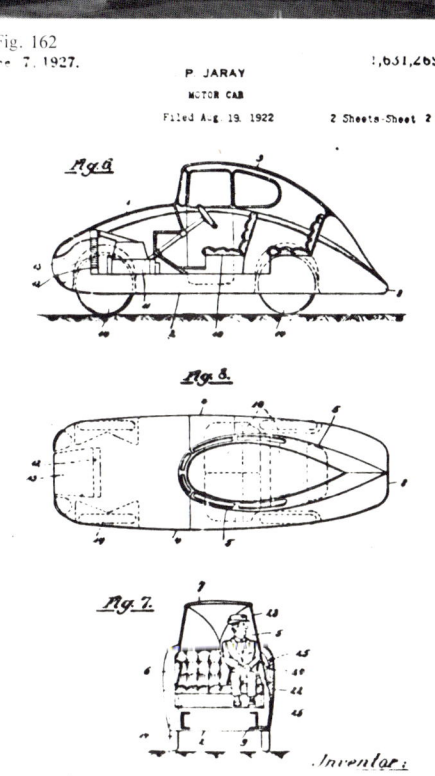
Fig. 162

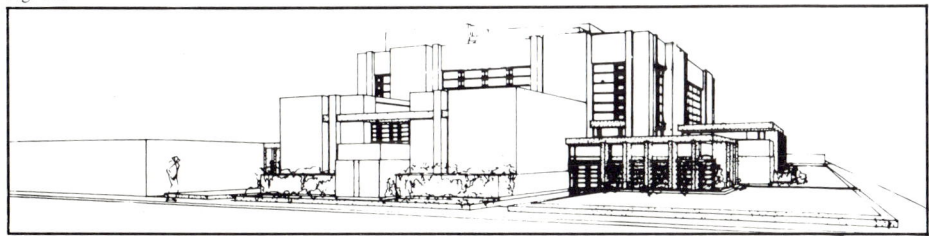
Fig. 160

ture, English translation of *Vers une architecture* by Le Corbusier.

«The modernist has always been the underdog, but when a distinctly modern structure like the new telephone building [Barclay-Vesey] wins the League's gold medal of honor, his position and that of the classicist have been reversed». RAYMOND HOOD, «Praise Architect Show», New York Times, 6 March 1927.

Proposal for Chicago Lakefront, 1923, Eliel Saarinen.

1924

Charles Ennis House, Los Angeles, 1924, Frank Lloyd Wright.

National Life Insurance Co. project, Chicago, 1924, Frank Lloyd Wright.

George G. Booth commissions Eliel Saarinen to develop the Cranbrook Educational Community, Bloomfield Hills, Mich., Site plan, 1924, Cranbrook School, 1925.

«City of Needles» project by Raymond Hood published *New York Times*, 28 Dec. 1924, Hugh Ferriss, delineator (*Fig.* 163).

«I wish we could all work with our own sense of discipline and be free as the devil». Raymond Hood, 1932 (?).

«His [Raymond Hood] life was a joy ride in which everybody got a thrill including the client». *Architectural Forum*, 1935.

«Building in the Modeling», drawing by Hugh Ferriss published in *The Manchester Guardian*, 22 Dec. 1924, on cover of *Sticks and Stones*, in December on the cover of *Pencil Points* and in *Vanity Fair*, Dec. «The New New York».

Sticks and Stones a Study of American Architecture and Civilization, 1924 by Lewis Mumford.

A shopping center, student project, University of Pennsylania, 1924, Louis Kahn (*Fig.* 164).

1925

Exposition des Arts Décoratifs, Paris, 1925.

«While some American architects had been aware prior to 1925 of the evolutionary Modern mode that was highlighted at the Paris Exposition des Arts Décoratifs, nonetheless the exposition was without doubt the decisive event in America's move toward architectural modernity. Its impact was felt almost overnight by architects in New York. The French forms and ideas found acceptance among many of New York's leading architects who had been trained in France as well as among the sophisticated New York public who traveled to Paris often and whose sympathies and cultural tastes largely tended to be pro-French».

Fig. 163

Fig. 164

Fig. 165

Fig. 166

Fig. 167

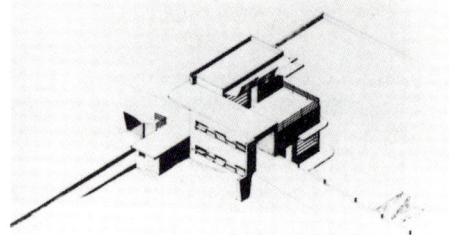

Fig. 168

Their spread was greatly facilitated by America's boom economy. New York department stores, their sales swelled by a burgeoning bourgeoisie, seized upon the new merchandise with a vergeance». *New York 1930*, ROBERT STERN, *et. al.*, New York, 1987, p. 27.

Tourist pavilion, Exposition des Arts Décoratifs, Paris, 1924-25, Rob Mallet-Stevens (*Fig.* 165).

«Titan City Exhibition», Wanamaker's department store, New York, October 1925, mural by Hugh Ferriss.

«Bridge Homes — A New Vision of the City», Raymond Hood, renderings by Hugh Ferriss, New York Times Magazine, 22 Feb. 1925.

Lovell beach house, Newport Beach, Calif., 1925-26, R.M. Schindler.

Adah Robinson studio, Tulsa, Okla. Design c. 1923-25, built 1926, Bruce Goff.

1926

Aisne-Marne Monument, France, 1926-32, Paul Cret (*Fig.* 166).

skyscraper regulation project, Chicago, Frank Lloyd Wright, 1926.

Metropolitan Opera House project, New York, 1926, Joseph Urban

skyscraper exhibition, New York, December 1926, organized by Alfred Bossom included Wm. Hohauser, H.W. Corbett, Sloan & Robertson, McKensie, Voorhees & Gmelin and Bossom.

1927

Jardinette Apartments, Los Angeles, 1927, Richard Neutra.

Country House for a Young Couple, project commissioned by *Architectural Forum*, 1927, William Lescaze (*Fig.* 167).

Ocotilla desert camp, near chandler, Ariz. 1927, Frank Lloyd Wright.

Dymaxion house, 1927, R. Buckminster Fuller ad for Saks Fifth Avenue, *Vogue*, 1927 Raymond Loewy.

Towards a New Architecture, translation into English by Frederick Etchell of *Vers une architecture* by Le Corbusier.

«Machine Age Exposition», 16 to 27 May 1927, Steinway Hall, New York, organized by *Little Review* editor, Jean Heap — Drawings by Ferriss, photos of Bauhaus and skyscrapers, Russian Constructivist work, etc. catalogue cover by Leger.

Chicago Board of Trade, 1927-28, Holabird & Root, sculpture on top by John Storrs.

Panhellenic Hotel, New York, 1927-30, John Mead Howells.

Park Avenue building, New York, 1927, Buchman & Kahn.

Chanin building, New York, 1927-30, Sloan & Robertson with Jacques Delamarre.

Fig. 169

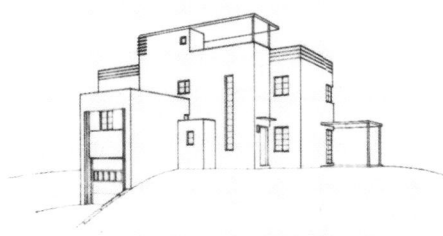

Fig. 170

Fig. 171

Fig. 172

1928

Lovell «Health» house, Los Angeles, commissioned 1927, built 1929, Richard Neutra.

Future American Country House — an American House in 1938, commissioned by *Architectural Record*, 1928, William Lescaze

village service station project, 1928, Frank Lloyd Wright.

Guaranty Laundry, Tulsa, Okla. 1928, Bruce Goff (*Fig.* 168).

Western Union building, New York, 1928-30 Voorhees, Gmelin & Walker.

Film Center building, New York, 1928-29, Buchman & Kahn.

Fuller building, New York, 1928-29, Walker & Gillette.

Chrysler building, New York, 1928-30, William Van Alen

«First International Exposition of Art in Industry», Macy's department store, New York, included rooms by Lee Simonson, Wm. Lescaze, Kem Weber, Ralph Walker, J. Hoffmann, G. Ponti.

«Exposition of Modern French Decorative Art», Lord and Taylor's department store, New York, interiors by F. Jourdain, designs of Chareau, Ruhlmann, Dunand, installation by E.J. Kahn.

«Life in New York City is just one modern exhibition after another...» *Good Furniture*, 1929.

1929

Elizabeth Noble apartment project, Los Angeles, 1929, Frank Lloyd Wright.

St. Mark's in the Bouwerie project, New York, 1929, Frank Lloyd Wright.

The Metropolis of Tomorrow, published 1929 by Hugh Ferriss (*Fig.* 169).

Modern Architecture: Romanticism and Reintegration, published 1929 by Henry-Russell Hitchcock.

Rex Cole showrooms, Brooklyn and Queens, N.Y. 1929-33, Raymond Hood.

Daily News building, New York, 1929-30, Howells and Hood.

Irving Trust building, New York, 1929-32, Voorhees, Gmelin & Walker.

The New School for Social Research, New York, 1929-30, Joseph Urban.

Toledo Scale Co. factory project, 1929,

Norman Bel Gueddes.

Kingswood School, Cranbrook Academy of Art, Bloomfield Hills, Mich. 1929-31, Eliel Saarinen.

Battledeck house, Highland Park, Ill., 1929-30 Henry Dubin (*Fig.* 170).

«The Architect and the Industrial Arts Exhibition», Metropolitan Museum of Art, New York, 1929, rooms by R. Hood — 15000 visitors at the opening, 186,000 estimate of total attendance.

Folger Shakespeare Library, Washington, D.C., 1929-32, Paul Cret.

Fig. 173

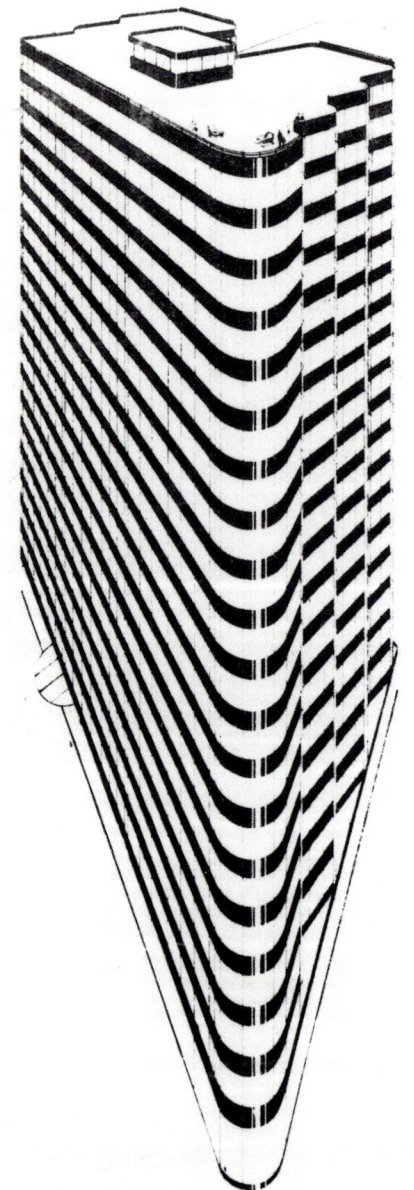

1930

P.S.F.S. building, Philadelphia, design 1928-30, finished 1932, Howe & Lescaze.

Frederick Vanderbilt Field house, New Hartford, Conn., 1930-31, Howe &

Fig. 174

Fig. 175

Fig. 176

Lascaze.

apartment project, Chicago, 1930, Bowman Brothers (*Fig.* 171).

bath houses, Hampton Bays, N.Y., 1930, William Muschenheim.

Empire State Building, New York, 1930-31, Shreve, Lamb & Harmon.

McGraw Hill building, New York, 1930-31, Hood, Godley and Fouilhoux.

R.C.A. Victor (now G.E.) building, New York, 1930-31, Cross and Cross

film set, *Just Imagine*, 1930, art directors, S. Gooson & R. Hammeras.

film set, *Wat a Widow*, Pathé set design, Paul Nelson (*Fig.* 172).

1931

Rockfeller Center, New York, designed 1928-35 R.C.A. building built 1931-33, Associated Architects (Hood, Corbett, *et al.*)

projects for the Museum of Modern Art, 1930-31, Howe and Lescaze

model house for *Ladies Home Journal*, 1931, Norman Bel Gueddes.

Capital Journal building project, Salem, Ore., 1931, Frank Lloyd Wright (prototype for Johnson Wax building, Racine, Wis).

Aluminaire House, Syosset, N.Y., 1931, Kocher & Frey (demonstration building for New York Architectural League Exhibition of 1931).

«Rejected Architects» exhibition organized by Philip Johnson in response to Architectural League exhibition, New York, 1931.

Airstream Trailer «kit», 1931, Wally Byam (*Fig.* 173).

The Brown Decades, published 1931 by Lewis Mumford.

«The way to the new architecture requires the weaving together of the several lines of initiative which were first started during the Brown Decades: the attempt at community planning which marked the building of Pullman, Ill., the experimental efforts towards new forms which was exhibited in Richardson, Sullivan, and above all Wright, the effort to integrate the playground and the park with the city as a whole which characterized the work of Olmstead and Elliot, and the effort to raise standardized industrial production to a higher aesthetic level which marked the work of the last generation of plumbing and kitchen utility manufacturers». (*The Brown Decades*, Dover 1955, pp. 180-81)

film set, *Easiest Way*, 1931, MGM, set design, Cedric Gibbons film set, *Palmy Days*, 1931, Goldwyn, set design, R. Dau & W. Pognay (*Fig. 174*).

1932

«Modern Architecture: International Exhibition», Museum of Modern Art, New York, February 1932 with catalogue.

International Style: Architecture Since 1922, published 1932 by H-R. Hitchcock and P. Johnson, preface by Alfred H. Barr.

«This uncertainty of direction is clearly demonstrated by two recent magazine articles, one on European and one on American architecture. The first, called *New Building for the New Age*, is illustrated by photographs of six buildings supposedly representative of "what is happening in architecture on the continent of Europe". They include Saarinen's pre-War Railway Station at Helsingfors; the bizarre Expressionist Einstein Tower (1920) at Potsdam and a ponderous department store, both by Mendelsohn; Tengbom's Concert Hall at Stockholm with its portico of tall decagonal columns surmounted by Corinthian capitals; a school by Dudok, one of the more advanced members of the conservative Amsterdam group; and a theatrical Danish church façade derived from Hanseatic Gothic prototypes.Could we have added the Romanesquoid Stuttgart Railway Station, a cubistic house from the rue Mallet-Stevens, a concrete church by the brothers Perret, and the neo-Barocco-Romanesque Town Hall of Stockholm, we would have nearly a complete list of the modern European buildings most familiar to the American public and, we are forced to believe, most admired by the large majority of American architects» (preface, p. 12).

VDL Research house, Los Angeles, 1932, Richard Neutra.

W.E. Oliver house, Los Angeles, design 1931, built 1933, R.M. Schindler.

Horizons, published New York, 1932 by Norman Bel Gueddes — streamlined designs for planes, trains, automobiles, etc.

Propeller-driven rail car, 1932, Raymond Loewy.

Hoover (Boulder) Dam, Boulder City, Nev., design c. 1930-32, finished 1936, Gordon B. Kaufmann, architect with Bureau of Reclamation Engineers.

1933

House of Tomorrow, «A Century of Progress», George Fred Keck (*Fig. 175*); Masonry house, «A Century of Progress», Andrew Rebory (*Fig. 176*); Century of Progress, World' fair, Chicago, 1933-34, board of design: Bennet, Burnham, Brown, Corbett, Cret, Holabird, Hood, Walker.

the *City of Salina*, streamlined train, Union Pacific, delivered 12 Feb. 1934

the Burlington *Zephyr*, streamlined train, Chicago, Burlington and Quincy, delivered April 1934

Federal Office Building, New York, 1933-35, Cross & Cross

town house, New York, 1933-34, William Lescaze

Malcolm Willey house, Minneapolis, project 1932, new design built 1934, Frank Llyod Wright.

Dymaxion Car Number One, 1933, R. Buckminster Fuller — a third version appeared at the Chicago exhibition in 1934

film set, *42nd Street*, 1933, Warner Brothers, art director, Jack Okey, dance sequences, Busby Berkeley

film set, *King Kong*, 1933, art directors, C. Clark & A. Herman.

Conclusion: by 1933 Modern Architecture was established in the United States, although this is not to say that period styles were banished: traditionalism and Modernism coexisted. The International Exhibition of 1932 at the Museum of Modern Art demonstrated that for the intellectual elite the International Style, as defined by Hitchcock and Johnson in their book, was the only intellectually respectable way to build. The Century of Progress fair in Chicago, on the other hand, demonstrated that the Moderne had become popular. In fact the two modes were not as separate as the intellectuals claimed. In any case, after 1933 Modernist, and Moderne, buildings appeared everywhere, especially in commercial buildings where seeming up to date was essential.

Background:

H.A. BROOKS, *The Prairie School, Frank Lloyd Wright and His Midwest Contemporaries*, 1976, W.W. Norton.
K.H. CARDWELL, *Bernard Maybeck, Artisan, Architect, Artist*, 1983, Peregrine Smith Books.
C. CONDIT, *The Rise of the Skyscraper*, 1952, University of Chicago Press.
M. GIROUARD, *Sweetness and Light, the Queen Anne Movement 1860-1900*, 1977, Oxford University Press.
H.R. HITCHCOCK, *The Architecture of H.H. Richardson and His Times*, 1961, M.I.T. Press.
R. LONGSTRETH, *On the Edge of the World, Four Architects in San Francisco at the Turn of the Century*, 1983, Architectural History Foundation M.I.T. Press.
S.T. MADSEN, *Sources of Art Nouveau*, 1980, Da Capo.
E. MCCOY, *Five California Architects*, 1960, Reinhold.
R. OLIVER, *Bertram Grosvenor Goodhue*, 1983, Architectural History Foundation M.I.T. Press, illustration, p. 227 bottom.

N. PEVSNER, *Pioneers of Modern Design from William Morris to Walter Gropius*, 1949, Museum of Modern Art.
V. SCULLY, *The Shingle Style, Architectural Theory and Design from Richardson to the Origin of Wright*, 1965, Yale University Press.

Chronology:

D. ALBRECHT, «The International Style Goes Holywood, How the Public Learned about Modern Architecture», *Skyline*, Feb. 1982, illustrations, p. 31.
D.J. BUSH, *The Streamlined Decade*, 1975, Braziller, illustration, p. 100.
S. COHEN, *Chicago Architects*, 1976, Swallow Press, Inc., illustrations, pp. 4, 86 right, 104 right.
Design in America, the Cranbrook Vision 1925-1950, 1983, Abrams.
A. DREXLER and T.S. HINES, *The Architecture of Richard Neutra, from International Style to California Modern*, 1982, Museum of Modern Art.
H. FERRISS, *The Metropolis of Tomorrow*, 1986, Princeton Architectural Press, illustration, p. 112.
D. GEBHARD, *Schindler*, 1980, Peregrine Smith, Inc., illustration, p. 44.

E.G. GROSSMAN, «Architecture for a Public Client: The Monuments and Chapels of the American Battle Monuments Commission», *Journal of the Society of Architectural Historians*, May 1984, illustration, p. 131, fig. 13
E.G. GROSSMAN, «Two Postwar Competitions: The Nebraska State capitol and the Kansas City Liberty Memorial», *Journal of the Society of Architectural Historians*, September 1986.
G. HILDEBRAND, *Designing for Industry, the ARchitecture of Albert Kahn*, 1974, M.I.T. Press.
H.R. HITCHCOCK, *In the Nature of Materials, the Buildings of Frank Lloyd Wright 1887-1941*, 1942, Duell, Sloan and Pearce.
A. IZZO and C. GUBITOSI, *Frank Lloyd Wright, Three Quarters of a Century of Drawings*, 1981, Horizon Press.
R. LANDAU and J. PHILLIPPI, *Airstream*, 1984, Peregrine Smith Books, illustration, p. 15.
T.A.P. van LEEUWEN, *The Skyward Trend of Thought*, 1986, AHA Books, the Hague, illustration, p. 132.
William Lescaze, Catalogue 16, Institute for

Architecture and Urban Studies, 1982, Rizzoli, illustration, p. 22, No. 22.
C. Robinson and R. Haag Bletter, *Skyscraper Style Art Deco New York*, 1975, Oxford University press.
V. Scully, *Louis I. Kahn*, 1962, Braziller, illustration, pl. 7.
R. Stern, G. Gilmartin and T. Mellins, *New York 1930, Architecture and Urbanism between the Two World Wars*, 1987, Rizzoli.
M. Tafuri, «The Disenchanded Mountain: the Skyscraper and the City» in *The American City*, 1979, M.I.T. Press.
Tulsa Art Deco, an Architectural Era 1925-1942, 1980, Junior League of Tulsa, illustration, p. 77.
C. Willis, «Zoning and *Zeitgeist*: the Skyscraper City in the 1920s», *Journal of the Society of Architectural Historians*, March 1986, illustration, fig. 10.
R.G. Wilson, D.H. Pilgrim and D. Taschjian, *The Machine Age in America 1918-1941*, 1986, Abrams, illustration, 6.59.

INTERVIEW WITH ALBERTO SARTORIS ON FEBRUARY 1988 IN COSSONAY-VILLE CONDUCTED BY J. RASPI SERRA AND N. ZANNI

Alberto Sartoris

1. *What was your position, both conceptual and cognitive, between the architectural culture in Italy and the modern movement (before 1925)? Relationship with Le Corbusier: introduction into Italy of new contents. What were the buildings which you admired?*

2. *What was your participation or of the more «informed» architecture to social, industrial, artisan problems... (Werkbund... Loos...)? What did your participation in these movements mean to you?*

3. *What foreign architectural forms were known in Italy before 1925 and what effect did they exert?*

4. *Gruppo 7: does its manifesto represent a common response to the problems of modern architecture? What meaning does the International Style have for you today?*
Do you think that the label of «rationalism» given to Italian architecture may still be valid today in a more logical historical panorama? In 1932 why did you call «functional» the architectonic forms gathered in your book? Where does the idea of the book come from and what has its history been?

5. *Between the 1930's and the 1940's was a lexical difference noticed in the architectural formulation in comparison with the former period? Was the architectural criticism aware that the structures of that decade, in their ordinary forms, referred to the modern language and tradition?*

6. *What examples of «classical» and of European architectural culture of the 1700's and the 1800's were known and applied eveywhere (Italy and abroad) and what was the degree of consciousness of their application in the 1920's and the 1930's?*

7. *Today, re-reading what has been written on you and on the period, do you consider «historical» the assertions that tend to split the cultural entities into tesserae of a mosaic which cannot be recomposed? On the contrary, how do you regard this research which attempts to find, in the assimilation of the forms of the past and of the «modern» contents, the real course of modern architecture and its true diffusion everywhere?*

8. *What is your reaction on having been included in the exhibition, «Everyday Masterpieces»? What is your point of view on this methodological research on the formal grammar of modern architecture?*

9. *What do you think about the* iter *and the forms of «Everyday Masterpieces»?*

10. *A comment on your work presented in this exhibition:*
a) Title
b) Iter *of the project*
c) Reference to the culture of mannerism and Ledoux in the dematerialization of the corner through the transformation of the theme in Gropius (Fagus, 1911-14) or in Mendelsohn (Berlin Tageblatt, 1921-23), to the classicism of Behrens in the facade, to Le Corbusier (Villa Citrohan) in the volume.

Are these references conscious or spontaneous?

1. Alberto Sartoris states that his position was already international in 1920, the year of the international exhibition of modern art in Geneva, where he met Marinetti, Van Doesburg and Gleizes. He was soon in contact with many exponents of the Modern Movement.

He had known the ideas of Le Corbusier through reading *Vers une architecture* (1923), and he had shared its opinions. But these same ideas were not thoroughly shared by many exponents of the Italian architectural culture of the epoch: «Unfortunately», he remembers, «Le Corbusier did not have a great formal influence in Italy».

Sartoris met Le Corbusier in Geneva in 1925, introduced by a mutual friend, the critic Lucienne Florentin. A propos of this Sartoris remembers the letter which Le Corbusier wrote to him to thank him for his intervention on his (L.C.'s) behalf during the competition for the League of Nations.

(See below the *scheda* (outline) written by the curators of the exhibition dedicated to Le Corbusier in the Maison Clarté of Geneva in 1987).

As for the buildings that he admired at that time, Sartoris remembers the work of the contemporaneous Rigotti, Ceppi, D'Aronco and Basile, exponents of a freedom with always individual characteristics, not a copy of the Viennese or German «Secessions».

He states, however, that the Secession was the most well-known foreign movement in Italy at that time.

The buildings of the past, among others, which he liked mainly were the Baptisteries of Parma and of Pisa, the former an «accomplished expression of integration of the arts».

Moreover, he does not forget the work of Alessandro Antonelli, whom he maintains to have been the first modern architect of the 19th century.

Finally, he insists on the fact that rationalism was not born in the 1900's, but that it has manifested itself in the works of artists of all epochs.

2. Alberto Sartoris' interest at that time was particularly directed to popular architecture and to the design of minimal houses. Possible examples are the «smallest house in the world» in 1925, defined «elementaristic» by Theo Van Doesburg; the minimal houses presented in 1928 at the MIAR exhibition in Rome; and in 1938 the planning, with Giuseppe Terragni of the workers' satellite quarter at Rebbio, a portion of which was carried out the following year in via Anzani in Como.

Besides the merely popular houses, he remembers that he studied «mixed» quarters, such as the variants of the town-planning arrangement of the esplanade of the Turin Stadium (1922-23-25) and the futurist quarter of Orbassano (1923-1926).

This propension was derived by him through contacts with German architects, then more engaged than others in research of social solutions.

Also, as far as problems of industrial production are concerned, Sartoris emphasizes that the Germans were always superior. In any case, *La casa bella* published an article by Alberto Sartoris on the standardization of the constructive elements in the building industry.

The crafts industry was instead a field in which the Italians dominated. Even Sartoris had come near the sector when, in 1925 he was nominated Commissioner of Piedmont for the IInd International Exhibition of the Decorative Arts at Monza, in which also the Piedmontese artisans showed their wares, where he organized the anthological show of the Maestro Annibale Rigotti. He then had the chance to meet Mme. Hélène De Mandrot (promoter of the Swiss section) who discussed with him her idea of organizing a convention of precursors of modern architecture in her castle of La Sarraz (C.I.A.M.).

In March, 1926, Senator Luigi Mangiagalli, president of the IIIrd International Exhibition of the Decorative Arts (Palazzo Reale, Monza, 1927) asked Sartoris to become a member of the Regional Committee (in which Pagano did not take part).

In the same year Alberto Sartoris had been appointed to draw up the project for the building of the Comunità Autonome Artigiane to be carried out in the Parco del Valentino in Turin. The first solution foresaw laboratories for the various branches of crafts, but they were no longer present in the project then built.

Sartoris remembers that since childhood he had lived in contact with artists and artisans. His father, a sculptor, had specialized in wood sculpture applied to interior architecture, creating both furnishings and wall compositions, in collaboration with architects of Switzerland and of other countries.

He ends by saying that Turin's ambience, in whose spirit he lived then, was particularly involved with industry and artisanship.

The interest for the avant-garde has always been grafted on the architectural and artistic thought of Sartoris. It is clear, however, that his activity, also as founder of movements later defined avant-garde, gave a precise imprint to his architectural choices. He likes, moreover, to insist on the absence of frontiers, which always characterized his own activity and his own interests, because he lived for a long time in an atmosphere such as that of Geneva which was strongly imbued with internationalism. Finally, the participation in avant-garde movements meant for him «the constant engagement with invention».

3. Sartoris states that the contemporary foreign architectural forms prevalently known in Italy before 1925, were those of the Viennese Secession and the School of Munich, forms revisited according to typically local and individual incidences. He reveals then that, in his opinion, the real founder of the Liberty style was Antoni Gaudi, then still unknown.

In reality, Sartoris, apart from exceptions, judges the environment of the Italian architects of that period as rather provincial, although he does not forget to point out the important role of Italian futurism in giving a new impulse to the arts.

The «style» mainly known to the contemporary architects was the neoclassical. For the spirit hovering over his formal solutions, Gigiotti Zanini was one of the 19th century heirs of neoclassical elements.

Moreover, Sartoris asserts that the architects of the early 1900's were the unwitting promoters of the post-modern for having applied the pure forms of neoclassicism to artificial, superficial, and decorative motifs.

4. Alberto Sartoris shares the points expressed in the manifesto of Gruppo 7, which he considers to have been the first organized Italian group. He points out the Europeanism which drove the exponents towards an architecture of international spirit, which was very close to his thinking. In his opinion the manifesto represented a partial but correct answer to important problems posed by modern architecture. He has written on Gruppo 7 and on Italian rationalism in, among others, *7 Arts* (1928), *Das Werk* (1928), *Monde* (a weekly of the Marxist writer Henri Barbusse, 1930), and in *L'équerre* (1932).

The expression «international style» is for Sartoris only a negative meaning that reflects the accusation made against the rationalist movement for creating an architecture good for every place. In reality, he counters that it is not a question of an architecture adaptable to all places, but of general principles, valid always and everywhere, which then on the site must find the most correct expression. This agrees with the statement that all great architectural currents of the past have an international character.

Italian architecture of the period under examination was rational, as is today that still responding to the principles of *The Elements of Functional Architecture*. Principles based on the fact that in architecture rationalism has always existed.

He sustains, moreover, the complete identity of «rationalism», «functionalism», and also «organicism». The three terms express an architecture based on the correspondence between architectural forms and function. The architectural examples presented in 1932 in *The Elements of Functional Architecture* were chosen as emblematic expressions of the new architecture: examples of works which with time would have become «classical».

The basic idea of the book was this: to present architecture that would have resisted, from the ideological point of view and from that of formal language, the corrosion of time. Today, in fact, on the occasion of the fourth edition, in both English and French, of the book, at a distance of more than 50 years, the emblematic meaning and the «presence» of the works illustrated are unchanged.

In 1926, Alberto Sartoris began the book (commissioned by Hoepli publishing house) after many travels during which he saw many of the works that he would then present, especially those of the German architects.

The collection of the photographic material presented many difficulties, both for the absence of adequate documentation of the architect's studies and for the problem in communications.

At the end of 1930 Sartoris wrote to Le Corbusier asking him for a preface. Le Corbusier replied on June 10th, 1931, with a text that has been published ever since the first edition of 1932.

5. Sartoris thinks that in some cases, as in that concerning Giuseppe Terragni, the language improved; in certain others (he prefers not to give names) it weakened. As to the second question, Sartoris states that for those who were in favor of it and defended rationalism, it was clear that the architecture of the decade 1930-1940 was still the expression of a new architecture, but for many others, always detractors like Piacentini and Ojetti, this was not equally true.

6. Examples of European architecture of the 1700's and the 1800's, admired by the architects between 1920 and 1940 were, according to Alberto Sartoris, the works of: Filippo Juvara, Benedetto Alfieri, Antonio Niccolini, Giuseppe Piermarini, Giovanni Antonio Antolini, Luigi Cagnola, Giuseppe Valadier, Pietro Bianchi, Ferdinando Bonsignore, Nicola Bettoli, William Kent, Robert and James Adam, John Wood, William Chambers, Claude-Nicolas Ledoux, Karl Friedrich Schinkel, Gottfried Semper, Eugène-Emmanuel Viollet-le-Duc.

Among the «classical» examples, to which the exponents of the architectural culture of the twenty year period 1920-1940 mainly referred, there are: Santa Sophia of Constantinople by Antonio of Tralles and Teodoro Belona, Romanesque architecture and the Comacini Masters (for their essentiality), Michelangelo, Palladio (whose work influenced architecture for more than three centuries), and Bernini.

7. «Summing up everything that has been said and written about me and the period, rejecting mistakes and inaccuracies, we must consider «historical» also the assertions which tend to break up, also for lack of information and of knowledge, the cultural entities of rationalism. These statements and these writings are tesserae which end with composing an organic mosaic of the aims of architecture».

Sartoris thinks that the research theme «Everyday Masterpieces» is an important and original complement tending to link modernity to the tradition as continuity — continuity which resolves itself through the metamorphosis of the styles.

8. Sartoris is happy that one of his works has been included in the exhibition «Everyday Masterpieces», because after having become acquainted with the method used in the research on the formal grammar of modern architecture, he completely shares the intentions of the curators.

9. Sartoris shares the idea of the *iter* traced by «Everyday Masterpieces», even if he thinks that it is not the only one possible. On the other hand, he thinks that the selection of the architecture presented is fruit of an obviously subjective critical operation, even if it is very interesting.

10. The «Building for the Comunità Autonome Artigiane» was awarded to Alberto Sartoris at the end of 1926 by the direction of the Comunità for the exhibition of the «Decennale della Vittoria», which would have taken place in the Parco del Valentino in Turin. It was Annibale Rigotti who introduced Sartoris to the direction. *La Stampa* of November 21st, 1927, reports the news of the nomination on the part of Mario Intaglietta, secretary of the «Federazione artigiana torinese», of an Artistic Council composed of: Alberto Sartoris, Gigi Chessa, Teonesto Deabate, Giuseppe Pagano, Edoardo Rubino, Mariano Berbardi (of *La Stampa*), Mario

Ceradini, Giorgio Ceragioli, Michele Intaglietta, Alessandro Orsi, Guglielmo Pacchioni (supervisor), Augusto Tellucini, Emilio Zanzi (of *La Gazzetta del Popolo*). On that occasion Mario Intaglietta made known the official intention of realizing a crafts show in the exhibition of 1928.

The Artistic Council nominated an Executive Committee made up of Sartoris, Pagano and Chessa, with the task of designing the artisan pavilions.

As in the case of the pavilion of *L'Esprit Nouveau* by Le Corbusier (World's Fair, Paris, 1925), which encompassed a tree, Sartoris was assigned a very wooded site and this, of course, made more difficult the drawing up of the project. This difficulty drove him to conceive of a project which, although not carried out, he considers emblematic of his architecture.

Alberto Sartoris only recently became acquainted with the original reasons for the failure of the first project: it was completely in contrast with the «style» of the pavilions designed by Pagano and associates, which he does not think were avant-garde compositions.

The meetings of this committee, as the preceding meetings of the council, took place in the headquarters of the «Federazione delle Comunità» in Turin.

The first project was especially defended by Annibale Rigotti, Felice Casorati and Gigi Chessa. After the rejection of this project, Sartoris drew others in more reduced dimensions and constructed, in 1928, the last of these with only three bays.

The building had a wooden structure; only the stairway tower was in reinforced concrete.

Alberto Sartoris is pleased about the comparison of his work to that of Ledoux, because if his work represents, according to some critics, the «manifesto» of Italian rationalist architecture, that of Ledoux is certainly very typical of his epoch.

As far as the dematerialization of the corner is concerned, Sartoris admits that he never thought of it. He remembers that he was asked to find a way of exposing ceramic works on the facade and on the flat roof, so that they were evident. This was the function of the corner's «small wings». It was not, therefore, a mannerist element, but a formal solution responding to a very precise function in the economy of the project.

Inside, on the ground floor, was the display of the artisan objects. On the first floor an «alloggio-tipo» (typical apartment) decorated with furniture produced by the Comunità, among others a white piano designed by Sartoris himself.

Since it was a building also with an advertising character, Sartoris molded and carved it from the outside, to the contrary of what Le Corbusier normally did.

ALBERTO SARTORIS
BETWEEN ART AND ARCHITECTURE
BIOGRAPHICAL NOTE

Alberto Sartoris was born in Turin on February 2nd, 1901, from artist parents. He completed his studies at Geneva, where he frequented the Accademia di Belle Arti and was a student of Henry Gallay, and at Turin and at Udine as a disciple and collaborator af Annibale Rigotti and Raimondo d'Aronco.

Architect and city planner, doctor in Sciences honoris causa from the *Ecole Polytechnique Fédérale* of Lausanne, essayist, critic and historian of art. He was professor in the Faculty of Letters and in the *Ecole Polytechnique* of the University of Lausanne, in the Accademia Cantonale di Belle Arti of Sion, in the *Athenaeum* school of architecture and in the Popular University of Lausanne. He has given courses of architecture, city planning and history of art in European and Middle Eastern universities. He is still today professor in the Department of Architecture of the *Ecole Polytechnique Fédérale* of Lausanne.

From 1920 Alberto Sartoris participated actively, often as founding member, in European movements of the artistic and architectural avant-garde. In particular, he adhered, although maintaining his independence, to the Italian futurist movement in

1920, year of the meeting in Geneva with F.T. Marinetti; he knew Fillìa in 1922 and had a strong influence on him in the field of architecture. Sartoris recognized that futurism had kindled in him «the ardor of the discovery, the faith of the invention, the Mediterranean creativity». Among the works of futurist inspiration is the «cappella-bar», whose first axonometric sketch is dated February 2nd, 1920.

Architect, with Felice Casorati, of the private theater of Riccardo Gualino (Turin, 1923-1925), author of the first rationalist building in Italy, the pavilion of the Comunità Autonome Artigiane (Turin, 1927-1928) and inventor of the house-studio Jean-Saladin van Berchem (Paris, 1930), he constructed in 1932 in Lourtier the first modern church in the mountains, cause of an international polemic. In the same year he designed, always in the Vallese, another emblematic work of rationalist architecture, the house for the viticulturer Morand-Pasteur and, in 1938, with Giuseppe Terragni the workers' satellite city of Rebbio, a fragment of which was realized the next year in Via Anzani in Como.

Founding member of the Congressi Internazionali di Architettura Moderna (CIAM), he is a signatory with Le Corbusier in 1928 of the Manifesto of La Sarraz. In the same year he is among the founders of the International Commission for the Realizzazione del Problema Architettonico Contemporaneo (CIRPAC) and of the Movement of functional architecture. He was, moreover, member of the *Union des Artistes Modernes* (Paris, 1930) and with Seuphor, Arp, Baumeister, Fillìa, Léger, Kandinskij, Mondrian, Gorin, Gropius, Le Corbusier, Pevsner, Prampolini, Russolo, Schwitters, Täuber-Arp, Vordemberge-Gildewart, Vantongerloo, founding member of the group *Cercle et carré* (Paris 1930), member of the *Abstraction-création* group (Paris, 1931-1936) and of the last group of *De Stijl* which gathered around van Doesburg in 1931, founder and animator of the *Gruppo di Como* which united abstract artists and architects (1935).

«But the contribution of Alberto Sartoris», writes Michele Cometa in 1987, «cannot be reduced to the mere enunciation of «avant-garde» axioms, certainly very efficacious, but which would prove nothing if they were not founded on a design praxis which made Sartoris a unique figure in the avant-garde sphere of those fecund years, which saw the triumph of Futurism and the birth of a new architecture. In fact, Sartoris succeeded in what would have been impossible for many of his companions to accomplish: the insertion of themes and European design formulae, I think particularly of the experience of the Dutch of *De Stijl*, in a pattern exquisitely Mediterranean or anyway southern».

From 1918 (exhibition of designs of descriptive geometry at the *Ecole des Beaux-Arts* of Geneva) he shows his works — designs of architecture, of city planning and of decoration, axonometry, collages, mosaics, furniture, serigraphs — in many countries. Among these exhibitions we note: in 1926 the collective «Views of Turin» which brought together painters, sculptors and architects of varying tendencies; in 1927 the preparation with Felice Casorati of the «Macelleria» in the sphere of the «Street of shops» at the Palazzo Reale of Monza and the show at the Rath Museum of Geneva «Artistes italiens contemporains»; in 1928 the exhibition at the Museum of Modern Art in New York, the decoration with Gigi Chessa of the Press Room at the Biennale of Venice and the participation, with 23 works, at the first show of futurist architecture, set up by Fillìa, in the Parco del Valentino in Turin, in which he won the first «Gran Premio di Architettura»; in the same year he designed the pavilion of the Comunità Autonome Artigiane on the site of the Exposition of the Decennale della Vittoria (Parco del Valentino, Turin) and presented various living typologies and his *minimal houses* in the first «Esposizione italiana di architettura razionale» (MIAR) in Rome; in 1929 he organized with Fillìa the futurist exhibition at the *Galerie 23* in Paris and the collective of twenty-one exponents of the *Novecento* in the Gallery Moos of Geneva; in 1930 he presented a group of contemporary Italian artists in the *Kunsthalle* of Basel and of Berne and took part in the first international exhibition of the group *Cercle et carré* in the *Galerie 23* of Paris; in 1931 he displayed in the second «Esposizione italiana di architettura razionale» and, in 1932, in the *Galleria del Milione* of Milan, on the occasion of the first publication of

Gli Elementi dell'architettura funzionale; in 1932 in Vevey the Jenish Museum and in 1933 the *Galleria d'Arte* in Via Veneto (directed by Pietro Maria Bardi) and the gallery *Al Bragaglia fuori commercio* (directed by Anton Giulio Bragaglia) dedicated a personal exhibition to him.

More recently anthological and retrospective exhibitions have taken place in the Galleria Martano of Turin in 1972; in Warsaw, in Poland, in 1975; at the Biennale of Venice in 1976; in Paris, East Berlin and West Berlin in 1977; at the Museum of Art and History in Münster, at the Museum of Modern Art in Paris and at the Politecnico Federale of Lausanne and of Zurich in 1978; at the Museo di Belle Arti of La Chaux-de-Fonds in 1979; at the National Gallery of Modern Art in Rome and at the Pavilion of Contemporary Art in Milan in 1979-1980; at the Gulbenkian Foundation in Lisbon in 1980; at the Accademia di Belle Arti of Porto, at the Royal Palace of Evora and at the Gallery of modern art of M.L. Jeanneret in 1981; at the Museum Diego Aragona Pignatelli Cortes of Naples in 1982 and, in the same year, in New York and in Boissano; in London, Turin, Carignano, Montreal, Martigny, Newark and Milan in 1983; in Paris, Carignano, Milan, West Berlin, Trieste and Lausanne in 1984; in Rio de Janeiro, Brasilia, Campinas, San Paolo, Boissano, Heidelberg and Como in 1985; in Stoccard, Madrid, Genoa, Lausanne, Santa Cruz de Tenerife, Buenos Aires, Savigliano, Frankfurt and Milan in 1986; in New York, Enna, Crema and Rome (Faculty of Architecture, University «La Sapienza») in 1987; in Atlanta in 1988.

Alberto Sartoris has moreover organized many exhibitions of Italian and foreign artists in Italy and abroad.

As an architect and urban planner he has conceived and designed more than 700 projects.

His bibliography includes about 1,500 titles: books of architecture, monographs and writings on the arts, essays and articles. Among these: «Annibale Rigotti» in *Artistes italiens contemporains* (Torino 1927), *Antonio Sant'Elia, architetto e urbanista* (Milan 1930), «Robert Mallet-Stevens, architecte» (Paris 1930), *Gli elementi dell'architettura funzionale* — a manifesto-book — (with preface by Le Corbusier, Milano 1932, 1935, 1942), *Introduzione all'architettura moderna* (Milano 1943, 1944, 1949), *Posizione dell'architettura e delle arti in Italia* (Firenze 1947), *Encyclopédie de l'architecture nouvelle* in three volumes (I, Milano 1948, 1957; II, Milano 1957; III, Milano 1954), *Giuseppe Terragni* (Como, 1949), *Emilio Pettoruti* (Roma 1952), *Léonard architecte* (Paris 1952), *Jean Gorin* (Venezia 1975), *La lunga marcia dell'arte astratta in Italia* (Milano 1980), *Benedetto e le second futurisme* (Paris 1981), *Metaphysic Architecture* in *Pamphlet architecture* (New York 1984), *Actualité du rationalisme* (Lausanne 1986), *Présence de l'architecture* (Milano 1986), *Magia de las Canarias* (Santa Cruz de Tenerife 1987), *Tempo dell'architettura, tempo dell'arte. Cronache degli anni '20-'30* (Milano, in press), the fourth edition of *Gli elementi dell'architettura funzionale* (Lausanne-New York, in press).

Sartoris has collaborated in reviews and journals of numerous countries. He was the chief editor of the *La città futurista* (Turin 1929), editor of *Raison d'être* (Paris 1929), of *Présence* (Geneva-Lausanne 1931), of *La città nuova* (Turin 1932) and president of the committee of *Architecture-formes & fonction* (Lausanne 1950). Moreover, he was critic of art and architecture of *Feuille d'avis officielle* (Geneva 1931) and of the daily, *Il Popolo di Brescia* (1939).

Artistic adviser of the Cooperativa Internazionale del Cinema Indipendente, he edited with Gropius and Rietveld the catalogue of the International Federation of Art Films (Paris 1960).

Many of his writings in French or in Italian have been translated into German, English, Spanish, Portuguese, Swedish, Turkish, Japanese, and Arabic.

He has given many lectures in various countries of the world; among these a cycle on architecture, city planning and integration of the arts in Latin America, between 1935 and 1936, and one having as theme the actuality of rationalism in Lausanne and Geneva in 1985, in Barcellona and Madrid in 1986 and in Bordeaux in 1987.

Alberto Sartoris was general secretary of the Società di belle arti *Antonio Fontanesi* (Turin 1923), vice-president of the *Le Corbusier* International Association, president of the permanent Swiss committee of the «Giornata mondiale dell'urbanistica», of the first international Congress of modern art and of the School of Altamira, member of the Belgian Society of Modernist Architects and Urban Planners.
He is still a member of the International Association of Critics of Art (AICA), of the French Society of Archaeology, of the International Center of Romanesque Studies, of the International Commission *Art et environnement* of East Berlin, of the Society of Swiss Painters, Sculptors and Architects (SPSAS). He is an honorary member of the Society of Swiss Engineers and Architects (SIA), of *Oeuvre* and of the *American Insistitute of Architects*, honorary member and correspondent of the Institute of the Canaries and of the *Royal Institute of British Architects*; member of the Academia Tiberina, of the Accademia di Belle Arti of Argentina, of the Royal Academy of Spain and of the Federation of Swiss Architects (FAS).

Prize of the Press Club of Turin in 1980, gold medal of the city of Turin in 1981, Oriol Bohigas and Antonio de Moragas have written that the work of Alberto Sartoris deserves a special mention. The lectures which he gave in Barcellona in 1949, for example, and others given in Spain and in the Canaries, have been defined as decisive for the process of development and transformation of Iberian architecture. The *architettura di carta* of Alberto Sartoris, the exhibitions which he has participated in or which he has organized have had a much greater incidence than his constructed works on the diffusion of rational architecture. In fact, the attention that he gives to a design as concretization of imagined structures in space is particular, and the privileged use of axonometry as a method of representation is well-known. In 1972 Cesare de Seta chose the axonometry of the interior of a stairway of the Jean-Saladin van Berchem house for the cover of *L'architettura razionale*, and an axonometric representation of *Notre-Dame du Phare* on the cover of Kenneth Frampton's book, *Modern Architecture: A Critical History* (1980), makes this work of 1931 an emblem of modern architecture. Alessandro Mendini has defined Alberto Sartoris in an article of 1985, «the precursor of designed architecture».

Numerous monographs, essays and articles have been published on the work of Alberto Sartoris, architect, city planner, designer, and critic. Among the authors of these writings: Ludwig Hilberseimer (1926), Alexandre Mairet (1927), Lucienne Florentin (1927), André Lurçat (1928), Raffaello Giolli (1928, 1936), Fillìa (1928), Robert Mallet-Stevens (1929), Arthur Korn (1929), F.T. Marinetti (1929), Theo van Doesburg (1929), Gustav Adolf Platz (1930), Arnold Kohler (1931, 1934), Pietro Maria Bardi (1932), Edmond Humeau (1932, 1947), Le Corbusier (1932), Michel Seuphor (1933, 1938), Anton Giulio Bragaglia (1933), Eduardo Westerdahl (1934), Carlo Belli (1935), Georges Linze (1936), P. Morton Shand (1936), Agnoldomenico Pica (1940), Gillo Dorfles (1947), Luis Felipe Vivanco (1951), Giulia Veronesi (1959), Luciano Patetta (1970), Alberto Abriani (1972), Cesare de Seta (1972, 1987), Marcello Fagiolo (1974, 1977), Marco Pozzetto (1974, 1987), Jacques Gubler (1975, 1978), Alberto Cuomo (1978), M. Alice Tavares Chicó (1978), Bruno Reichlin (1978, 1979), Paolo Angeletti (1979, 1987), Gaia Remiddi (1979, 1987), Salette Tavares (1980), Paolo Portoghesi (1982), Alessandro Mendini (1985), Christian Leprette (1987), Riccardo Mariani (1987), Michele Cometa (1987), Giancarlo Priori (1987), Gino Agnese (1987), Alberto Longatti (1988).

Today Alberto Sartoris is still engaged in designing activity. Recent works include the «Lesieur» factory at Dunkerque (1984), the industrial complex «La Beyrie» in Biarritz (1987-1988), and on the way to realization is the insertion of a quarter, «city within the city», in the historical center of Carignano.

Edited by M. Sommella

INTERVIEW WITH DENISE SCOTT BROWN ON 10 MAY 1988 IN PHILADELPHIA

The trajectory of Denise Scott Brown's career has touched the history of Modern architecture at some of its critical moments:

When she was two years old in 1933, her parents built an International Style house in Johannesburg. Its designer, Norman Hanson, was one of the first Modern architects in South Africa. «I can recall playing on the flat roof and the sound of my grandmother's heels clacking on the treads of our staircase, which was of black-and-white tile and had tubular steel balustrades and a half-round half landing.»[1]

She was at school at the Architectural Association in London in the early 1950s, when Brutalism, the most influential architectural movement after the Second World War, was at the point of ignition: «in 1953 the Smithsons became known in London and Le Corbusier's Maisons Jaoul were published».

She worked in Rome in 1956 for Giuseppe Vaccaro, the architect of the Central Post Office in Naples (catalogue **10a**), at a time when this architecture was out of favor.

She entered the University of Pennsylvania in 1958, meeting Kahn when his most important building of the '50s was going into construction. She also made contact with the new «social planners» (the name not yet coined), most especially Herbert Gans and Paul Davidoff: «Something unusual was buzzing around the planning department. I think it was the New Left.»[2] At Penn, in 1960, she began her collaboration with Robert Venturi, as he was developing ideas that would, with the publication of *Complexity and Contradiction in Architecture*, burst apart the hegemony of the Modern Movement.

«In 1966, on a trip between the West and East coasts, I stopped off in Miami Beach to see the Fountainbleau Hotel... [and] photographed hotels on the beach and on Ocean Avenue... But looking through my collection of slides I became aware that there was more to Miami Beach than the large hotels on the shoreline. A neighborhood of less bombastic edifices was visible at the edges of my photographs. These cubist-looking stucco buildings seemed to fill a large sector of the Beach.

«It was not until late 1972 that my husband and I returned to Miami Beach... During this trip we drove further south than I had been before and discovered a whole neighborhood, South Beach, filled with the buildings I had seen peeking in at the edges of my slides: street after street of smaller hotels, painted pastel colors or white, Cubist in shape and Jazz Modern in styling.»[3]

The interview began with our presenting three questions:
What do you, as an architect, find interesting and useful in the buildings we are exhibiting, our «Everyday Masterpieces»?
A - Compositionally - they integrate Modern and Classical: learning the *right* lessons from Classical architecture.
B - Urbanistically - they fit into traditional urban settings as in Miami Beach or the Grand Concourse in the Bronx.

C - Socially - their architects and clients tended not to be from the intelligentsia or the upper class.

DSB - These sound like summary questions that belong at the end of a discussion, can we answer them later?

TK - O.K. Another major question then: Is this a kind of pre-Postmodern architecture? These architects were doing, in 1935, what architects in 1975 said they were doing, and I wonder, as somebody who is well acquainted with this and also well acquainted with the 1975 version, whether you find the earlier architecture really more meaningful? To me, it's much better than the recent attempts have been — maybe because the architects were trained in the Classical tradition, so that for them traditional architecture was the background, whereas for us, now, the Modern is the background? What can one learn from this architecture?

DSB - Let me try to understand it first in terms of its history, then to relate it to what we've wanted to do, and then to think of it in the abstract.

The early-Modern turn away from history was part of an ethos. The new direction was propounded by a particular group of very young architects, who were radical for their time and in tune with certain avant-garde art movements. The first images that emerged from their thinking were austere, and were tied to statements about society that practicing architects couldn't really accept, because they undermined the values of the very people who pay architects. This was always the problem with an avant-garde in architecture.

But at that time aesthetic sensibilities began to change.

Despite the radical philosophies avant-garde Modern architecture initially stood for, in the wake of the movement people's eyes changed. My theory is that sensibilities change because of social movements. You begin to want to see differently because something has happened in society. I think the early Moderns saw differently and acted differently, at least in part because of changes that came about before and during World War I. The «*art moderne*» or «modernistic» architects (as we called them) followed a little later, I would surmise, when the change in eyes had become more general. The *Modernes* didn't want a symbolism of left-wing radicalism, so they attempted to be more accommodating to prevailing values than were the Moderns. For this reason, we might find their work interesting today, in a time when architects try to work with, rather than fight against, societal forces.

Now the Deconstructivists may be trying once again to break down the system. But maybe not...

TK - Now, they're trying to recover the...

DSB - ...nostalgia for the Modern.

TK - They're trying to put themselves into 1925.

DSB - Maybe they're merely trying to maintain something else. There's a general feeling, now, of let's maintain, let's rehabilitate, let's conserve.

TK - You were comparing Art Deco architecture translated to Miami Beach with the architecture of the people who studied in Philadelphia in 1960 and then went back home to Texas or Africa and tried to practice what they had learned in a different context.

DSB - They had to adapt, which isn't easy, but the Deco architects did it very well.

TK - What is it about this architecture: this stuff is around the world, it's done by thousands of architects — they can't all be geniuses — so there must be something about the architecture, or about the time when it was done...

FAB - ... or about the training?

TK - ... that made it work, but which doesn't work anymore. It's the same as the Shingle Style: thousands of people could build in the Shingle Style. They all did it well — or the Greek Revival.

DSB - Or Georgian architecture in England. All these styles, including Deco, made good pattern book architecture. Maybe they were easier to copy. In Deco there *are* definitely recognizable elements, as there are in Georgian architecture and, as in Georgian architecture, people made personal arabesques on those elements, did them their own way.

Another thing: this building I'm looking at [1211 Pennsylvania Avenue, **1c**] is modest in size. In South Beach nothing is very big, but even the much bigger hotels are not really very big. Deco architecture makes composition of small-scale elements, which are then aggregated in certain spots to suggest a larger scale, but that aggregation isn't very big either. Maybe the whole is more manageable because of its modest size. Taming a skyscraper may be harder.

TK - Except that in the '20s they could do it. We were noticing, while driving through Philadelphia today, there are quite a few more buildings from the '20s than I had realized. What is the building at the point where you turn into the Ben Franklin Parkway?

DSB - Suburban Station: a very beautiful Deco building. These architects were trained in traditional skills. They were probably the last architects who were. Although they intended to keep away from traditional construction and to evolve new techniques for an industrial era, their training gave them skill and suavity in the way they handled both design and construction.

TK - Maybe they still had the craft skills. Nobody has those anymore.

DSB - Yes, yes.

TK - The Modern Movement's desire to wipe out history actually succeeded.

DSB - It wiped out skills. Modern architects took a long time to develop relevant skills (those who weren't, like Mies van der Rohe, trained in traditional construction). Part of the trouble with latter-day Modern architecture is that it isn't very skilled.

FAB - I think that crafts take a long, long, long time to die. Certainly in the construction industry, to diverge a little bit, you see that the Italian craftsmen are always masons, masons and plasterers, and they deal with stone. German craftsmen, the Northern craftsmen, deal with wood.

DSB - But, take today's average American architects, who go to undergraduate school for their cultural preparation then have two and a half years of graduate training in architecture: they cannot, in that time, acquire skills. They can hardly develop design skills, and they don't learn much about construction at all.

FAB - I want to get back to something you said when we were looking at 1211 Pennsylvania Avenue (**1c**). You said «the grandeur was skin deep,» and you made a remark about this being a builder architect's response to a practical problem, meaning somebody used a certain stock sized window and stock sized door.

DSB - More than that — I meant to suggest that within the building there isn't room for the double volume hall that the facade suggests... The double volume was indicated symbolically on the outside to denote urban grandeur; inside, the architect met the problem of function, which is to have as many apartments as you can. The melding of the needs of inside and outside is quite poignant.

FAB - What is it that allowed architects to do that? Is it that they were still adept at what became looked down on, which is composition?

DSB - They were adept at composition, but they also weren't burdened with ideals about being true to function and structure. Modern architects couldn't bring themselves to do «facade architecture.» As a student, when I saw a building like that, I called it a fake.

TK - Also, they weren't interested in being original.

DSB - No.

TK - Although one can almost recognize Hohauser's buildings in Miami Beach, you don't have the sense that that was his aim. We recognize them because he repeated himself.

DSB - He may, himself, have been scornful of what he was doing. Has anyone ever talked with Hohauser?

FAB - No, we didn't talk with him. Tony Robins, who's the assistant director of research at the New York Landmarks Preservation Commission, interviewed Marvin Fine, who used to be chief designer for Horace Ginsbern. He was trained under Paul Cret in Philadelphia, and then he worked for the architect of the Woolworth building, for Cass Gilbert. He designed gargoyles, and he wanted to do something

TK - more. No, he wasn't looking down on what he was doing. He was very free; he was very facile with the tools of design.
TK - This [1791 Grand Concourse, **52c**] isn't one of his buildings, but it's the style that he worked in.
DSB - It is really amazing. Bob would love it.
TK - Do you know the Grand Concourse?
DSB - No.
TK - You should go and go soon because daily there are less, but it is a miraculous street of these things. There was a study done by Hunter College of the Bronx Art Deco. It's a district like Miami Beach. It's equally dense.
DSB - It's also Jewish, presumably.
TK - I call it the Jewish style. Mendelsohn is one of the most important sources. I'm convinced Mendelsohn and Dudok were the two people that the American architects paid attention to when they developed this style.
FAB - Again, I want to get back to something you said previously. You spoke of this sense of thinness, the sense that the decoration and the devices are only skin deep. It's something you found in Las Vegas, in the Stardust.
DSB - Yes.
FAB - Do you think that there is something either particulary American or Modern about this? What is it that they share?
DSB - It seems to me that in Deco everywhere there is a sense of thinness, of the skin being stretched. Wrap-around windows help give this impression, and so does sculpture. Deco architectural sculpture is often in *bas relief*; it's only shallowly carved, yet it suggests surfaces behind surfaces.
FAB - Yes, this corner [1211 Pennsylvania Ave.] is exfoliated.
DSB - If there had been a panel of decoration here, it would have had leaves in front and then leaves behind and leaves behind them again, but the whole would have been not more than half an inch deep. The Cubist zigzag patterns are the same. I think they played with the notion of being on the surface yet suggesting depth, just as the Cubist painters did. Deco furniture, too, plays tautness against layered depth. That was a Deco theme, but it also goes very well with merchant builder's architecture, where you can't allow depth in the skin because it costs too much. The builder doesn't want to take inches, precious inches, out of the apartment; so, in this architecture, the inside pushes as far as it can to the outside, the outside impinges as much as it can on the inside, and the facade is held in tension.
TK - Isn't this a characteristic of vernacular architecture? If you took, say, Georgian architecture in England, is it so different from the previous Gothic style? Except maybe for the position of the windows the buildings are the same. The architecture was also skin deep, in a sense. In other words, it was really a builder's architecture; the architect probably had nothing to do with how it was built. In New York, the law established that you could build six stories without fireproofing, so they built six stories. These things are givens, and the architect just put the living room in the corner.
FAB - What do you think of this idea? How come this architecture is, in fact, so international? We keep talking about Miami Beach, but we can see this architecture in Heliopolis and Cairo, in Europe, everywhere.
DSB - It is certainly Mediterranean, isn't it? Le Corbusier *was* influenced by the architecture of the Mediterranean. That is where the sun is bright. Strong shadows can be easily created. These horizontal elements cast a nice clean shadow [1211 Pennsylvania Ave.]. Not much use doing that in England because shadows there are rarely visible. In England you use recesses and niches to create shade. Gothic architecture relates well to a northern climate. I think Deco architects could have reasoned that Mediterranean-like climates would go well with Deco buildings. Another thing that's typical of a lot of Mediterranean architecture is windows that are holes punched in the wall. A good sense of proportion can give you a good opening in a wall, and Deco architects punched their openings very well. In this example, breadth of wall is played against the articulation of windows. This makes it possible for

human beings to use the building. In some Deco "Fascist" architecture there's such a dependence on breadth you couldn't insult the building with windows. Some of those are marvelous, too, but they don't make good apartment buildings.

TK - Another aspect of this style is that it has different modes for different functions. The official buildings are the least transformed into the Modern, and the commercial buildings are the most Modern with the fewest Classical remembrances. I think the function of the building, in that sense, determines the degree of Modernity.

DSB - *Moderne* differs from Modern in its symbolism, its symmetry, its layering, and the play of wall versus opening.

FAB - You were talking earlier about the elements. They played with a very few, defined sets of elements. I think you were looking at these horizontal lines and you were also looking at these thin columns.

DSB - The horizontal lines are, in part, borrowed from De Stijl.

FAB - But they're done in a different way here; they're done in a very symmetrical way; they're very grounded.

DSB - Exactly, very differently from how it was done by Rietveld.

FAB - As you were using the word elements, I was thinking, is it that in fact these architects used these elements the way they were taught to use the orders? In other words, using this fixed set of design words, so to speak, and recombining them in some way, the way they used the orders, although in a slightly different way.

DSB - Not as differently as Rietveld would have done it, but they are different. I was thinking of that auditorium in Los Angeles that you have.

FAB - You mean the Pan Pacific Auditorium [**25a**].

DSB - Yes. In a way, that facade uses an order, its elements are very streamlined and they're jumpy, not calm, but they are a kind of equivalent of a distortion of, a Classical order.

FAB - I was wondering if, in fact, these architects were not using these elements, overlaying them, on the discipline of Classical architecture. The orders are very much the way you compose a building. If you take the way they used the round bay or the way they used horizontality or the way they used these little lines, I'm wondering if it was not possible for them to do that successfully because they had the discipline.

DSB - They had a lot of training in how to relate the elements of architecture, even if they subsequently did it in a different way.

TK - We have become interested in developing in this exhibition what we call «Heraldic Elements». How do you see this?

DSB - Do you mean the flagpole?

FAB - Yes, it used to occur in a lot of buildings.

TK - It's a recurring motif, as on the Karl Marx-Hof in Vienna [**21b**].

DSB - Very often they were placed symmetrically, one on either side.

FAB - Or one in the center.

DSB - Also, the theme of the balcony rail that is a strip of concrete floating above the building — [Safi villa, **25b**] there are many like that in Yugoslavia. And these flagpoles, you see a lot of them in Johannesburg.

TK - Are they anthropomorphic.

DSB - The whole question of what is anthropomorphism in design is fascinating. I think they're certainly there to give human scale, to mediate between the scale of the city and the scale of the individual. They are like huge statuettes on the top. In Russia they could have been statues of workers. Architects, as esthetes, will, whatever they say, use symbolic elements for their compositional as well as their representational value — to achieve aesthetic aims, often to give salt and savor to what would otherwise be bland.

FAB - To give a kind of density...

DSB - Yes, but also to give contrast. And symmetry. Associating facade elements symmetrically gives them greater strength. Combining them closely, rather than spreading them across the facade, reinforces them. It makes small elements strong, while we still want them small.

FAB - Composition.

DSB - Yes. What do you need to do to mediate between the urban scale and an individual? I think the Moderns didn't consider that very much, but the Beaux-Arts architects certainly did, and so did the *Modernes*. Human scale, as viewed by Modern architects, meant associating one person with the whole building. The Modern aim to "articulate the facade to the scale of the human being" can result in large, boring buildings, if there is nothing between the scale of the individual and that of the overall building. In Deco architecture there are aggregated intermediate scales, call them group or community scales, between the unit and the whole.

FAB - Do these make better urban buildings than Modern buildings, than strictly Modern buildings, because of this intermediate scale which speaks to the street?

DSB - Sometimes and sometimes not. It's true that, near the end, Modern architecture didn't take enough notice of the relation of buildings to the street and CIAM urbanism was anti-street, but I think most of Le Corbusier's buildings are wonderful urban things.

TK - This building [UOP Fragrances, catalogue **9a**] sits out in the middle of nowhere, in Long Island City, yet it commands this little space so that it makes a place, which the more conventional Modern buildings don't succeed in doing.

DSB - Yes. I think the Moderns reacted against traditional architecture's use of articulation to suggest hierarchies of scale. When Modern architects abandoned eclecticism, they flung off the notion of going from the scale of the nation, to the community, to the individual, because they found it more interesting to juxtapose the little and the very big. I think that was one of the thrills of Modern architecture. You didn't set a cornice at the top of the building, you just ended it.

TK - I think that the Modern architects in the '20s were able to disregard the past because it was so present they didn't miss it. Now we have lost so much.

DSB - Particularly in Europe, but the Europeans who had the greatest romance with the machine came from peasant societies. America did not have that romance because the reality was right upon them.

TK - I think that's why what was done in America in the '50s and '60s was so awful. People didn't realize they were going to miss it. They cleared out New Haven; they cleared out Stamford...

DSB - It's true. I agree with that. But I think we have to be careful because we'll find that we'll sound quaintly old-fashioned when the '50s come back into fashion.

TK - Right!

FAB - Ha, ha, ha — some of the '50s.

TK - You said that when you were first in architecture, you despised *Moderne* and worked for the pure Modern. If you tried to remember back to how you felt then I think you'll agree that you didn't think about all these things we've been talking about.

DSB - Absolutely. Peter Smithson has said the Brutalists caught a whiff of the powder of the Modern revolution. It was a very exciting revolution, and it was the right revolution for the Moderns. What we've always maintained was that it's not the right revolution for us: things have moved since then.

FAB - Well, I don't know that it was a right revolution for France, because French culture, like Italian culture, is steeped in, absolutely penetrated by classical culture, and for architects to be told, and to think and be convinced, that it's wrong, is like cutting both their arms and head at the same time and still trying to design.

DSB - But think of the impact of the industrial revolution; they had to accept a very, very big change in society. They also had to accept the depredations of an incredibly destructive war. I feel their grasping the nettle of industrialization was a way of surviving then, and the truth is, we build today using the methods they evolved; we haven't gone back on those. We don't build the way Medieval society built. If you consider what are the conventional systems of building now, you'd have to agree that they're basically Modern. Early Modern architects had a big job to do to internalize the industrial revolution, and to deal with the wholesale destruction around them. If they evolved philosophies that related to these needs, that was right for them. We've internalized their revolution now; we're not going backward. When we build a decorated facade, the rest of the bulding is still a Modern building.

FAB - Do you think that those people then, our «Everyday Masters», were, in a sense, putting their heads in the sand? What is it they were doing? They were not saying we need to be revolutionary, so they were not grappling with the question.

DSB - Take an analogy with the immigrants to America. The first generation came over because they were in revolt. They were looking for a new world. The first ethnic immigrants, the first Italians or Irish who came here, came because they were rebels; the next came because they had a brother here. The Deco architects are the people who had a brother. They internalized some of that revolution and then they made it able to be accepted by the market.

FAB - So they're not polemical anymore. They go through this process of assimilation.

DSB - Yes and then they tamed the revolution.

FAB - They brought both things together.

DSB - Le Corbusier would say they prettified his work. He was horrified by that...

TK - They popularized it. J.M. Richards in his book [*An Introduction to Modern Architecture*] talks about the «nasty modernistic villas».

DSB - Yes, yes, the Moderns, seeing what *Moderne* had done, cried «But this is not what we meant!» And that's what Bob and I said about Postmodernism: This is not what we meant. They prettified it.

FAB - This is interesting: «That is not what we meant.»

What is it that we should have asked you that we haven't asked you?

DSB - Let's look at your three questions as a summary:

Compositionally: Well, we talked about many aspects of Deco composition. Urbanistically: Miami Beach Deco accepts its grid and builds within it. It maintains existing height lines. It does the right thing by making a nice little front door and a nice little front yard with a few palm trees, and then the streets evolve nicely from that. Because it was built before there were too many cars, and because old people don't use cars, the Deco District has not been broken down by parking lots. It's maintained its integrity.

TK - We went to Miami Beach at Christmas expecting to see two or three Art Deco hotels, and when we got there, we discovered this whole city, which was mind-boggling, and I had the feeling I was in Tony Garnier's *Cité Industrielle*.

DSB - Yes.

TK - And I learned since that the lot sizes are the same: 15 meters, 50 feet.

DSB - That's very interesting.

TK - They also did this thing; they created an inner-block space [Kesandra and South Shore apartements, **50b**].

DSB - These are marvelous. You get them in California as well. They predate Deco. I think they're wonderful, for their scale and their economy of means. So, urbanistically, I think the Deco buildings, much more than the Modern, fit into a tradition. The composition of individual buildings suggests community on the front and individuality at the back and the sides. Deco architects had a nice urbanistic sense.

Socially: I suspect Deco architecture is, to a large extent, Jewish architecture, for what that means. South Beach, which was the retirement place of Eastern European garment workers from New York, is now, as the Deco District, being invaded (in the sociological sense) by perhaps the spiritual, if not the actual, grandchildren of its original occupants. Both groups cleave to the cheery humaneness of its environment.

With all its improbable streamlining, its zigs and zags, its symmetries, its ornamental arabesques and its architectural attitudes, the Deco District is very proper and middle-class. It has a modesty to it. It is domesticated Deco.

---

[1] Denise Scott Brown, «A worm's eye view of recent architectural history», *Architectural Record*, February 1984, p. 79.

[2] *Ibid*, p. 75.

[3] Denise Scott Brown, «My Miami Beach», *Interview*, September 1986, p. 156.

NEW YORK FROM CLASSIC TO MODERNE: LOCAL ARCHITECTS REMEMBER

In the years following World War I, New York City emerged in the eyes of the world as a great modern metropolis. Architecturally, that new identity found expression in a change from the traditional classical styles of the Beaux-Arts to the modernistic of the so-called Art Deco or Moderne. Most of the architects who worked in the latter styles had been trained or apprenticed in the former. Sooner or later they fell under the sway of the great monuments of 1920s New York, and became part of a mass movement that saw the city transformed from the classicism of the turn of the century to the modernism of the Jazz Age.

The three architects whose interviews are recounted below were all active in New York in the 1920s and 1930s. Each began work in traditional styles of one kind or another, and then evolved towards the modernistic. None was a giant in the field, none designed a major skyscraper, but each drew from and contributed to the city's changing image. Modern New York cannot be imagined without their work.

The architects' interviews reveal varging levels of awareness of the influence of the frends of the period on their work. Their thought on the subject ranges from straightforward denial of any outside influence, to quite specific acknowledgements of monuments and architects important to their development. Nevertheless, all three evolved in the same general direction, from the classical to the modernistic.

Israel L. Crausman

The Bronx owes much of its typical post-World War I look to Israel L. Crausman (b. 1899), one of the dozens of architects who designed the thousands of apartment houses, movie theaters, stores, and garages that transformed a rural county into a dense urban conglomerate almost overnight. Crausman's work falls directly into the mainstream of standard New York and American design of the period, yet he seems to have been largely unaware of his relationship to the larger context, and of the three architects interviewed he had the least to say on the subject of his stylistic development and models.

Like many of his colleagues, Crausman did not have the advantage of advanced architectural training. A teenage immigrant from Russia at the outbreak of World War I, he took a B.S. degree in engineering from Cooper Union in 1919, and set up his own office in the Bronx the following year.

During the 1920s Crausman designed several of the hundreds of theaters which sprang up in the Bronx during the great national theater-building boom of the years between World War I and the Depression. His work reflected the standard eclecticism of the times. The theater of which he was most proud, the Avalon (Burnside and Anthony Avenues; 1928, demolished) built in memory of his father, followed the lead of the Broadway theaters of the day, particularly those designed for the Shuberts by Herbert Krapp. The ornament of its plain brick front was drawn from classical sources, and included such typical details as a parapet balustrade crowned

Israel L. Crausman

Ca. 1931 Israel L. Crausman rendering. Bronx, N. Y.

with decorative urns. The decorative plasterwork of its interior, derived from 18th century Adamesque models, had been standard for theaters on or off Broadway for two decades. In a 1982 interview, Crausman described a similar theater, the Oxford (Jerome Avenue and 185th Street, 1928) as being «in a beautiful classic interior design».

In the 1930s, Crausman abandoned his 1920s classical repertory for the lively, colorful Bronx Modern that gradually transformed the dreary grey of the Grand Concourse and points west into one of the country's great collections of modernistic buildings. Instead of terra-cotta urns and swags, his apartment house designs featured such lively details as curving corner casements, Aztec-inspired rooflines, and - (streamline-curve) balconies.

In retrospect the influence of the great 1920s monuments of Manhattan on Crausman's development seems plausible, but when asked Crausman recalled no connection. He «...never went to Manhattan to look at their designs... Every architect had his own ideas about how he would decorate his buildings», he said, and he would not admit to any influence on his work, nor could he say why his style changed from the classic to the modernistic.

Louis Allen Abramson

A broader perspective emerges from a series of 1980 interviews with Louis Allen Abramson. A decade older than Crausman, Abramson also had a limited architectural education, but developed a more sophisticated awareness of his architectural surroundings.

Abramson (1887-1985), born in New York, began studying civil engineering at Cooper Union, found it boring and left. He also had a brief stint at the Mechanics Institute on West 44th Street. Abramson recalled that his introduction to architecture came through a job at the turn of the century as an office boy for John Duncan, one of New York's preeminent late 19th century Beaux-Arts practitioners. Duncan had completed most of his famous work by that time, including Grant's Tomb, but was still active designing the fashionable limestone-fronted, English-basement town houses that he popularized for the banker's palaces of Midtown Manhattan. After

Louis Abramson

Automat, New York v. 1930.

leaving Duncan, Abramson went West «to find my fortune». He stayed in Seattle for a few years, then returned to New York. Abramson took extension courses at Columbia University, spent a short time as a draftsman in the office of Louis Gerard, and then went out on his own.

Abramson recalled learning two important lessons from his early days with Duncan, whom he remembered chiefly as a bon-vivant who treated his teen-aged apprentice very kindly. The first: «I can only tell you what I subconsciously absorbed (from him): quality». The second: «(through him) I was introduced to (the work of) McKim, Mead & White». Duncan's great admiration for the premiere practitioners of classical styles in New York made a strong impression on the young Abramson, who was filled with: «...admiration of what they had done. And that never left me, never. Each time I'd go by the University Club on Fifth Avenue, I'd stand and figuratively bow. I did love that building. When they started to destroy the Penn Station I used to go over there and cry. To me it was perfection, perfection. And then I'd walk, at times I'd commute to Grand Central. I had admiration for it, but in a totally different sense. Penn Station was... I don't know how I can really say it. I felt meek in the presence of that building... I recall once, and I don't know if you will recall it, as you walk in from the Seventh Avenue side, where the bronze letters, tablets, on either side... the spacing of the letters themselves impressed me. It was done as a master would do it. In fact that inspired me once to get a book of architectural lettering and study it».

In his early days, Abramson was also «an admirer of Cass Gilbert». In later years Gilbert, particularly through his designs of the late 1920s and 1930s, survived as a stubborn Beaux-Art relic in a modernistic age, but at the time Abramson «admired his modernity, if one may use that expression, his breakaway from the classical school».

Abramson's early experience in the office of Louis Gerard, a New York agent of Paul Cret, kept him in thrall to Beaux-Arts practices. He spent countless hours doing charcoal studies of shadow falling on cornices, both for Gerard and for other architects' offices to which Gerard rented him out.

Abramson's first independent work was a YWHA on Central Park North just west of Fifth Avenue. He smiled when describing its interior: «The auditorium was Stanford White's Italian. That was the influence». From «White's Italian», Abramson moved on in the 1920s to the eclecticism typical of the decade. An office building of his design on Maiden Lane (1927) recalls the Gothic detailing of Cass Gilbert's Woolworth Building.

Abramson too broke with the past in the 1930s, with the design of a series of modernistic restaurants, including two Horn & Hardart Automats, six Longschamps restaurants, and Ben Marden's Riviera.

Abramson designed his two Automats in 1931. For the first, on West 33rd Street, he conceived a terra-cotta faced, modernistic, two-story facade with the blocky modern reliefs, abstract grillework, stylized floral patterns, and dramatic indirect lighting so typical of the period. Similarly modernistic friezes, reliefs, and ornamental metalwork adorned the otherwise simple interior. The Horn & Hardart representative that Abramson worked with had very specific requirements for such things as kitchen layouts and hygienic concerns, but Abramson recalls only one piece of instruction from him on design matters: «We like Modern», said the representative, «not Moderne». Abramson thought this statement amusing, had no idea what the man meant, and simply designed what he liked.

Later that same year Abramson designed one of the most extravagant of all New York's Automats, on West 181st Street in Washington Heights. Its facade included such wonderfully modernistic details as the name «HORN & HARDART» superimposed over a polychromatic glazed terra-cotta band of stylized floral patterns, and zig-zag metal and glass pylons lit from within. It was for the interior, however, that Abramson reserved his most extraordinary effects, introducing into his work the use of large-scale illustrations: to crown the two-tiered restaurant, whose walls were adorned with terra-cotta grillework, geometric glass light fixtures, and floral reliefs, he created a set of extravagant colored glass ceiling and wall panels illustrating the icons of Modern New York. In the ceiling panels the Chrysler and Empire State Buildings (modernistic skyscrapers completed in 1930 and 1931 respectively) rose towards each other, their spires meeting electrically over a central schematic diagram of the Manhattan street grid. On the end wall a female figure (whose allegorical significance Abramson could no longer remember) rose from flames through the center of the George Washington Bridge, straddling the mighty Hudson. The Washington Bridge, completed the same year as the Washington Heights Automat, provided the logical symbol for Abramson's restaurant. In his words, he had «a great deal of fun» with the design.

Abramson continued the happy collaboration of architecture and illustration in his Longchamps chain. Beginning in 1934, he worked with painter Winold Reiss on six branches of the restaurant, each arranged around a different pictorial theme. In a Longchamps of 1936, Abramson's plate glass and satin finished chromium exterior, and streamline — and S-curved interior, was adorned with Reiss's images of "the historical contrasts» of New York City — Pilgrims and Skyscrapers on the facade, and portraits of famous old New Yorkers inside.

Abramson remembers two occasions when the question of older versus newer style came up with a client. One was for Hillside Hospital, where he was asked to prepare two possble designs, one «traditional» and one «contemporary». He did, and to his relief Hillside chose the «contemporary» version.

The second instance concerned Abramson's most extraordinary commission, which came with very precise stylistic instructions. Ben Marden's Riviera (1937) in Fort Lee, New Jersey, was to be a combination dinner theater, bar, cafe and lounge. Marden instructed Abramson to make his complex look like George Washington's Mt. Vernon home, as traditional a model as could be imagined. Abramson told Marden not to worry, and kept him away from the site as long as possible.

Ben Marden's sat on a dramatic outcropping of the Palisades, overlooking the Hudson River, in what is now the Palisades Interstate Park. Abramson designed a great semi-circular restaurant, its upper portion an unbroken band of glass affording breathtaking views of Manhattan through the cables of the George Washington Bridge. A huge, S-curved bar with indirect ceiling lighting, porthole windows, and a curving entrance bay, made for an extraordinarily contemporary design, an effect enhanced a year later by the addition of abstract murals on the walls framing the stage. These Abramson commissioned from Arshile Gorky, hardly a traditionalist. (Marden had asked for «dancing girls», and accepted the murals only after asking the opinion of Joey Addams, who approved). On clear nights, the roof of the complex could be rolled back to open the restaurant to the sky.

Marden didn't find out what had happened to his Mt. Vernon until construction was well underway. Whatever his initial feelings, in the end his public relations people put out flyers boasting that the Riviera's advanced modern style was ahead of the plans still being developed for the upcoming 1939 World's Fair.
What inspired the change in direction that left "Stanford white's Italian" behind for the modernistic approach of Abramson's work in the 1930s? Like Crausman, Abramson was reluctant to ascribe any role to the influence of specific contemporary monuments or architects. While acknowledging the impact of white on his early designs, he said of his later works only that: "I was designing according to my own tastes, my own inclinations, and while I admired a great deal of contemporary... work being done... if it influenced me I wasn't consciously aware of it".

Marvin Fine

Of the three interviewed, the architect who most clearly articulated the influence of period trends on his work was Marvin Fine (1904-1981). Chief designer for the firm of Horace Ginsberg (later Ginsbern) & Associates, among the most prominent in the development of the Art Deco apartment buildings of the Grand Concourse, Fine described the impact of major architects and monuments on his work in a 1980 interview.

Unlike Crausman or Abramson, Fine had a sophisticated architectural education, at the University of Pennsylvania. «Penn was a Beaux-Arts school, and my critic was Paul Cret. And Paul Cret was a real exponent of the Ecole des Beaux-Arts».

After graduating from Pennsylvania in 1924, Fine took a position with the office of Cass Gilbert, where he was put to work on drawings for the new New York Life

1936 Marvin Fine Design, Bronx, N.Y.

Marvin Fine.

Insurance Company headquarters on Park Avenue South. His job was to develop drawings of gargoyles, calculating the varying effects of light and shadow: «First you made little drawings, then you developed it quarter-scale, then half-scale, then three-quarter, then half-full size, and then full-size. We used to work on the floor. When we finished the gargoyles, we used to send them to the boss. He used to check them and see if he liked them. And if it passed the secondary boss, then it went on to the chief designer, who put it onto the overall composition of the elevation, and then it was sent on to Cass Gilbert for his comments. And occasionally he would take a big red sanguine chalk and zing it all on, he didn't like the format and so forth. That was what happened».

While working for Gilbert, Fine tried to stay in touch with the Beaux-Arts method by attending an informal atelier conducted by Burnham Hoyt. «About ten men, from all the universities, they came from all around, and we all went in and we chipped in and employed Burnham to give us criticism, and we worked in the evenings. And we loved working under Burnham, because he was a hale fellow well met, and we were not kids, you know, we felt that we were men. We were all graduates, we were all full of vim and vigour and right out of architectural school. But none of us wanted to really give up school completely. We still wanted to do *projets*. And our *projets* were things that he created».

Fine felt the lack of such experience working in Gilbert's office. He did have contact with Cass Gilbert, and considered him a... «terrific guy, terrific. Just terrific. And he went abroad a great deal. And we used to send a lot of our drawings over to him. And he used to send them back, corrected».
But Fine felt the lack of any prospects for further growth: «I had been working on these gargoyles all this time and it started to bug me. And I said, "you know, I'm not learning any architecture this way". And my immediate boss said, "your best bet is, get into a small firm and learn what the dollar amounts to", because I was completely unconscious of what construction costs were, or anything, didn't know if I was designing something that cost a thousand dollars or a million dollars. Directly out of school, you're all imbued with Beaux-Arts...».

Taking the advice, Fine left Gilbert's office to work for Horace Ginsberg, and stayed with the firm for the rest of his working life. Ginsberg may have been the most prominent of all the apartment house developers on the Grand Concourse: «In fact they used to call it the "Ginsberg Gables". And Horace was very very brilliants a brilliant man. Very brilliant architect. He could design an apartment house on the back of an envelope, have the complete layout in his mind, and just scribble a few little things and come in and develop the whole thing...».

Ginsberg left the exterior designs of his buildings to Fine, and it was Fine who developed the characteristic look of «Ginsburg Gables».

One of the first apartment houses Fine designed for Ginsberg was the Park Plaza (1929-31), an eight-story complex at 1005 Jerome Avenue near West 164th Street. The drawings show that Fine originally conceived the building's facade in traditional classical style, adorned with the usual urns and swags. At a certain point, however, he changed his approach, and the Park Plaza became Ginsberg's, and possibly the Bronx's, first «Art Deco» building. He designed the large building as a series of five blocks, separated by recessed courtyards, and faced in light brick. Its striking modernistic effect derives from the arrangement of the windows in vertical shafts of windows and recessed spandrels, and from bands of ornamental polychromatic terra-cotta. The scenes within the bands are typical of the period: panels of flamingos flanking a fountain and backed by a sunburst, alternating with panels in which the rays of a rising sun shine out from behind a Bronx apartment house. Photos of the original version of the building (the Park Plaza was destroyed in a fire while under construction and had to be rebuilt several stories shorter) show large and small chevrons lining the cornice level.

Fine, un like Crausman or Abramson, had no doubt at all about the influences on his stylistic evolution: «I think I met Bill Van Alen originally at some architectural meeting. ...he gave a lecture, a talk, and he impressed me. And I got the, just a hankering to follow his work and look at it. And I enjoyed it».

The chevrons that once lined the cornice level of the Park Plaza, and the projecting figures of birds and squirrels above the terra-cotta bands, bear a striking resemblance to the ornament on William Van Alen's Chrysler Building. Even if Fine had not heard Van Alen lecture, or read of his exploits in the architectural press, he would have know the Chrysler Building, one of the outstanding modernistic monuments of Manhattan, because he watched it rise down the block from his office on East 42nd Street.

But there was more at work than just the Chrysler Building: «And then I also enjoyed the work, at that particular time, of, um, oh, little guy, little grey-haired fellow — worked on the Radiator Building... Raymond Hood».

It was in fact Hood's great striped 1929 headquarters for the Daily News that replaced Fine's office. Moving across the street, he then watched the Daily News Building rise. Fine «... met Raymond Hood. And he, his work, and his style, made me design all of these apartment buildings with the vertical shafts...», of recessed windows and spandrels so typical of the modernistic buildings of the late 1920s and 1930s. They were prominent elements in Hood's design for the Daily News and, earlier, the American Radiator Building. Fine «... developed his style, his vertical style. And all up the Concourse you'll see all the buildings we designed, with the colored brick, change of brick in between the spandrels... That I got directly from him».

Even as Fine turned away from the Beaux-Arts to the modernistic style of Van Alen and Hood, however something of his earlier training persisted. The modernistic metal gates on the Park Plaza were inspired by the work of Samuel Yellin: «I think he was probably the greatest designer of wrought iron. And he gave us some lectures at the University of Pennsylvania... And when I ever came to design wrought iron, I always used Samuel Yellin as my guiding light. In fact I had several criticisms from him, on work that I had designed and sent down to Philly. Great guy».

The most telling detail, however, shows up in a curious scene in the otherwise modernistic terra-cotta banding of the Park Plaza. The details of the scene are classical: a figure kneels before a temple, with an arcade in the background. The inspiration came from a French book of wrought iron ornament: «A lot of details I developed having seen that particular book... There was one that had an architect presented, carrying a building to the Acropolis, a fellow kneeling down. And I remember developing this thing, and the idea, the architect of today, presenting his building to the

Acropolis and saying, you know, well, what do you think? Kid, kid's thoughts».

Even as he helped turned the Bronx towards the modernistic future, Marvin Fine looked to the personification of the classical past for approval.

FOLK MODERN/
MODERNE SAUVAGE

Three famous monuments can establish the category: its naivete and its force. The Chrysler building in New York by William van Alen (1928-30), the Hoover factory outside London by Wallis, Gilbert and Partners (1932 and 1935) and the Coca Cola bottling plant in Los Angeles by Robert Derrah (1936-37).
They are a far cry from the work of the Heroic Period or the sophisticated Art Deco of Paris — or for that matter from the subtleties of Rockefeller Center, although the naive, *sauvage* element lurks in all the Art Deco/Moderne of America, as it does also in much of the work of Frank Lloyd Wright and such lesser promulgators of the «goofy» as Bruce Goff, Eero Saarinen, Paul Rudolph, *et al.* Bunshaft's pavilion for Wonder Bread at the New York World's Fair of 1939/40, a youthful work of a master of sophisticated technology, clearly demonstrates how close the «high» and «low» are in America.
But the work being presented here is limited to that of the *petits maitres,* to those like Horace Ginsbern who built numerous small apartments throughout New York, including on the Grand Concourse in the Bronx, and Henry Hohauser who worked in Miami Beach. These are two names from the innumerable anonymous masters of small works around the world — from Jeddah, Saudi Arabia to Portland, Oregon. One of today's controversies centers on the question of the value and interest of popular culture. If a middle ground position can be taken, one might show that quality and cultural level are distinct matters, as for example the adjectives «big» and «red»: something can be big and red; not red and big; red and not big; not red and not big as well as all the variable range in between. Thus a high culture work can be good or bad as can a low or popular work. The movies of Buster Keaton, the Marx Brothers and Fred Astaire can be cited as examples of high quality at the popular level.
Another of today's controversies centers on the question of Modernism's acceptability to the public. It is a tenet of some who support a version of Post-modernism that Modernism is bad because it has never been publicy accepted, or perhaps that it has never been publicly accepted because it is bad. Again, a middle position, while arguing that a work's modernness and its quality are distinct attributes, might cite the large body of modern work at the popular level to contradict the assertion that modernness and popularity are incompatible. This book presents a small part of the vast extent of this work — and work of noticeable quality.
We have chosen to focus our attention on these buildings both because they give us pleasure, ie. they are beautiful, and for the suggestions they offer to designers today. Twenty-five years ago these buildings were despised by architects of the *avant garde* as modernistic, as merely parading modern forms on traditional modes of building. In a word, as superficial.
At the same time, these architects deplored the absence of a modern vernacular, something equivalent in their eyes to the buildings of «primitive» peoples, whether peasants on a Greek island or «natives» of Africa. What wasn't understood was that this vernacular existed but in an inaccessible form: inaccessible because the «advanced» professional, to prove his sophistication, had to keep ahead of it. (Perhaps

what distinguishes the vernacular of today from that of the past is the speed in catching up. Previously stylistic change, what Morse Peckham has called «nonfunctional stylistic dynamism» which has displayed a rather constant rate of change over recorded history, has tended to be restricted to the upper levels of society, but the rise of democracy has made the pleasures of novelty available to a larger part of the population).

The aspect of the Modern Movement most widely deplored today is its planning, its wish to replace the city of streets and squares with buildings standing free in a continuous park. Today the *avant garde* proposes a return to traditional typologies. This amounts to adopting the methods of our *petits maitres* who worked within the existing urban pattern, merely styling conventional construction in Modernistic motifs. To make the point more emphatic, our Folk Modern works, such as those in ''The New 'Quartier''' could easily be fitted into Leon Krier's project for La Villette (one such P.T.T. is already there) or Culot's Brussels, could even offer suggestions for how the «Reconstruction of the European City» might be undertaken.

''«Appearance», wrote Nietzsche, «belongs also to *reality;* it is a form of its being», allowing identical events to be calculated through their «semblance» (Francesco Dal Co, «Criticism and Design», *Oppositions* 13, p. 2).

The study of contemporary architecture might well take this text as its motto. For by asserting the «reality of appearance», Nietzsche allows us to see that the formal «images» produced by the act of designing might be separate entities in themselves, autonomous from, yet equally valid as the procedures that engendered them. The traditional way of analyzing the development of architectural culture has emphasized a «reality» that has to be sought beneath the «surface» of events, or has seen the architectural form as a determined response to another reality based in economics, politics, or society; in all cases it has tried to tie an appearance back to its presumed cause. Following Nietzsche's argument, however, it should be possible to concentrate on just this appearance — the *image* of architectural design — as a reality of its own. Such a «reading», carefully conducted, of the images or formal manifestations of architecture might provide a more certain account of how architectural culture exists than any reconstruction of how that form was produced by the various modes of design activity''.

If we are to possess that «architectural culture» so often spoken of these days, we should include the work of these *petits maitres* within our ken.

THE PAST PRESENT

The novelty of the 20th century is the «new» idea of the past: not an imitation but a new language. The value of memory inaugurates a new culture of remembrance, a free interpretation of antiquity, a new mark of tradition.

«Classical» becomes synonymous with the essentiality that is a stylistic reduction, interest in geometric volumes, essential form in a building. Everything becomes classical in the ambiguity of the modern[1].

It is not, therefore, only the recall of the symbol of the temple. The lesson of the «new» past (18th cent.) gives double meanings to the image that is used also in the «temples» of labour. The temple becomes a factory according to the symbolism inaugurated in the new Doric City at the beginning of the 19th century — celebration of the new civilization of the machine for a young mythical age[2] —: buildings are no longer distinguished by their style.

The great architectural revolution of the 18th century, in its discovery of free interpretation, has opened the way to the infinite possibilities of being classical[3]. It is the new past to which one goes back. The «rule» has only historical value.

The rigorous search for rational essentiality exalted Paestum and the Doric order, encouraging a return to elementary geometric forms in architecture — as in the work of Ledoux — or to the extreme reduction of vocabulary, tending to simplify form to its structural essentiality — as in the work of Soane.

The symbolic-theoretical conception of Ledoux is transformed in the interpretation of Gilly on the basis of a new structural conception in which the primitive concept of the hut, theorized by Laugier becomes the modern structural essence.

The use of simple forms realised throught basic geometrical elements in this work by Gilly (see e.g. *Fig.* 9) was a step towards the structural rationality typical of many subsequent works of architecture in Germany: Schinkel's modern interpretation of the Doric temple in the Neue Wache took the form of a cube adorned with a colonnade (see e.g. *Fig.* 2).

The return to the ancient in Boullée is a free rendering: exaltation of geometric volumes (cube, pyramid, truncated cone, cylinder, sphere). This feeling is in Le Corbusier: «The light plays on pure forms, and repays them with interest. Simple masses develop immense surfaces which display themselves with a characteristic variety according as it is a question of cupolas, vaulting, cylinders, rectangular prisms or pyramids. The adornment of the surfaces is of the same geometrical order. The Pantheon, the Colosseum, the Aqueducts, the Pyramid of Cestius, the Triumphal Arches, the Basilica of Constantine, the Baths of Caracalla.
Absence of verbosity, good arrangement, a single idea, daring and unity in construction, the use of elementary shapes. A sane morality»[4].

The past is not history, but it is a source of inspiration, a vital spring. It is the idea of transforming and transgressing according to the way shown by the architects of remembrance - Soane, Ledoux, Boullée, Gilly, Schinkel.

The past is a way to remember in order to imagine the world again. The past is the origin of the modern. The past *is* the modern. It is tradition as invention of the new view of the antiquity: it is the knowledge of that gold dust seen by Louis Kahn[5].

The memory is refracted in the most diverse forms of the lexicon and emerges always different, contrasted. From the uniqueness of the example various ways are opened to interpretation: only by returning to the origins through the paths of memory is it possible to discover the meaning of an epoch and the historical truth beyond critical superimpositions. This is the opportunity given to history.

Loos, Hoffman, Tessenow: in them the interpretation of the antique reemerges as formal essentiality, chromatic unity, reduction of the design, geometric symplicity. The return to the Classical and to the temple in the architecture of Behrens, Le Corbusier and Wright assumes a different form: from the image of pure geometry to the timber gable applied to volumetric masses.

By the years 1910-1912 the idea of memory had been formulated and a new direction for architecture was opened.

A rich vitality is gained in the non-codification, in the possibilities of opposites, in the variety of solutions.

Everyday architecture resonates with the same contradictions, experiencing them in its free reflection on the multiplicity of interpretations already accumulated by tradition; this is the legacy of the past.
The true of the new memory is the error: error as new invention of the past.
«*Error* has made man so deep, sensitive, and inventive that he has put forth such blossoms as religions and arts» (F. NIETZSCHE, *Human, All-Too-Human,* n. 29, pp. 44-45).

J.R.S.

---

[1] See: VENTURI, Ital. ed., 1980, *passim*.
[2] See e.g. LE CORBUSIER, (1923) 1952, p. 83.
[3] For the relations between architectural exemples of the 18th and 19th centuries and modern ones see: KAUFMANN, (1933) 1973; (1952) 1982; (1955) 1966; PEVSNER, 1968; SUMMERSON, (1963), 1983; NEUMEYER, 1984; EISENMAN, 1987, p. 168.
[4] LE CORBUSIER, (1923) 1952, pp. 146-147.
[5] See NORBERG - SCHULTZ, 1980, p. 114.

TRADITION AND INNOVATION IN MODERN ARCHITECTURE

«After the secessionist cycle, we return to a new, deliberate barbarity, which looks with one eye at the theater of Marcellus, the temples of Paestum and the walls of Hadrian's villa, and with the other, at Sullivan's skyscrapers»[1].

According to Giuseppe Pagano, one of the protagonists of Italian «rationalism», the 20th century aims to follow the same road as the architects and theorists of the 18th century, who suggested, after Paestum, a return to essentiality of form... Soane, Ledoux, Laugier, Gilly, Weinbrenner. It was the Doric Style's natural capacity to comply with the need for simplification of form, that led to the success of the neo-Doric — whose influence penetrated as far as the history of contemporary architecture.

During the 20th century, simplified and geometrical forms influenced building activity at all levels, even that of so called mass architecture. In the myriad of anonymous buildings constructed by anonymous builders (whose figurative impact remains ever determining), in the urban physiognomy of large important areas of the historical context, the link between tradition and innovation is highly significant.

The problem of tradition vs. innovation had already been posed in the 18th century. The language of the orders, that is, of the elements of architecture *par excellence*, was reconsidered in an extreme attempt at simplification and in the attainment of a better equilibrium between contrasting terms: the recognizability of linguistic membership (to classicism) and the opening to novelty that architecture requires. Stylistic simplification was not the only means adopted, since it was intersected by volumetric scansion of the building.

The problem was (and remains) how to define the building's bodies so as to render them legible, measurable, and includable in an urban context, considering on the one hand, the new habitability requirements and the technical support offered by industry, and on the other, the need to give the city form with a strongly defined, connotated architecture. Yet again, it was a matter of guiding the eye by means of segmentation of the work into bodies (bodies more or less distinguished by traditional elements), organizing them into lots so that the eye does not wander over an undifferentiated surface.

In the past the use of the orders gave meaning to all the other architectural elements. Doors and windows were understood as elements of composition. Can architecture give up a rule? Are not rules such as these what give architecture its distinctive character?

The long-standing success of classicism resides in the fact that, even if rigidly disciplined, it nonetheless allows tremendous freedom to use an unlimited variety of expressions[2].

There are instances of variations allowing certain building typologies, which for reasons of size, economic constrictions, constructional methodologies and purpose would otherwise be excluded, to re-enter the framework of classical architecture: for example, the superimposition of orders, the use of attics and bases, giant orders, orders interrupted by a gallery, twin columns, rusticated, ringed, and enclosed columns and enclosed pronaoi. Such elements — as we have seen — can be transformed (omitted, alluded to, emphasized) because, in keeping with general classical principles and with the fundamental perceptive rules, they can be variously applied to different contexts and their many aspects.

The normative code, on the contrary is made up of binding, informing principles that serve as hallmarks of the system itself and are thus not modifiable (in the sense that they cannot be modified, if not by modifying the system itself).

The beholder can recognize the syntax even if the elements in themselves are so limited and simplified that they are unrecognizable. The context or the isolated recall of a sole parastas on the sides of an enormous facade very often serve as clue[3].

With regard to the now urgent problem of the increase in size of buildings and cities, the giving of form to the visual product (while meeting the need for functionality in architecture in the industrial age) must not be neglected.

The monumental becomes, then, a unmistakable urban mark (see the Oud project for the new Amsterdam town hall); the 'jump in scale' guarantees the maximum habitability. Loos emphasizes the problem of 'out of scale' building, in his project for a skyscraper in the form of a Doric column, presented for the Chicago Tribune Competition.

The comparison, made by Berlage during his journey to America (1912), between the towers of San Gimignano and the skycrapers of Downtown, highlights the possibility of shifts from the small to the large and vice versa, with extreme facility, giving rise to "surprising combinations", such as the invention of the giant order that ascends through several storeys attributed by Berlage to Palladio[4].

The 'jump in scale', from small to large and vice versa, which has been present in the minds of artists since the times when the lamps of the catacombs were made in the form of a basilica[5], becomes the central theme of the manipulation of classical elements, as long as it remains possible to decode the deviations from the original, bringing them back within a system which it has taken centuries to establish. It is a system whose rituality allows the bringing of collocation of transgression into the mainstream of tradition.

But Berlage states that "modern architecture yearns to express itself through the composition of volumes"[6]. And it is in everyday architecture that we find the synthesis between classicism and modernism, the 'modernist classicism', according to Tom and Charlotte Benton's definition, "We can distinguish it from the 'stripped' classicism to be found in such buildings as Speer's New Chancellery, or Troost's Haus der Kunst where explicit references to the full repertoire of classical forms are retained". This style "shares with the stripped classicism the rules of symmetry, proportion, grandeur and 'correctness'. But it absorbs from the Modern Movement a new sense of space, a treatment of walls as surfaces rather than load-bearing masses, and a completely 'modern' approach to materials"[7].

The typology — as we have seen — of the curved building in a corner lot reflects for example, 'modernist' intonations in the fluidity of unitarily curved volumes and 'classicist' intonations because the volumes are suitably highlighted by primary elements, such as balconies and terraces. In this dialectic between modernism and classicism the gap is bridged between the apparent abstraction attributed to the modern movement and the expressive needs proclaimed by the academics.

Apart from the transformation of the elements, the other evident aspect of the renewed lexicon is the progressive geometricization of the forms, which solves the artisan's problems. The industrial mentality is such that the architect, when he designs, must consider the impossibility of leaving the manipulation of 'ornamental' forms to the creativity of the artisan. These forms must be linear and essential so that they can be easily chain produced.

John Soane had already intuited this: in Tivoli Corner of the Bank of England, an exact copy of a portion of the Temple of Vesta at Tivoli, the capitals, the most ornate of the prototype, have schematic forms, so as to be easily reproduced in series.

The reproduction of typical wood forms in stone and vice versa, and from these to new materials — a recurrent theme in 18th century theory and developed by Adam and Soane — has allowed an ever greater rationalization of the forms themselves, according to the same principle that every 'omissive' stylization can in some way respond to classical relationships and harmonies[8].

The return of the architrave and of the orthogonal squaring typical of the Greeks and the Egyptians, on the other hand, is substantially due to the use of reinforced concrete in the more recent phases of the Modern Movement.

The problem was to find the *best form* together with the use of new materials and techniques.

This was the principal aim of the search for linguistic renewal, ever in that sector of 20th century architecture which seems more subversive of tradition, and that in effect is characterized by the vast resort to motifs clearly inspired by the conning-towers of ships or airports, the living quarters of ocean liners, the cockpits of airplanes... New forms, 'technically' adapted to the new materials: aerodynamics can become a criterion of value substituing that of classicism.

The quest for architectonic forms suited to the constructive characteristics of the new materials, leads to the establishment of a set of criteria by which to measure their functionality and worth according to proved standards set by specific avantgarde sectors. These new criteria, in their modernist impetus, may replace those proposed by classicism; however it is precisely in their explicit contraposition to the 'eternal' values of classicism that their connection with the tradition should be seen; they represent the other side of a necessary dialectical relationship which belongs to the old cliché *"la querelle des Ancients et des Modernes"*.

N.Z.

[1] From the lecture, «Aspetti e tendenze dell'architettura contemporanea», held by G. PAGANO in Turin, 1928, in MELOGRANI, 1955, p. 53.
[2] CHITHAM, 1987, p. 132.
[3] See ZANNI, 1980, pp. 284-295 and 1984, pp. 45-90.
[4] BERLAGE, 1985, p. 122.
[5] On this subject see e.g. P. TESTINI, *Le catacombe e gli antichi cimiteri cristiani in Roma*, Bologna 1966, p. 214.
[6] BERLAGE, 1985, p. 115.
[7] BENTON, 1978, p. 25
[8] ZANNI, Cat. *La fortuna di Paestum...*, 1986, vol. II, pp. 285-289.

THE ARCHITECTURE OF THE MACHINE

The myth of machines and of technological progress has been one of the components of western thought since the first Industrial Revolution. But it is with the advent of electricity and its application that the image assumes a completely original force, producing, on one hand, new families of objects, and on the other, the belief of finally and definitively being able to have an unlimited energy source.
The literary fervor of the novels of Jules Verne and especially the *Nautilus* of *Twenty Thousand Leagues under the Sea* (1870), testify to this, but even more so does the ironical mythicizing of Thomas Alva Edison in novels like *L'Eve future* by Villiers de l'Isle-Adam (1886).
But, in addition to the literary and fantastic imagery, the new source of energy, electricity, makes possible things unthinkable up to that time. The phonopraph and the electric light bulb are only two of the many objects through which man on the threshold of the century shows that he can dispose of inexhaustible sources of energy at his discretion. The object *princeps* of all this is the Turbine, the Dynamo, that produces this electricity. It is merely a utilitarian object, but one which, precisely because of its capacity to produce energy, became symbol and catalyst of a new epoch and, as a symbol of dynamism, assumes aesthetic value.
The historical avant-gardes of the first years of the 20th century, particularly Futurism, mark a decisive step in this direction.
When the «machinist» inspiration refers to the objects which produce movement, the formal principle links itself to objects whose aspect is merely that of things — pylons, cables, plates — which help to make them work, disposed according to the most economic aggregation possible.
«We must invent and rebuild *ex novo* our Modern city like an immense and tumultuous shipyard, active, mobile and everywhere dynamic, and the modern building like a gigantic machine. Lifts must no longer hide away like solitary worms in the stair-wells, but the stairs — now useless — must be abolished, and the lifts must swarm up the façades like serpents of glass and iron. The house of cement, iron and glass, without carved or painted ornament, rich only in the inherent beauty of its lines and modelling, extraordinarily brutish in its mechanical simplicity, as big as need dictates, and not merely as zoning rules permit, must rise from the brink of a tumultuous abyss; the street which, itself, will no longer lie like a doormat at the level of the thresholds, but plunge storeys deep into the earth, gathering up the traffic of the metropolis connected for necessary transfers to metal cat-walks and high-speed conveyor belts»[1].
This involves the existence of a «functionalism» made of continually concatenated volumes, of forms, of colors, and of materials that are coordinated not casually but according to a principle that proceeds from that of the volumetric aggregations used previously in architecture or in engineering. The assumption of this principle as aesthetic principle, as the historical avant-gardes do, leads to a new «picturesque» aesthetic form, in which the criterion of distributive utility is replaced with that of functionality.

To the past as source of esthetic emotion, to the picturesque vertigo of the past, it is now possible to add the vertigo of the future, progress itself as a process, as esthetic act and formal value.

The two compositional processes, that deriving from the Dynamo and that coming, though with deep modifications, from the aggregative principles of the beginning of the 19th century, and especially from Durand, are very clear to contemporaries. It is important for the position of Tessenow, who opting for simplification in the purist sense of the architectural language, cannot in any way achieve the form of the machine, even though he accepts the principles of compositional clarity.

«If we think of a showy and particularly insignificant ornament, and at the same time we think of a copper wire carrying high voltage current, we have before us two possible and antithetical forms of human engagement: in the first case, we have a supremacy of the form, without anything essential behind it; in the second case, we have an almost total absence of form, with a very evident content: after all, we can accept neither one nor the other of these two solutions, we seek a form which is alive in each of its parts, but we also seek a form that knows how to fully express what is alive»[2].

Beside this poetics of the machine, another important process, directly linked with modern progress, develops as well: the industrial production of architecture. An important date is 1907, the year Behrens joins AEG and Muthesius founds the Werkbund. Behind these two events there is a long evolution which has already created the elements of the new architecture. In particular there are the new frame construction and reinforced concrete which was replacing iron, that is, structure where the load bearing skeleton and the wall panels were separate. In fact, in the first half of the 20th century, beginning with Perret's theorization on the Greek and gothic of Choisy, and with the studies of engineers such as Hennebique, the basis for industrial construction had been laid.

On one hand this involved the development of an esthetic theory of purism, in particular the position of Loos, and on the other hand a different interest in the building process which was then transforming spatial and productive models from industry. The problem was to face both the demand for more goods and for the formal and functional quality of these goods, among which the house was the most important. The Werkbund responded to this demand with proposals often very different in formal results which divided the organization.

This same problem was shared by movements more tied to the linguistic revolution, from Futurism to *De Stijl,* which had important contacts between themselves, in relation to the possibility of realizing architecture with standardized elements. From this point of view the rediscovery of Greek and classical architecture, as architecture of modular elements, was a logical consequence, and its circle of influence went from the classicism of Oud to that of Le Corbusier. The observations of the latter on the Parthenon are well-known:

«Phidias would have loved to have lived in this standardized age. He would have admitted the possibility, nay the certainty of success. His vision would have seen in our epoch the conclusive results of his labours. Before long he would have repeated the experience of the Parthenon»[3].

The industrial transformation of architecture and the house leads, in the end, to the re-examination of social needs and of the «real» requirements of space for human functions. It is the EXISTENZ MINIMUM, the module that becomes the fundamental instrument for the planning of new quarters. But in this the compositional process almost inverts itself and, in the pure geometric form of the parallelepiped and of the cube, carves the prototypes of the optimal distributive dispositions.

The studies of «existenz minimum» borrow models of spatial and social relationships from the industrial production of vehicles. Still again the spectrum of the quotations, recalling automobiles and steamships as formal and functional models, is very vast. It already begins in the 1910's and finds in 1923 with Le Corbusier's «machine pour habiter», its best known slogan.

Everybody asserts with conviction and enthusiasm: «The motor-car marks the style of our epoch!» but the Breton bed is sold and manufactured every day by the antique dealers.

Let us diplay, then, the Parthenon and the motor-car so that is may be clear that it is a question of two products of selection in different fields, one of which has reached its climax and the other is evolving. That ennobles the automobile. And what then? Well, then it remains to use the motor-car as a challenge to our houses and our great buildings. It is here that we come to a dead stop. "Rien ne va plus". Here we have no Parthenons»[4].

But it is with large building production that architecture as a machine for living assumes more decidedly, in prefabrication, its productive and industrial connotations. Architecture is rational and functional like a machine, but it is also produced like a machine.

This new form of building production, moreover, is only the application of Taylor's principles to one of the main human activities: the production of space for one's own existence. But this involves new planning and formal problems: «The concept of standardized construction means in the first place the elaboration of the solution — the most simple, the most functional, and the most apt for use on a large scale — of every building problem, from the detail to the type of the house. Each unnecessary variation, each deviation must be eliminated»[5].

In fact, precisely the theme of architecture as machine when it appears as a pure compositional mechanism, leads to such silence in the geometrical rigor and in the exasperated and repetitive modularity, that the problem of form returns, already in the 1930's, in a different key.

«To give the objects geometrical forms means: to standardize, to mechanize». «Yet we do not want to mechanize the objects themselves, but only the way of producing them. We do not have to give form to our individuality, but to the individuality of the objects. Their aspect must coincide with the objects themselves»[6].

The disputes of those years are well-known. The houses are by this time machines full of other machines, elevators, electric lights, refrigerators... but often they do not express anything other than the mere function of living, programmatically anonymous and as reproducible as cars, steam-ships, or trains. As these, they are deprived of «Aura».

Nevertheless, beginning exactly with the process of optimization and standardization of the new linguistic and functional forms — from the circular balconies to the stairway turrets, from the pilasters to the strip windows, from the portholes to the 'Three Lines' — a new repertoire of forms grows up, also characterizing the Everyday Architecture of those years, which separates them, with infinite «variations», independently from the industrial character of the constructive process of the single buildings.

A final aspect which must be emphasized is the landscape, dotted by new objects born to make the world of the machines work: gas pumps, garages, train stations. These announce, in their typological repetitiveness, the unfolding of a process of standardization which goes well beyond the linguistic and architectural one.

P.M.M.

---

[1] A. Sant'Elia, *L'architettura futurista. Manifesto*, Milan, 11 July 1914, translation from Banham, *Theory and Design in the First Machine Age*, 1960, Praeger, N.Y. p. 129.
[2] H. Tessenow, *Osservazioni elementari sul construire*, (1916), Milan 1987, p. 89.
[3] Le Corbusier, *Towards a New Architecture*, 1970, Praeger, N.Y., Washington. D.C., p. 135
[4] Le Corbusier, *op. cit.*, pp. 130-131
[5] H. Schmidt, «Costruzione standardizzata», 1931, ms. in *Contributi all'architettura 1924-1964*, (1965) Milan 1974.
[6] H. Häring, «Wege zur Form», *die Form*, October, 1925, cit. in Hilberseimer.

ESSENTIAL BIBLIOGRAPHY

Abbati V., "Le luci della città. Luce ed architettura", *Domus*, IV, 47, novembre 1931, pp. 32-33.

Achenbach S., *Erich Mendelsohn*, Berlin 1987.

Ackerman J.C., "The tuscan / rustic order: a study in the metaphorical language of architecture", *Journal of American Society of Architectural Historians*, XLII, 1, 1983, pp. 15-34.

Alpern A., *Apartments for the affluent. A Historical Survey of Buildings in New York*, New York 1975.

American Architecture: Innovation-and-tradition, edited by D.G. De Long, H. Searing, R.A.M. Stern, New York 1986.

Andersson H.O., Bedoire F., *Swedish Architecture Drawings 1640-1970*, Stockholm 1986.

"Arched and Columns: The Debate between Piacentini and Ojetti", 1933, *Modulus. The University of Virginia School of Architecture Review*, 1982, pp. 7-17.

Argan G.C., "Introduzione a Wright", *Metron*, 18, 1947, pp. 9-24.

Argan G.C., *Walter Gropius e la Bauhaus*, Torino 1951.

Argan G.C., *Progetto e destino*, Milano 1965.

Argan G.C., *Libera*, Roma 1975.

Art Nouveau Architecture, edited by F. Russel, New York 1986.

Baldessari L., *L'architettura moderna in Italia*, Rovereto 1939.

Banham R., "Ornament and Crime. The Decisive Contribution of Adolf Loos", *Architectural Review*, February 1958, pp. 85-88.

Banham R., *Architettura della prima età della macchina*, (1960) Bologna 1970.

Banham R., *Ambiente e Tecnica nell'architettura moderna*, (1969) Bari 1978.

Barbieri U., *J.J.P. Oud*, Bologna 1986.

Behne A., *L'architettura funzionale*, (1926) Firenze 1968.

Behne A., *Eine Stunde Architektur*, (1928) Berlin 1984.

Benton T. Ch., "Towards Modernist Classicism", *werk archithese*, 23-24, nov.-dez. 1978, pp. 23-27.

Berlage H.P., "Über moderne Baukunst", *Zeitschrift des österreichischen Ingenieur-und architekten-Vereines*, 1911, n° 21, pp. 321-326.

Berlage H.P., *Amerikaansche reisherinneringen*, Rotterdam, 1911.

Berlage H.P., *Architettura urbanistica estetica,* Bologna 1985.

Bernabei G., Gresleri G., Zagnoni S., *Bologna Moderna 1860-1980*, Bologna 1984.

Birkner O., *Bauen und Wohnen in der Schweiz 1850-1920*, Zürich 1975.

Boesiger W., Girsberger H., *Le Corbusier 1910-65*, Zürich 1967.

Bonfanti E., Porta M., *Città Museo e Architettura. Il gruppo BBPR nella cultura architettonica italiana 1932-1970*, Firenze 1973.

Borsi F., *L'Ordre monumental: Europe 1929-1939*, Paris 1986.

BOSSAGLIA R., *L'art Deco*, Bari 1984.

BOULLÉE E.L., *Architecture. Essai sur l'Art*, edited by J.M. PÉROUSE DE MONTCLOS, Paris 1968.

BRAHAM A., *L'Architecture des Lumières, de Soufflot à Ledoux*, Paris 1982.

BRULHART A., "Maurice Braillard et la Cité Vieusseux", *werk archithese*, 23-24, nov.-dez. 1978, pp. 49-51.

BRULHART A., FREY P., *19-39. La Suisse Romande entre les deux guerres*, Lausanne 1986.

BUCCIARELLI P., HÖGER F.: "Il verbo espressionista", *Eupalino*, 8, 1987, pp. 40-51.

C.E., "Cesare Pascoletti e l'opera sua", *La panarie*, XI, 62, marzo-aprile 1934, pp. 104-111.

CAMPBELL J., *The German Werkbund. The Politics of Reform in the Applied Arts*, Princeton, 1978 (trad. it. *Il Werkbund tedesco*), Venezia 1987).

CANELLA G., GREGOTTI V., "Il Novecento e l'architettura", *Edilizia moderna*, 81, dicembre 1963, pp. 1-108.

CANESI G., CASSI RAMELLI A., *Architetture luminose*, Milano 1941.

CARLI E., "Il genere architettura rurale e il funzionalismo", *Casabella*, XV, 107, novembre 1936, pp. 6-7.

CAVALLOTTI C., "Architetti italiani: Pietro Lingeri", *Comunità*, XI, 50, giugno 1957, pp. 68-72.

CECCHERELLI C., "Recenti opere di architetti lombardi e delle Venezie", *Architettura e Arti Decorative*, IV, fasc. II, 1924-25, pp. 299-313.

CENNAMO M., *Materiali per l'analisi dell'architettura moderna*, Napoli 1973.

CENNAMO M., *La 2ª Mostra del MIAR e la polemica del 1931*, Napoli 1976.

CHITHAM R., *Gli ordini classici in architettura*, Milano 1987.

COCCHIA C., *L'edilizia a Napoli dal 1918 al 1958*, Napoli 1961.

COLLINS G.R. e Ch. C., "Monumentality: a Critical Matter in Modern Architecture", *Monumentality and the City*, IV, Spring 1984, pp. 15-35.

COLLINS P., *I mutevoli ideali dell'architettura moderna*, (1965) Milano 1973.

CONRADS U., *Manifesti e programmi per l'architettura del XX secolo*, Firenze 1970.

CONTESSI G., *Umberto Nordio. Architettura a Trieste 1926-1943*, Milano, 1981.

CRESTI C., *Architettura e fascismo*, Firenze 1986.

CRUSVAR L., "Il sistema urbano nella Trieste degli anni '30", in Cat. *Gli affreschi di Carlo Sbisà e la Trieste degli Anni Trenta*, Trieste 1980, pp. 51-99.

DAL CO F., *Teorie del Moderno. Architettura Germania 1880-1920*, Roma-Bari 1982.

DAL CO F., "The Stones of the Void", *Oppositions*, 26, Spring 1984, pp. 98-116.

DAL CO F., *Abitare nel moderno*, Roma-Bari 1985.

DAMIANI L., *Arte del Novecento in Friuli. Il Novecento: mito e razionalismo*, II, Udine 1982.

DE FEO V., *U.R.S.S. Architettura 1917-1963*, Roma 1963.

DEPERO F., *Fortunato Depero nelle opere e nella vita*, Trento 1940.

DE SETA C., *La cultura architettonica in Italia tra le due guerre*, Roma-Bari 1983.

DE SETA C., *Architetti italiani del Novecento*, Bari 1987.

DI GADDO B., *Villa Borghese. Il Giardino e l'architettura*, Roma 1985.

DOIG A., *Theo van Doesburg. Painting into Architecture, theory into practice*, Cambridge, New York 1986.

DREXLER A., *Mies van der Rohe*, New York 1960.

DRUDI GAMBILLO M., FIORI T., *Archivi del Futurismo*, I-II, Roma 1958-1962.

DUBOY PH., LEQUEU, *An architectural Enigma*, London 1986.

DUBUT L.A., *Architecture civile. Maison de ville et de campagne de toutes formes et de tous genres...*, Paris, an XI (1803).

"Due opere di Pietro Lingeri", *Domus*, IV, 48, dicembre 1931, pp. 36-44.

DURAND J.N.L., *Recueil et parallèle des édifices de tout genre anciens et modernes remarcables dessinés sur une meme échelle*, Paris an IX (1800).

DURAND J.N.L., *Partie graphique des cours d'architecture*, Paris 1821.

DURAND J.N.L., *Precis des leçons d'architecture données à l'Ecole Royale Polytechnique...*, I, II (1802-1805) Paris 1823-1824.

Durand J.N.L., *Lezioni di architettura*, edited by E. D'Alfonso, Milano 1986.
Dudok W.M., "En gewijd aan het Raadhuis - Ontwerp voor de gemeente Hilversum en mitgevoerde projecten, van architect W.M. Dudok... Antwerpen", *De Sikkel*, 1924 (*Wendingen*, ser 6, no. 8, 1924).
Dudok W.M., "En gewijd aan het gebouw van de Bijenkorf te Rotterdam, van architect W.M. Dudok... Antwerpen", *De Sikkel*, 1930 (*Wendingen*, ser 11, n. 8, 1930).
Erhard L., "Die neuzeitige Tektonik", *Zeitschrift des Österreichischen Ingenieur - und Architekten - Vereines*, Wien, n. 49, pp. 769-775.
E.N.R. (E.N. Rogers), "Stazione Marittima di Trieste", *Rassegna d'architettura*, IV, 4, aprile 1932, pp. 154-159.
Eisenman P., *La fine del classico*, Venezia 1987.
"Esempi da fuori", *Domus*, IV, 48, dicembre 1931, pp. 53-57.
F.R., "Corriere architettonico. I padiglioni italiani alla Mostra della Stampa di Colonia e di Barcellona", *Architettura e Arti decorative*, IX, fasc. VII, 1930, pp. 322-325.
F.W. "Der Internationale Wettbewerb für den neuen Zeitungspalast der 'Chicago Tribune'", *Zeitschrift des Österreichischen Ingenieur - und Architekten - Vereines*, 1923, nn. 3-4, pp. 13-17.
Fanelli G., *De Stijl*, Bari 1983.
Felice C.A., "La nuova sede dei "Cannottieri Lario" in Como architettata da Mantero", *Domus*, IV, 46, ottobre 1931, pp. 70-73.
Ford J. and Morrow Ford K., *The Modern House in Amerika*, New York 1940.
Forti A., *Angiolo Mazzoni architetto tra fascismo e libertà*, Firenze 1978.
Foucault M., *Microfisica del potere*, (1971) Torino 1977.
Frank J., *Architettura come simbolo*, (1931) Bologna 1986.
Frühlicht, 1920-1922 Gli anni dell'avanguardia architettonica in Germania, Milano 1974.
Gerettsegger H., Peintner M., *Otto Wagner*, Milano 1985.
Giacumacatos A., Godoli E., *L'architettura delle scuole e il razionalismo in Grecia*, Firenze 1985.
Giedion S., *Space, Time and Architecture*, (1941) Cambridge Mass 1967.
Giedion S., "The need for a new Monumentality, *Monumentality and the City*, IV, Spring 1984.
Gioseffi D., *La falsa preistoria di P. Mondrian e le origini del neoplasticismo*, Trieste 1957.
Gioseffi D., *Udine: Le Arti*, Udine 1982.
Godoli E., *Il Futurismo*, Bari 1983.
Gramsci A., "Il razionalismo nell'architettura" (Q.I), in *Letteratura e vita nazionale*, Roma 1975, pp. 48-49.
Grandi M., Pracchi A., *Milano, guida all'architettura moderna*, Bologna 1980.
Grassi G., *La costruzione logica dell'architettura*, Padova 1967.
Grassi G., *Architettura e formalismo*, in L. Hilberseimer. *Architettura a Berlino negli anni venti*, Milano 1981, pp. 7-30.
Gravagnuolo B., *Adolf Loos*, Milano 1981.
Gregotti V., *New directions in Italian architecture*, New York 1968.
Gregotti V., "Milano e la cultura architettonica tra le due guerre", in cat. *Il Razionalismo e l'architettura in Italia durante il Fascismo*, Venezia 1976, pp. 16-21.
Gropius W., *The New Architecture and the Bauhaus*, New York - London 1937.
Gruppo 7 (Il), "Architettura", *Rassegna Italiana*, dicembre 1925, pp. 849-851.
Gruppo 7 (Il), "Architettura (II). Gli stranieri", *Rassegna Italiana*, febbraio 1927, pp. 129-137.
Gruppo 7 (Il), "Architettura (III). Impreparazione - Incomprensione - Pregiudizi", *Rassegna Italiana*, marzo 1927, pp. 247-252.
Gruppo 7 (Il), "Architettura (IV). Una nuova epoca arcaica", *Rassegna Italiana*, maggio 1927, pp. 467-472.
Gubler J., *Nationalisme et internationalisme dans l'architecture moderne de la Suisse*, Lausanne 1975.
Gutkind E., "Estetica tecnica nelle moderne costruzioni tedesche" in *Architettura e Arti Decorative*, III, 1923-1924, fasc. VI, pp. 268-276.

Guttry (de) I., *Guida di Roma Moderna. Architettura dal 1870 ad oggi*, Roma 1978.
Haerdt G., "Una nuova casa di Joseph Franck", *Domus*, IV, 43, luglio 1931, pp. 48-49.
Heidegger M., *L'epoca dell'immagine del mondo*, in *Holzwege*, Frankfurt-am-Main, 1950 (ed. it. *Sentieri interrotti*, a cura di P. Chiodi, Firenze, 1968, pp. 71-101).
Hamlin T., *Greek Revival Architecture in America*, New York 1944.
Hilberseimer L., *Architettura a Berlino negli anni venti*, (1967) Milano 1981.
Hitchcock H.R., Johnson Ph., *Lo stile Internazionale*, (1932) (1966), Bologna 1982.
Hitchcock H.R., *L'architettura dell'Ottocento e del Novecento*, (1958)Torino 1971.
Howarth T., *Ch. Mackintosh and the Modern Movement*, (1952) London 1977.
"Il primo mercato rionale coperto", *Rivista mensile della Città di Trieste*, VIII, 1, gennaio 1935, pp. 1-8.
Jencks Ch., *What is Post-Modernism?*, London-New York 1986.
Johnson Ph., *Mies van der Rohe*, New York 1947.
Johnson Ph., *Writings*, New York, 1979
Joedicke J., *Die Weissenhofsiedlung, the Weissenhof colony, La Cité de Weissenhof, Stuttgart*, Stuttgart 1984.
John Soane, London-New York, 1983.
"Joseph Hoffmann", *Domus*, IV, 39, marzo 1931, pp. 46-49.
Junghanns K., *Bruno Taut 1880-1938*, Milano 1984.
Kaufmann E., *Da Ledoux a Le Corbusier, origine e sviluppo dell'architettura autonoma*, (1933) Milano 1973.
Kaufmann E., *Tre architetti rivoluzionari. Boullée Ledoux Lequeu*, (1952) Milano 1982.
Kaufmann E., *L'architettura dell'Illuminismo*, (1955), Torino 1966.
Kemp J., *American Vernacular*, New York 1987.
Krafft J. Ch., N. Ransonette, *Plans, coups, élévations des plus belles maisons et des hotels construits à Paris et dans les environs...*, Paris s.d.
L'abitazione Razionale. Atti dei Congressi CIAM 1929-1930, Padova 1971.
"L'architettura moderna in Italia", edited by P. Montesi, *La casa*, 6, s.d.
"La casa del Combattente in Trieste", *Architettura*, XIII, V, maggio 1934, pp. 271-277.
"La casa della Giovane Italiana a Gorizia", *Edilizia moderna*, VIII, genn. marzo 1937, pp. 66-67.
Labò M., "Pagano scrittore: cronaca e documentazione", *Casabella, Costruzioni*, XVII, 195-198, dicembre 1946, fascicolo speciale, pp. 59-65.
"La Triennale di Monza. Mostra Internazionale delle arti Decorative", *Architettura e Arti decorative*, IX, fasc. XI, luglio 1930, p. 481.
Le Corbusier, *Verso un'architettura*, (1923) Milano 1973, 1986.
Le Corbusier, *Quando le cattedrali erano bianche*, (1936) Faenza 1975.
Le Corbusier, *Precisions sur un état présent de l'architecture et de l'urbanisme avec un prologue americain, un corollaire brésilien suivi d'une température parisienne et d'une atmosphère moscovite*, Paris 1930.
Ledoux C.N., *L'architecture considérée sous le rapport de l'art, des moeurs et de la législation*, I (Paris 1804) Nördlingen 1981; II (Paris 1847) Nördlingen 1984.
Lenarduzzi L., "Razionalismo e memoria storica nell'architettura di Ermes Midena", *Arte in Friuli-Arte a Trieste*, 10, 1988, pp. 169-184.
Lenzi L., "I garages", *Architettura e Arti decorative*, VII, fasc. X, giugno 1928, pp. 440-470.
Libera A. Piacentini M., "Discussioni artistiche. Del razionalismo in architettura", *Rassegna italiana*, marzo 1928, pp. 437-441.
"L'Italia che si rinnova", *Domus*, VII, 73, gennaio 1934, pp. 4-9.
Loos A., *Parole nel vuoto*, Milano 1986.
Loukomski G.K., "Il ritorno dell'architettura classica in Russia", *Rassegna di Architettura*, V, 4, aprile 1933, pp. 175-179.
"Luciano Baldessari", *Controspazio*, 2-3, (numero speciale), febbraio-marzo 1978.
Magnago Lampugnani V., *La realtà dell'immagine. Disegni di architettura nel ventesimo secolo*, Torino 1982.

Malkiel Jirmounsky M., "Le architetture nuove in Francia", *Dedalo*, XII, X, ottobre 1932, pp. 780-816.

Mallet - Stevens R., "Il pubblico e l'architettura", *Edilizia moderna*, VIII, 25, aprile-ottobre 1937, pp. 1-3.

Mantero E., *Il razionalismo italiano*, Bologna 1984.

Mariani R., *E 42. Un progetto per l'Ordine Nuovo*, Milano 1987.

Masera P., "Cento case in Milano", *Edilizia moderna*, VII, 21-22, aprile-settembre 1936, pp. 76-89.

Melis A., "L'esposizione di Torino del 1928", *Architettura e Arti Decorative*, VII, fasc VIII, 1928, pp. 372-381.

Melograni C., *Giuseppe Pagano*, Milano 1955.

Mendelsohn E., *Das Gesamtschaffen des Architekten*, Berlin 1930.

Michelucci G., "Contatti tra architetture moderne e antiche", *Domus*, V, 51, marzo 1932, pp. 134-137.

Mies van der Rohe, "Hochhaus Project für Bahnhof Friedrichstrasse in Berlin", *Frühlicht* 1 (1922), pp. 122-124.

Minnucci G., "Moderna architettura olandese", *Architettura e Arti Decorative*, III, fasc. XI, 1923, pp. 492-522.

Minnucci G., "L'architettura e l'estetica degli edifici industriali", *Architettura e Arti Decorative*, V, fasc. XI-XII, 1925-26, p. 481.

Modern Architectur in Noorwegen, Zweden, Finland, Denemarken Duitschland, Tsjechoslowakije..., Amsterdam 1927.

Mohrmann K., "Architettura moderna a Berlino", *Dedalo*, XII, VIII, agosto 1932, pp. 627-653.

Monck E., *Built in USA: 1932-1944*, New York 1944.

Moos von S., "Vor Gebrauch schütteln", *werk archithese* 23-24, nov.-dez. 1978, pp. 4-8.

Mourdant Crook J., *The Dilemma of Style*, London 1987.

Morton Githens A., "Recent American Group Plans: Monumental Groups", *Brickbuilder*, XXI, 11, November 1912, p. 283.

Mumford L., *Architettura e cultura in America dalla Guerra Civile all'ultima frontiera. The Brown Decades*, (1931) Venezia 1977.

Mumford L., *Roots of Contemporary American Architecture*, (1952) New York 1972.

Münz L., Künstler G., *Adolf Loos. Pioneer of modern architecture*, London 1966.

Muthesius H., *Kultuur en Kunst*, Amsterdam 1911.

Muzio G., "Alcuni architetti d'oggi in Lombardia", *Dedalo*, XI, XV, agosto 1931, pp. 1082-1119.

Nerdinger W., *Walter Gropius. Opera completa*, Milano 1988.

Nietzsche F., *On the Advantage and Disadvantage of History for Life* (1874), translated, with an Introduction by P. Preuss, Indianapolis, Cambridge, 1981.

Nietzsche F., *The complete works*, edited by O. Levy, Edinburgh 1909-1913, vol. VII, *Human All-too-Human* (1878), translated by H. Zimmern, with introduction by J.M. Kennedy 1909.

Nietzsche F., *Ecce Homo* (1888-1889), translated with an introduction by R.J. Hollingdale, London 1979.

Norberg Schulz Ch. with Digeroud J.G., *Louis I. Kahn*, Roma 1980.

Norberg Schulz Ch., *Genius Loci*, Milano 1986.

Numero Unico Futurista Campari, 1931.

"O.N.B. Gorizia. Palestra. Teatro", *Rassegna d'architettura*, II, 8 agosto 1930, pp. 299-301.

Oud J.J.P., "Het monumentale Stadsbeeld" (*De Stijl*, I, 1, ottobre 1917, pp. 10-11), *Lotus International*, 16, settembre 1977, pp. 51-52.

Oud J.J.P., "Kunst en Machine" (*De Stijl*, I, 3, gennaio 1918, pp. 25-27), *Lotus International*, 16, settembre 1977, pp. 52-53.

Oud J.J.P., "Architectonische beschouwing bij bijlage VIII", *De Stijl*, I, n. 4, February 1918, 39-41.

"Il Padiglione della Stampa", *Casabella*, VI, 8-9, agosto-settembre 1933, pp. 14-17.

Padiglione della Stampa, V triennale di Milano, stralcio dal catalogo generale, Milano 1933.

Pagano G., "I benefici dell'architettura moderna. A proposito di una nuova costruzione a Como", *La casa bella*, III, 27, marzo 1930, pp. 11-14.

Pagano G., "La tecnica e i materiali nell'edilizia moderna", *Edilizia moderna*, IV, 5, aprile 1932, pp. 34-43.

Pagano G., "Partenone e Partenoidi", *Domus*, XX, 168, dicembre 1941, pp. 26-31.

Pagano G., *Architettura e città durante il fascismo*, edited by Cesare de Seta, Bari 1976.

Papini R., "Le arti a Parigi nel 1925", *Architettura e Arti Decorative*, V, fasc. V, 1925, pp. 201-233.

Papini R., "L'architettura europea e il concorso di Ginevra", *Architettura e Arti Decorative*, VII, fascc. I-II, 1927-28, pp. 31-79.

Papini R., "Alcuni architetti giovani in Roma", *Dedalo*, XII, II, febbraio 1932, pp. 133-163.

Patetta L., *L'architettura in Italia 1919-1943. Le polemiche*, Milano 1972.

Payne Knight R., *An Analytical Enquiry into the Principles of taste*, (3rd. ed.) London 1806.

Pérouse de Montclos J.M., *Étienne-Louis Boullée (1728-1799)*, Paris 1969.

Pérouse de Montclos J.M., "De la ville rustique d'Italie au pavillon de banlieu", *Revue de l'Art*, 32, 1976, pp. 23-36.

Perspectives in Vernacular Architecture, II, edited by C. Wells, Columbia (Mo) 1986.

Persico E., *Tutte le opere (1923-1935)*, a cura di G. Veronesi, Milano 1964.

Persico E., *Scritti di architettura (1927-1935)*, a cura di G. Veronesi, Firenze 1968.

Pevsner N., "Richard Payne Knight", *Art Bulletin*, XXXI, 4, dec 1949, pp. 293-320.

Pevsner N., "Karl Friedrich Schinkel", in *Studies in Art, Architecture and Design*, I, London 1968, pp. 175-243.

Pevsner N., *L'architettura moderna e il design da William Morris alla Bauhaus*, (1968) Torino 1969.

Piacentini M., "Prima Internazionale architettonica", *Architettura e arti decorative*, VII, fasc. XII, 1928, pp. 544-562.

Pica A., *Nuova architettura italiana*, Milano 1936.

Pica A., "Architettura tedesca moderna", *Emporium*, febbraio 1937, pp. 75-89.

Pica A., *Nuova architettura nel mondo*, Milano 1938.

Pica A., *Architettura moderna in Italia*, Milano 1941.

Pinottini M., "Nicolay Diulgheroff", in *L'estetica del Futurismo - revisioni storiografiche*, Roma 1979, pp. 73-77.

Ponti G., "Giudicare lo Stile Moderno", *Domus*, V, 53, maggio 1932, p. 241.

Ponti G., "Perchè oggi tanto interessa l'architettura", *Domus*, V, 55, luglio 1932, p. 395.

Ponti G., "Ieri e oggi", *Domus*, V, 58, ottobre 1932, pp. 580-581.

Porphyrios D., "Reversible faces. Danish and Swedish Architecture 1905-1930", *Lotus International*, 16, settembre 1977, pp. 35-41.

Portoghesi P., *Dopo l'architettura moderna*, Roma-Bari 1984.

Portoghesi P., "L'EUR ha cinquant'anni", in Cat. *E 42, L'Esposizione Universale di Roma, Utopia e scenario del Regime*, II, Roma 1987, pp. 9-14.

Pozzetto M., "Umberto Cuzzi architetto", *Iniziativa isontina*, 1974, 2, p. 29.

Price U., *On the Picturesque: with an essay on the origin of taste and much original matter*, by Sir Thomas Dick Lander, Bart., (1794), Edinburgh - London 1842.

Quilici V., *Adalberto Libera, l'architettura come ideale*, Roma 1981.

Ragghianti C.L., *Mondrian e l'arte del XX secolo*, Milano 1962.

Ragghianti C.L., "Architettura liberatrice", *Critica d'arte*, XVI, ns., fasc. 105, sett. 1969, pp. 3-92.

Rava C.E., "Dell'Europeismo in architettura", *Rassegna Italiana*, 1928, pp. 133-138.

Rava C.E., "Panorama del razionalismo. I. Svolta pericolosa", *Domus*, IV, 37, gennaio 1931, pp. 39-44.

Rava C.E., "Panorama del razionalismo. Spirito latino", II, *Domus*, IV, 38, febbraio 1931, pp. 24-29.

Rava C.E., "Specchio del razionalismo. Necessità di selezione, III (parte I)", *Domus*, IV,

39, marzo 1931, pp. 36-40.

Rava C.E., "Specchio del razionalismo. Necessità di selezione, III (parte II)", *Domus*, IV, 40, aprile 1931, pp. 39-44; 88.

Rava C.E., "Specchio del razionalismo. Di un'architettura coloniale moderna, IV (parte I)", *Domus*, IV, 41, maggio 1931, pp. 39-43; 89.

Rava C.E., "Specchio del razionalismo. Di un'architettura coloniale moderna, (parte II)", *Domus*, IV, 42, giugno 1931, pp. 32-36.

Rava C.E., "Specchio del razionalismo. Giovani architetti nordamericani", V, *Domus*, IV, luglio 1931, pp. 33-36, 88.

Rava C.E., "Specchio del razionalismo. Conclusione", VI, *Domus*, IV, 47, novembre 1931, pp. 34-40.

Rava C.E., "Prodromi di un nuovo romanticismo", I, *Domus*, VI, 72, dicembre 1933, pp. 634-635.

Rava C.E., "Prodromi di un nuovo romanticismo", III, *Domus*, VII, 74, febbraio 1934, pp. 56-57.

Rava C.E., "Prodomi di un nuovo romanticismo", *Domus*, VII, 77, maggio 1934, p. 35.

Ricci G., *La cattedrale del futuro, Bruno Taut 1914-1921*, Roma 1982.

Rietdorf A., *Gilly Wiedergeburt der Architektur*, Berlin 1940.

Rittich W., *La nouvelle architecture allemande*, Berlin 1941.

Rocco G., "Le scuole di Hilversum", *Rassegna di architettura*, II, 6, giugno 1930, pp. 213-224.

E.N.R. (E.N. Rogers), "Stazione Marittima di Trieste", *Rassegna d'architettura*, IV, 4, aprile 1932, pp. 154-159.

Rosemblum R., *Trasformazioni nell'arte. Iconografia e stile tra Neoclassicismo e Romanticismo*, (1967) Roma 1984.

Rossi A., "Adolf Loos, 1870-1933", *Casabella*, XXIII, 233, 1959, pp. 5-53.

Rossi P.O., *Roma. Guida all'architettura moderna 1909-1984*, Bari 1984.

Rothschild R., "Rapporto sull'architettura olandese", *Edilizia moderna*, VII, 17, aprile-giugno 1935, pp. 26-33.

Rothschild R., "Architettura in Danimarca", *Edilizia moderna*, VIII, 24, gennaio marzo 1937, pp. 14-21.

Salvagnini S., *Il teorico, l'artista, l'artigiano del Novecento. Bontempelli, Terragni, Sironi*, Verona 1986.

Samonà G., *La casa popolare degli anni '30*, a cura di M. Manieri Elia, Venezia 1982.

Samonà G., "Le funzioni dell'ornato nell'architettura moderna", *Rassegna d'Architettura*, II, 3, marzo 1930, pp. 87-95.

Santuccio S., *Luigi Moretti*, Bologna 1986.

Saporiti F., *Architettura in Roma 1901-1950*, Roma 1953.

Sartoris A. "Le ragioni dell'architettura razionale", *Domus*, agosto 1930, pp. 35-70.

Sartoris A., *Gli elementi dell'architettura funzionale*, Milano 1932.

Sartoris A., *Introduzione all'architettura moderna*, Milano 1944.

Sartoris A., *Encyclopédie de l'Architecture nouvelle. Ordre et climat américains*, Milano 1954.

Sartoris A., *Costruzioni Monumentali*, in *La nuova architettura*, a cura di L.C. Fillia, Torino 1931, ripubblicato in *La nuova architettura e i suoi ambienti*, a cura di R. Gabetti, Torino 1985, pp. 57-63.

Sartoris A., *L'actualité du Rationalisme*, Paris 1986.

Scalvini M.L., Sandri M.G., *L'immagine storiografica dell'architettura contemporanea da Platz a Giedion*, Roma 1984.

Schmidt H., *Contributi all'architettura, 1924-1964*, (1965) Milano 1974.

Schwarz F.A., "Aspetti della moderna architettura navale: "Bremen" "Atlantique" "Victoria"", *Rassegna d'Architettura*, IV, 4, aprile 1932, pp. 161-169.

Schwarz F.A., "Brevi note sull'Estetica delle forme meccaniche", *Rassegna d'Architettura*, IV, 4, aprile 1932, pp. 171-173.

Schwarz F.A., "La nuova stazione di Cincinnati", *Rassegna d'Architettura*, VI, febbraio 1934, pp. 69-74.

SCOPPETTA U., *Picturesque. Aurora del giardino romantico. Un pittoresco paradosso che non disdegna l'artificio*, tesi di laurea, Università di Salerno, Facoltà di Lettere e Filosofia, a.a. 1986-1987.

SCOTT BROWN D., "La ville en tant que moyen de comunication", *werk archithese*, 33-34, sett.-ott. 1979, pp. 34-39.

SCULLY V., "Romantic Rationalism and the Expression of Structure in Wood: Downing, Wheeler, Gardner and the Stick Style", *Art Bulletin*, XXXV, 2, June 1953, pp. 121-142.

SCULLY V., *The Shingle Style. Architectural Theory and Design from Richardson to the Origins of Wright*, New Haven - London 1955.

SCULLY V., "The Nature of the Classical in Art", *Yale French Studies*, 19-20, 1958, pp. 107-124.

SCULLY V., *Frank Lloyd Wright*, New York 1960.

SCULLY V., *The Shingle Style and the Stick Style*, (revised edition) New Haven - London 1971.

SCULLY V., *Architettura moderna*, (1961) Milano 1985.

SCULLY V., *American Architecture: The real and the ideal*, in *American Architecture. Innovation and Tradition*, New York 1986, pp. 5-23.

SCURATI MANZONI P., *Il razionalismo. L'architettura dall'Illuminismo alla reazione neoespressionista (XVIII-XIX-XX secolo)*, Milano 1966.

SEKLER E.F., *Josef Hoffmann, The architectural work*, Princeton, New York 1985.

SHAND TUCCI D., *Built in Boston*, Boston 1978.

SOANE J., *Plans, Elevations and Sections of Buildings...*, London 1788.

SOMARÈ E., *Aldo Andreani architetto-scultore*, Milano 1937.

STROUD D., *The Architecture of John Soane*, London 1984.

SUMMERSON J., *Il linguaggio classico dell'architettura*, Torino 1970.

SUMMERSON J., *The classical language of architecture*, (1963) London 1983.

SUMMERSON J., *The Architecture of the Eighteenth Century*, London 1986.

SZAMBIEN W., *Jean-Nicolas-Louis Durand 1760-1834. De l'imitation à la norme*, Paris 1984.

TAFURI M., DAL CO F., *Architettura contemporanea*, I, II, Milano 1979.

TAUT B., *Modern Architecture*, London 1929.

TENTORI F., *Architettura e architetti in Friuli nel primo cinquantennio del Novecento*, Udine 1970.

Terragni, Poesia della razionalità, a cura di F. MARIANO, Roma 1983.

TESSENOW H., *Osservazioni elementari sul costruire* (1916; 1953), Milano 1987.

The Architecture of the Ecole des Beaux-Arts, edited by A. DREXLER, London 1984.

The Classical Tradition and the Modern Movement, 2nd Int. A. Aalto Symposium, Helsinki 1985.

TREIBER D., *Frank Lloyd Wright*, Paris 1986.

"Trent'anni dopo il Palazzo Stoclet", *Casabella*, VIII, 91, luglio 1935, pp. 4-9.

Trentasei progetti di ville di Architetti italiani, Milano-Roma, s.d.

"Una villa a Gorizia", *Domus*, 80, agosto 1934, pp. 17-19.

"Un club sul lago di Como dell'arch. Piero Lingeri", *La Casa Bella*, IV, 48, dicembre, 1931, pp. 11-15.

"Unterbrochene Stadt la ville interrompue", *werk architese*, 23-24, nov.-dez. 1978.

Venezia e la sua laguna (T.C.I.), Milano 1947).

VENTURI R., *Complessità e contraddizioni nell'architettura*, (1966) Bari 1980.

VERONESI G., *Luciano Baldessari architetto*, Trento 1957.

VOYCE A., *Russian Architecture*, New York 1948.

VONDER MÜHLL H.R., *Padiglioni*, in *La nuova architettura* a cura di C. FILLIA, Torino 1931, ripubblicato in *La nuova architettura e i suoi ambienti* a cura di R. GABETTI, Torino 1985, pp. 241-243.

WANGERIN G., WEISS G., *Heinrich Tessenow 1876-1950*, Essen 1976.

WATKIN D., *Thomas Hope 1769-1831 and the Neoclassical Idea*, London 1968.

WEBER E., *Art deco in America*, New York 1985.

WHITTICK A., *European Architecture in the Twentieth Century*, II, p. III, *The Era of*

Functionalism, 1924-1933, London 1953.
Whittick A., *Eric Mendelsohn*, London (1940) 1956.
Wright F. Ll., *Ausgeführte Bauten und Entwürfe von Frank Lloyd Wright*, Berlin 1910.
Wright F.Ll., *Una autobiografia*, Milano 1985.
Wright F.Ll., *Buildings Plans and Designs*, New York 1963.
Wright F.Ll., *Gli anni della formazione, studi e realizzazioni*, introduzione di V. Scully, Tübingen-Milano 1986.
Zanni N., "Simone Cantoni e l'impiego del binato", *Arte Lombarda*, 55-57, 1980, pp. 284-295.
Zanni N., "Giulio Romano e l'istituzione dell'ordine rustico come sistema", *Boll. C.I.S.A.*, XXIV, 1982-1987, pp. 221-235.
Zanni N. "Dal Palladianesimo al Modernismo, Robert Adam, John Soane, Giovanni Muzio", *Arte in Friuli-Arte a Trieste*, 8, 1984, pp. 45-90.
Zanni N., "Ledoux a Trieste: "Gloriette" all'Acquedotto", *Arte in Friuli-Arte a Trieste*, 10, 1988, pp. 83-90.
Zardini M., "Progetto per una biblioteca pubblica a Latina", in *Casabella*, XLVIII, 50, nov. 1984, pp. 4-13.
Zevi B., *Giuseppe Terragni*, Bologna 1980.
Zevi B., *Erich Mendelsohn*, Bologna 1982.
Zukowsky J., *Mies Reconsidered: His Career, Legacy, and Disciples*, Chicago 1986.

DICTIONNARIES

Dizionario biografico dei meridionali, a cura di R. Rubino, s.l., 1974.
Dizionario di Architettura, a cura di N. Pevsner, H. Honour, J. Fleming, Torino 1981.
Dizionario Enciclopedico di Architettura e Urbanistica, voll. 1-6, Roma 1968-1969.
Enciclopedia dell'Architettura moderna, Milano 1967.
Macmillan Encyclopedia of Architects, voll. 1-4, New York 1982.

CATALOGUES

Cat. *Angiolo Mazzoni (1894-1979)*, Bologna 1985.
Cat. *Anni Trenta*, Milano 1982.
Cat. *Architectures en Allemagne: 1900-1933 exposition*, Paris 1979.
Cat. *Architettura Giapponese. Mostra fotografica*, Istituto Giapponese di Cultura Roma, Roma 1987.
Cat. *Architettura moderna. L'avventura delle idee 1750-1980*, Milano 1985.
Cat. *Architettura nel paese dei Soviet 1917-1933*, Milano 1983.
Cat. *Autour de David. Disegni neoclassici del Museo di Lille*, Roma 1984.
Cat. *Berlin 1900-1933: Architecture and Design. Architektur und Design*, Berlin-New York 1987.
Cat. *Friedrich Gilly 1772-1800*, Berlin 1984.
Cat. *Gli affreschi di Carlo Sbisà e la Trieste degli anni Trenta*, Trieste 1980.
Cat. *Il Werkbund*, Venezia 1977.
Cat. *Il razionalismo e l'architettura in Italia durante il fascismo*, Venezia 1976.
Cat. *L'arte a Parma dai Farnese ai Borbone*, Bologna 1979.
Cat. *La colonna Traiana e gli artisti francesi da Luigi XIV a Napoleone I*, Roma 1988.
Cat. *La cantieristica a Trieste e gli anni Trenta*, Trieste 1980.
Cat. *E 42. L'Esposizione Universale di Roma, Utopia e scenario del Regime*, I, *Ideologia e programma per l'"Olimpiade delle Civiltà"*, Venezia 1987.
Cat. *E 42. L'Esposizione Universale di Roma, Utopia e scenario del Regime*, II. *Urbanistica,*

architettura, arti e decorazione, Venezia 1987.
Cat. *La fortuna di Paestum e la memoria moderna del dorico 1750-1830*, I-II, Firenze 1986.
Cat. *Le Arti a Vienna, dalla Secessione alla caduta dell'Impero absburgico*, Venezia 1984.
Cat. *Le Corbusier Pittore e Scultore*, Milano 1986.
Cat. *Luciano Baldessari*, Milano 1985.
Cat. *Nordic Classicism 1910-1930*. Helsinki 1982.
Cat. *Paestum and the Doric revival 1750-1830*, Firenze 1986.
Cat. *Pizzigoni. Invito allo spazio progetti e architetture 1923-1967*, Milano 1982.
Cat. *Ricostruzione Futurista dell'universo*, Torino 1980.
Cat. *The age of Neoclassicism*, London 1972.
Cat. *The architecture of Adolf Loos*, London 1987.
Cat. *Vienna Rossa*, Milano 1980.

PHOGRAPHIC REFERENCES

Bari, Priv. coll. Carmelo Calò Carducci: 38b
Berlin, Technische Hochschule, Charlottemburg: 56c
Berlin, Technische Universität Charlottemburg: 40a
Cossonay-Ville, Archivio Sartoris: 7a
Dresden, Sächsische Landesbibliothek: 3b
Dublin, National Library of Ireland, Murray Coll.: 24c
Florence, Foto Alinari: 8b
Genève, Frederich Boissonaz: 10b
Gorizia, Archivio Schiozzi-Brandi: 56b
Karlskrona, Marin Museum: 27d
Lille, Musée des Beaux-Arts: 22b
London, Sir John Soane's Museum: 9b; 14b; 37a
London, National Monument Record: 19b; 28b
London, Victoria and Albert Museum: 37a
Milan, Davide Campari S.p.A.: 29b
Milan, Triennale: 6b
Moscow, Archivio Černichov: 44b; 45a
Moscow, Gnima: 3a; 5b; 15b; 43b; 46b
Naples, P. Mascilli Migliorini: 16a
New York, T. Killian - F. Astorg Bollack: 1b; 1c; 2a; 2b; 4b; 5a; 6a; 8a; 9a; 9c; 12b; 13a; 13b; 13c; 14a; 15a; 16b; 17a; 17b; 18a; 19a; 20b; 22a; 23a; 24a; 25a; 25b; 26b; 27a; 27b; 28a; 28d; 30a; 30b; 30c; 31a; 31b; 32a; 33b; 34a; 34b; 35a; 36a; 36b; 36c; 37b; 41a; 41b; 42b; 45b; 47a; 48b; 48c; 49a; 49c; 50a; 50b; 51a; 51b; 52a; 52c; 53a; 53b; 54a; 54b; 55a; 55b; 56a; 57a; 57b
Paris, Archives de Seine et Marne, 48a
Paris, Bibliothèque Nationale: 10c; 21a; 42c; 43a
Paris, E. Moreno: 28c
Paris, Musée Carnavalet: 23b
Parma, Accademia di Belle Arti: 40c
Potsdam, Sans-Souci, Staatliche Schlosser: 7b
Rome, Archivio Busiri Vici: 39c
Rome, Archivio G. Del Debbio: 21c
Rome, Archivio Leda Cattini Vaccaro: 10a
Rome, Archivio Paola Libera: 4d; 42a
Rome, L. Morelli: 12a; 33a
Rome, Studio Moretti: 47b
Rovereto, Musei Civici Archivio Mazzoni: 35b
Salerno, Dipartimento Analisi delle Componenti Culturali del Territorio, Fisciano: 12a; 24b; 28c; 33a
The Hague, Rijksdienst Beeldende Kunst, Van Doesburg Collection: 1a
Trieste, Archivio Iona: 14c
Trieste, Archivio Pozzetto: 44a
Trieste, Foto Gasparo: 4a; 11a; 21b
Venezia, D. Chinellato, E. Vassallo: 40b